PUBLIC
INTIMACIES

TALK SHOW PARTICIPANTS
AND TELL-ALL TV

D0914823

THE HAMPTON PRESS COMMUNICATION SERIES

Communication Alternatives
Brenda Dervin, *supervisory editor*

PUBLIC
INTIMACIES

TALK SHOW PARTICIPANTS
AND TELL-ALL TV

PATRICIA JOYNER PRIEST, PH.D.

HAMPTON PRESS, INC.
CRESSKILL, NEW JERSEY

Printed in the United States of America

Portions of this volume were previously published in "Pulp Pulpits: Self-Disclosure on Donahue," *Journal of Communication*, 44(4), pp. 74-97.

Library of Congress Cataloging-in-Publication Data

Priest, Patricia Joyner.
    Public intimacies : talk show participants and tell-all TV /
Patricia Joyner Priest.
        p.   cm. -- (The Hampton Press communication series)
    Includes bibliographical references and indexes.
    ISBN 1-57273-002-1. -- ISBN 1-57273-003-X (pbk.)
    1. Talk shows--United States. 2. Donahue (Television program)
I. Title. II. Series.
PN1992.8.T34P75   1995
791.45'6--dc20   95-3929
                                                          CIP

Hampton Press, Inc.
23 Broadway
Cresskill, NJ 07626

Cover design: Karen Davidson
Cartoonist: Rob Shepperson

DEDICATED
to my beloved husband, Neal,
Renaissance man of the postmodern age,
who listened patiently, endlessly, and contributed immensely

CONTENTS

CONTENTS

PREFACE

I swayed on a tightrope, disparate audiences waiting on either side, as I worked to make this book accessible both to fans of daytime talk shows and to scholars. I sometimes teetered precariously toward one group or the other, but I tried always to maintain a sense of balance.

Readers who find talk shows compelling yet may shy away from books whose table of contents contain off-putting words such as counter-hegemony, take heart! You will probably find that you know many of the characters whose stories are told in this volume, and you will also find useful information, I believe, about bringing your issues into national forums such as *Donahue* or *The Oprah Winfrey Show*. You may, however, want to skim through Chapters 9 and 11 in which, I will admit, I veered most toward the scholarly types.

I believe scholars will find this work unusual in many ways—for its emphasis not on audiences but on television participants, for its interdisciplinary nature, and the no-holds-barred, on-the-record comments from informants. I hope that this book will alter readers' thinking about this porous television site, where a wide range of outsiders can step in to participate—briefly and warily.

As I grappled with the slippery phenomenon of daytime talk shows, many wonderful people have inspired and assisted me. What a long, strange trip it's been. I would especially like to thank the many talk show participants who discussed their experiences on television with me. I was unbelievably fortunate that they were so articulate, honest, and generous with their time and information.

I also wish to thank my friends and family who put me up as I traipsed around the country: Jackie and Greg Smith, Melissa Wright, Mary Towle and Kristy Notor. Carl and Sylvia Priest ably kept watch over the "wildebeests" while we were away.

My publisher at Hampton Press, Barbara Bernstein, has been a jewel—amazingly friendly and always accessible. My transcriptionist, Madeline Hawley, and my indexer, Sharon Neff, could not have been nicer.

My thanks to many fine people I met while at the University of Georgia: our dear friends Dave and Jillian Burns, the wonderful and mul-titalented Kristen Smith (who assisted me at many nerve-wracking moments), Doug Barthlow, Larry Etling (who passed along many useful articles), and Melinda Hawley (whose dissertation served as a helpful—though daunting—template).

Many others at UGA deserve special thanks. Alison Alexander, chair of the Telecommunications Department, provided office space and encouragement even during the long, dry spells. David Hazinski's generous and crafty advice kickstarted new rounds of good fortune. Myrna Powell, ever cheerful, helped at many critical points.

Joseph Dominick helped guide my dissertation, a seemingly never-ending story, to its completion. I probably interrupted him, as my grandmother would say, fifty'leven times. His droll humor made working with him a pleasure. My gratitude also goes out to James Fletcher, whose encyclopedic knowledge, close editing, good cheer, and computer assistance proved invaluable. Dean Krugman encouraged me to pursue this project from its earliest glimmerings of existence. David Shaffer led me through the maze of self-disclosure literature. And very special thanks are due Jill Swenson. Her endless enthusiasm continually buoyed me, and I was inspired by her insistence on excellence, her intellectual curiosity, and her social consciousness. My thanks to each of these remarkable people. This project is strengthened by their participation.

Thanks, too, to Dr. Shah, Dr. Priest, and "Dr." Sylvia, who helped me live to write this.

The women of the Athens area rape crisis center warrant a heap of thanks for teaching me, among many other things, how to listen carefully and nonjudgementally. Hilary Ruston and Lorraine Fuller, especially, have helped sustain me in a thousand ways.

Lastly, to my dear family: a million, heartfelt thanks. To my wonderful mother, who has stood by me every day of my life. Her strength and grace have shaped my life enormously. To my sister Kim, whose intellect has always challenged me and who has always listened generously. To Jackie, the big sister I have always looked up to, who inspires me in her search for truth. To Daryll, brother and friend, who bore with me as I practiced storytelling. And to my dad, whose memory I will always cherish.

And Neal, I simply could not have done it without you.

Patricia J. Priest
Athens, GA
December 1994

CHAPTER ONE

PRIVATE TALK IN PUBLIC PLACES

Several years ago a startling interaction on *The Oprah Winfrey Show* caught my attention. Oprah was in the midst of a gut-wrenching interview with a woman who had killed her father after enduring years of sexual abuse. The program ground to a halt when the woman, the sole guest that day, politely refused to disclose the horrific details. Oprah's response was awkward, and the show seemed to teeter precariously, as conversations sometimes do when a norm has been broken. Yet it seemed so very normal to decline: The studio audience was leaning forward to listen, as was an audience of millions at home.

Seeing the informal rules shattered by the guest that day galvanized my interest in this peculiar genre and launched this examination of talk show guests' willingness to step into what appeared to me then to be a very public confessional booth. Quite commonly, of course, talk show panelists are perfectly willing to disclose the most intimate of details. On two separate shows during April 1993, for example, panelists on *Sally Jessy Raphael* tearfully recounted detailed accounts about the devastating sexual and emotional abuse perpetrated by family members, with victims actually confronting their abusers on one harrowing episode.

A parade of new characters passes through each day, flinging out their most intimate stories like Mardi Gras beads to members of the audience, and I wanted to know why. I traipsed across the country interviewing people the likes of whom I had never met—or at least that I was never aware of having met—a transsexual lesbian, a "sex priestess," prostitutes, a "vigilante dad," swingers (in their swinging headquarters, no less), and many other off-beat or tragic types. I wanted to know why

1

they had been willing to discuss juicy tidbits such as, in the case of the transsexual, the inevitable questions about the deconstruction of her penis, and I wondered whether participants were simply game to do whatever it took to get on television, like contestants on *The Gong Show*.

I also sensed even then, however, that something more serious was transpiring, despite the oftentimes tacky nature of the genre. The paradox became apparent early on: Although many participants seemed somewhat nutty and so very vulnerable, there was a powerful declaration in their voices in a determined seizing of the national consciousness, despite the din of criticism that swirled around them. Then, too, there were those searing images from shows on incest, drunk driving, and breast cancer that would not leave me.

This public talk about private horrors is not new. In the 1950s, women who provided the most moving stories of their lives' hardships won prizes such as refrigerators and washing machines on the long-running radio and television program *Queen for a Day*.[1] Similarly, *Strike it Rich* doled out money and gifts to the destitute and needy who were willing to step forward and relate their woeful life stories.[2] On current daytime talk shows, however, the rewards are far less tangible, and the disclosures are generally much more explicit.

The lineup of panelists on *Donahue* the week of May 3, 1993 provides an encapsulated example of the intimate nature of the disclosures on talk shows. The topics that week are roughly representative of *Donahue* and the genre as a whole. Monday's titillating show title was "Mormon sex secrets." Tuesday's show featured three sisters who had had liposuction and three who were contemplating the procedure; stomach-churning footage of fat suctioning was shown. Wednesday's central guest was a polygamist, who was joined on stage by several of the women he had duped. The next day's panelists were teens whose high school teachers had lured them into sexual encounters and later, in some cases, forced them to get abortions when they became pregnant. Friday's guests were teenagers who had been inappropriately placed in mental hospitals by their parents.

Donahue is only one of a host of programs on which such disclosure occurs, and other shows of the genre are perhaps more intimate in nature, on aggregate, because of *Donahue's* occasional treatment of political and racial issues that do not center on self-disclosure. During the first six months of 1993, for example, the program covered the crisis in the former Yugoslavian republics and aired several shows about the Rodney King verdicts in Los Angeles.[3] However, the general tone of the show for approximately four of five days is characterized by intimate revelations from panelists.

The dynamics of daytime talk shows dictate that almost any question is fair game. For example, the *Donahue* audience asked whether a "former homosexual" who is now married had been tested for the AIDS virus and whether he still had gay fantasies; and a *Donahue* audience member interrogated a woman who married her former husband's brother about whether she had slept with him before she divorced. The studio audience asks a variety of other intimate questions beyond the scope of the topics the panelists have agreed to discuss, such that a broad stream of disclosure is often expected of those who consent to appear.[4] Even if a guest were to refuse to utter a single word on the program, however, disclosures are summarized on screen with phrases such as "Married couple who swing" or "Treated for sexual desire problem." These shorthand labels for the disclosures are also provided in the listings in *TV Guide* and in promotions for upcoming episodes.

Callers and studio audience members also enter into the conversation with divulgences of their own.[5] Less frequently, hosts also self-disclose, as did Oprah Winfrey in a powerful revelation in 1985 during a show taping that she is a survivor of repeated incidents of acquaintance rape that occurred during her childhood. Jenny Jones made guest appearances on a variety of shows to talk about the health problems associated with her breast implants. After Sally Jessy Raphael's daughter died in 1992, Sally thanked viewers for their outpouring of sympathy and showed a short photo montage of Alison's life. The various male hosts, however, rarely disclose intimately. A prominent exception is Geraldo Rivera, who made the rounds of the talk show circuit to discuss his years of philandering (and to promote his new book, appropriately entitled, *Exposing Myself*). Celebrities also routinely use television talk shows as forums for discussing such problems as alcoholism, drug addiction, and eating disorders.

The tell-all nature of these programs makes them popular with American viewers. Nielsen figures for the week ending May 8, 1994 ranked *The Oprah Winfrey Show* fourth among syndicated shows with a 9.1 rating (approximately 9 million households). Reruns of popular programs such as *Married with Children* and *Roseanne* have knocked

Donahue and *Sally Jessy Raphael* out of their several year position within the top 15 syndicated offerings. Ratings for both *Sally Jessy Raphael* and *Donahue* are roughly half that of Oprah's.[6] *Donahue* has been a national show since 1969 and often ranked first among syndicated programs before the advent of *The Oprah Winfrey Show*, which quickly secured the top daytime talk show spot after it debuted nationally in 1986. Many new shows crowd the field each year, with the total figure topping 19 in 1993.

Daytime talk shows have been largely neglected as an area of inquiry in communications research. Their sensational nature, characterized by critics as "nuts 'n' sluts" and "freak of the week,"[7] may cause them to be overlooked as if they were of little consequence. However, as Donal Carbaugh points out, programs like *Donahue* are noteworthy because "One cannot find places in history where millions have gathered daily, to talk."[8] These discussions often reverberate into the lives of viewers, occasionally forming the basis for face-to-face conversations and perhaps altering the norms for appropriate levels and topics of disclosure used in nonmediated interactions.

This highly popular genre depends on a steady stream of participants willing to discuss intimate topics that reveal varying degrees of deviancy. *Donahue* requires approximately 30 guests per week.[9] On *Donahue* alone, which has taped over 6,000 shows, many thousands have stepped forward to self-disclose on television during the quarter century the program has been on the air.

Who are these people willing to tell all to millions? One survey found that Americans "are more terrified of appearing before an audience than they are of insects, darkness, heights, illness, or elevators."[10] Self-disclosure on television would seem to be even more unnerving, because the topics often concern taboo or embarrassing areas of personal life. However, as I discuss in the pages that follow, the opportunity to appear on television is a draw for some such that misgivings or social anxiety are diminished or set aside.

This book represents an attempt to answer a variety of questions about daytime talk shows: Why do people choose to appear to discuss subjects normally considered stigmatizing? Also, are participants highly invested in television as an important part of their lives? Similarly, before their appearances, were they enthusiastic fans of the talk show genre and the various program hosts? And what in the world happens to them when they return to their communities, now that their various peccadillos—or worse—have been revealed?[11] To get at these questions and others, I conducted interviews with a wide-ranging group of talk show participants to capture an insider's view of what the opportunity to be on a talk show meant to people who were asked to self-disclose on air.[12]

I chose to focus primarily but not exclusively on *Donahue* because of methodological exigencies. Furthermore, the program's longevity (25 years on the air as of 1993) and its prototypical form make it an important site for investigation into the odd genre of daytime TV talk shows. I do, however, discuss the wider talk show terrain, from *Ricki Lake* to *The Oprah Winfrey Show*, because many of the people I interviewed had appeared on several programs.

Virtually nothing is known about talk show participants except for tidbits provided by scattered anecdotal evidence.[13] Researchers in diverse fields have carried out more than 1,400 self-disclosure studies[14] since Sidney Jourard, in 1958, first hypothesized about the relationship between self-disclosure and mental health.[15] Researchers have yet to utilize the findings and theoretic underpinnings of this vast body of work in their investigations of mass-mediated communication.[16] Disclosures on television talk shows are often extremely personal, despite the fact that the discloser is speaking not to intimates but to an audience of millions. Here, the focus is on how and why self-disclosure is employed in this novel and sometimes risky way by talk show guests.

The programs' staffs offer potential participants an unusually active role on a medium characterized largely by its one-way flow of information. Although the spectacle nature of the genre may sometimes rival the silliness of *Let's Make a Deal* and other game shows, those who appear on daytime talk shows take a personal role in the national dialogue that occurs on such programs. Both genres allow the public to step in as contestants, but the stakes are, for many, much higher on talk shows. Participation entails a price—the self-disclosure of matters normally withheld because of their painful nature or their potential to discredit the discloser.

Programs in this genre provide one of few forums onto which "ordinary" people—rather than solely the stars and experts who vie to promote their latest ventures—can step to center stage and discuss their lives. Many participants are members of stigmatized groups who are put on display, much like carnival freak shows that showcase and commodify the "bearded lady" and other oddities. As I discuss in later chapters, the role of television in the lives of these outgroup members often is different in important ways that induced them to step up to these electronic soap boxes.

The resulting exposure to a variety of groups outside the margins of society may have a significant effect on the public's attitudes toward members of such groups. The focal point here, however, is the impact on the participants themselves. People asked to appear generally have very little information at their disposal when making important decisions about whether to participate.[17] The contested nature of the daytime talk show forum makes it a fairly risky site on the dial.

Although countless studies have investigated television viewers, few have examined the view from the other side of the screen.[18] In other words, what is it like to be inside the "box"? Situating the focus of study from this vantage point increases understanding about a slippery new idea put forth by Cecelia Tichi and others that stepping inside the set, getting in, represents access to a desired landscape and a strange form of "reality." Participants' feelings about themselves are of particular interest after they have been "there," after they have pulled aside the curtain, revealing Oz at work.

NOTES

1. *Queen for a Day* was an odd show in which several contestants vied for the top honor—to be "Queen for a Day" and rake in the many prizes awarded. Winners were showered with gifts such as a new fashion wardrobe, lingerie, three dozen roses, and a variety of other consumer items. Sometimes the gifts, donated by the show's sponsors, seemed glaringly inappropriate, given the dire life circumstances faced by the winners (see Brown, 1977).

2. Brooks and Marsh, 1979, called this program the worst show in TV history. Public assistance services in New York City decried the show and claimed the producers lured the destitute from around the country to New York City, where they sometimes waited for weeks with the hope of striking it rich on the program.

3. Self-disclosure often surfaces in these shows as well. For example, in an episode featuring Officer Briseno, one of the men found innocent in the federal trial for the Rodney King beating, Briseno frequently mentioned that he had cried over the incident. Donahue also pointed out that Briseno had been seeing a psychiatrist.

4. A common question asked by the audience is "Were you abused as a child?" Donahue's most frequent question asked regardless of the topic seems to be "Are you drug free?"

5. In an episode of *Montel Williams* pertaining to childhood sexual molestation, which aired in April 1993, Montel asked one audience member to stand and comment on the topic, noting that she had been crying throughout the show. She was, in fact, a survivor and was essentially "outed" by Montel's urging. Normally, however, disclosures appear to be freely offered by audience members.

6. When I write of hosts Oprah Winfrey and Sally Jessy Raphael throughout this book, I occasionally refer to them by their first names, although I use Phil Donahue's surname when mentioning him. I recognize the gender bias of this usage, but I adhere to it because it reflects the way audiences generally refer to the hosts. The bias is part of larger societal patterns in which women are often addressed by their first names, and men by their last. I believe this public and press usage also indicates viewers' perceptions of greater intimacy with the female hosts. Furthermore, the programs' titles play a role in this uneven usage. Donahue's title simply displays his surname, while Oprah's opening credits first indicate *Oprah*! before the screen scrolls to the full title, *The Oprah Winfrey Show.*

7. Kneale, 1988, p. 25.

8. Carbaugh, 1989, p. 2.

9. Givens, 1989.

10. This survey was cited in Hilton and Knoblauch, 1980, p. 76.

11. The intent is manifestly similar to that often undertaken by researchers in the uses and gratifications field of communication theory. Katz et al., 1974, defined the field's focus: "The social and psychological origins of needs, which generate expectations of the mass media or other sources, which lead to

differential patterns of media exposure (or engagement in other activities), resulting in need gratifications and other consequences, perhaps mostly unintended ones" (p. 20). The qualitative methodology used here, however, is quite different from those generally utilized by uses and gratifications researchers.

12. A qualitative approach to the phenomenon was chosen largely because of the counterintuitive nature of the behavior. Geertz, 1973, spoke of the quest to "bring us into touch with the lives of strangers" (p. 16) and argued that this can be accomplished through a close examination of the participants' interpretations of their actions. Additionally, the underlying view here is in line with Carey's (1989) definition of communication as "a symbolic process whereby reality is produced, maintained, repaired and transformed" (p. 23). The study of self-disclosure in the fields of social psychology and speech communication consists almost entirely of experimental manipulations. In my view, self-disclosure on television, as with other forms of social behavior, seems too complex to pin down with such methods. Schickel, 1985, wrote of television: "It must be doing something to us, this demanding, overgrown Venus's fly trap that we have planted in the corner of the living room. And, of course, it is. The problem is that it has worked on us slowly, undramatically, in ways that are not measurable through conventional social science techniques. A subjective medium, it can be approached only subjectively" (p. 9).

13. Only one experiment has directly addressed the topic of videotaped self-disclosure. In an interview with David Sohn, author Jerzy Kosinski described his unpublished research in which he found that 9- to 14-year-old children were willing to detail incidents of masturbation and shoplifting while they were being videotaped that they had been unwilling to reveal off camera. This suggests that the presence of the television camera, contrary to expectations, may prompt disclosure from some people.

14. Hill and Stull, 1987.

15. Jourard believed that adequate levels of self-disclosure were necessary for good mental health and for relationship development.

16. Haag's (1993) description of Oprah Winfrey's patterns of discourse briefly mentions the self-disclosure literature. She argues that Oprah's intimate manner is grounded in women's communication styles.
17. There are several books that are oriented toward practical considerations pertaining to appearing on and gaining access to the shows. These include works by Hilton and Knoblauch, 1980; Mincer and Mincer, 1982; Prone, 1984; and Rein et al., 1987.
18. Kuehn's (1976) participant observation of the backstage behavior of game show contestants is an interesting exception. He found that a subculture took shape among the participants and that show business norms that focused on looking good were quickly adopted.

CHAPTER TWO

"TELL-ALL" TELEVISION

Television talk shows are a carryover from the early days of radio and have flourished as a staple in syndication because the format is relatively inexpensive to produce, flexible to schedule, and traditionally less encumbered by broadcast standards than network shows.[1] Profits are very high in this genre, with production costs of approximately 15 million dollars per year, and profit margins anywhere from roughly fourfold for *Donahue* ($90 million in 1991) to tenfold for *The Oprah Winfrey Show*.[2] Clearly, stripping away the veneer of propriety sells.

Donahue represented a different kind of talk show when it debuted in Dayton, Ohio in 1967 because of the program's emphasis on audience involvement and current issues rather than show business chitchat.[3] Donahue's first week of programming was highly unusual in its day: his very first guest was atheist Madalyn Murray O'Hair. On Tuesday's show, bachelors conversed about what kind of women they found attractive; Wednesday's program featured a baby's birth; Thursday, Donahue examined the funeral industry; and the week wrapped up with a discussion of anatomically correct dolls.[4] These off-beat topics were originally a consequence of the difficulty of luring big name celebrities to Dayton.[5] The formula worked, however, and the audience participation, issues-oriented television talk genre was born.

The controversial nature of some episodes prompted several stations to offer half-hour versions in late-night time periods in the early years of the show's history.[6] Stations occasionally refused to air an episode entirely, as did about 20 percent when programs showcasing a birth and an abortion were sent to participating stations.[7] Although the show has been the subject of sporadic controversy during its 25 years on the air, critics contend the program has become increasingly tawdry.[8] In 1993, a Christian dentist in Dallas began a campaign to pressure advertisers to pull their ads from *Donahue* unless the show aired in a late-night time period, when children would be less likely to be present in the audience.[9] Some advertisers did pull their campaigns, but the show still airs during the daytime. Parental advisory labels that warn of frank discussions of adult themes have become more common.

Donahue and other shows of the genre broadcast what appears to be an everexpanding, unbounded array of topics. Executive producers from various programs assembled on a November 21, 1991 episode of *The Joan Rivers Show* claimed that one topic they would not broach is bestiality, although two producers noted that they had received letters from enthusiasts who wished to tout its pleasures on national TV.

Where Do They *Find* These People?

The genre's boundaries are to a large measure defined by what aspects of their lives people are willing to disclose. Oprah Winfrey receives 4,000 letters each week, many of which are from people clamoring to appear.[10] Approximately 50 percent of Sally Jessy Raphael's guests are culled from viewer mail.[11]

The shows also take a proactive stance, vying to beat out the competition to procure potential guests for their shows when headline-grabbing scandals such as the "Spur Posse" hit the news. Producers also generate ideas and then seek willing participants through organizations as diverse as rape crisis centers, sperm banks, or clubs for swingers. Psychologists invited to appear because of their therapeutic specialty or new book often tap their more attractive and vivacious clients to testify to their expertise.

Producers also pour over resources such as *The Yearbook of Experts, Authorities, and Spokespersons*, an annual volume chock-full of people willing to speak on every conceivable topic. Inclusion in this yellow pages of experts costs those listed upwards of $250. A similar source of talk show guests, the *Radio-TV Interview Report*, is published twice monthly and also derives from ads paid for by people longing to appear. A new national registry lists more than 1,000 people eager for exposure in public forums.[12] Potential talk show participants pay the registry $3 a month to be listed in the data bank.[13]

Several shows routinely broadcast recruitment messages.[14] For example, in August 1993, Sally Jessy Raphael asked, "Are you a mother who was raped by her son?" A toll-free number was then provided for women willing to disclose about this taboo subject. Oprah Winfrey made a plea at the end of a show in January 1992 for people to come forward on her show to talk about their tendencies to abuse their children. She urged viewers to call her staff "if you want to be courageous enough to ask for help."

Producers also ask audience members at show tapings if they have topics they would like to suggest. Here, too, the subjects for future episodes are often revealed in case those present might be willing to discuss the topic publicly. At a show taping for *Montel Williams*, for example, the crowd waiting to file in was asked if they made their spouses pay for sex. Audience members at *The Jerry Springer Show* are often asked to indicate on a form whether a list of situations applied to them. One day the list included questions like "Do you know a parent who thinks they have a nerdy kid who deserves a makeover? and "Are you or have you been in an unusual relationship?"

The procurement process, then, works both ways: the producers work to come up with topics and secure guests willing to discuss them, while many viewers, like moths, throw themselves at the flickering glare of the TV screen, trying to get in. The end result, shaped by producer gate-keeping as well as availability of participants willing to disclose, is an array of topics ranging from pregnant women with bulimia to—fill in the blank, it has probably been done.

Increasingly, scholars are theorizing about the degradation of the public sphere[15] and the blurring of public and private arenas of behavior.[16] Talk show guests are essentially cashing in on a marginalizing element of their lives for the chance to participate in these high profile forums. The genre's characteristic mix of private and public requires a similarly unusual melding of theoretical positions for explication. Wayne Munson described the genre's odd amalgamated characteristics:

> Like the term itself, the "talk show" fuses and seems to reconcile two different, even contradictory, rhetorics. It links conversation, the interpersonal—the premodern oral tradition—with the mass-

mediated spectacle born of modernity. It becomes, among other things, a recuperative practice reconciling technology and commodification with community, mass culture with the individual and the local, production with consumption.[17]

Throughout this book, seemingly disparate fields of scholarship will be pieced together in new ways to reflect these disjunct conjunctures. This work lies at the intersection of the fields of self-disclosure, mass communication, social activism, and sociological theories about deviance. The phenomenon situated in this overlapping portion of these diverse fields is what might be called *television disclosure*, the revelation of intimate information broadcast on television. The talk show literature that follows provides a useful first stitch, whereas later, threads of other disciplines will be interwoven to better encompass the peculiarities of telling all on television.

The Talk Show Literature

Considering the constant stream of participants willing to disclose intimate details in public and the widespread enthusiasm of viewers, the genre has attracted surprisingly scant attention from scholars. Wayne Munson's recent book, *All Talk*, provides a sweeping historical look at radio and TV talk shows, which he describes as quintessentially postmodern forms because of their myriad boundary-shattering characteristics.[18]

Several works have analyzed the public dialogue that occurs on the programs to determine the norms and patterns displayed. Donal Carbaugh's discourse analysis of a year's programming on *Donahue* elucidates the underlying motifs that characterize both the show and larger themes in American culture. These include the rights of individuals to express their opinions and to make choices for their own lives. Importantly, Carbaugh described the distinct norms operating on the program:

> Since honest (open, truthful and direct) speaking is identified, praised and promoted, it is sometimes used as the proper way of saying the wrong things. By speaking this way, a speaker can reveal information that may seem untoward and thus bring discredit to one's self, community or country, yet do so in a way that is redeemable socially.[19]

Carbaugh argues that society's need for information is served by the disclosures of the speakers, who are rewarded by tolerant listening and praise for their honesty.

Bryan Crow's study of Dr. Ruth's now-defunct *Good Sex* television show on the Lifetime channel focuses on the conversational dynamics of the intimate phone calls heard on the program. Crow notes that most callers followed unarticulated conventions, which include concisely summarizing the problem and accepting a brief answer as sufficient. In addition, Crow points to the paralinguistic and linguistic cues Dr. Ruth used to foster a sense of intimacy. He describes the host's role in providing a safe forum for disclosure:

> Dr. Ruth's frankness is projected and contained by her use of clinical rather than colloquial terminology, by a persona of innocence, affability, and liberal Judeo-Christian morality, by the assurance that her expertise is the result of professional training and clinical practice rather than personal behaviour, and by the gatekeeping presence of her co-host.[20]

Crow's characterization suggests that the host's style and personality may play an important role in prompting intimate disclosure.

Jane Banks also analyzed Dr. Ruth's program and speculates about the sociocultural implications of the show: "For some of her callers, Westheimer may have taken the place of an earlier confessor, even to the granting of absolution, and in some ways, shows like Westheimer's have replaced the function of institutions like the parish church."[21] Banks discusses the educational, interpersonal, and therapeutic functions that seemed to be served by the show both for callers and the audience and notes that the multiple functions provided a sort of legitimate cover so that viewer interest in the show appears less prurient. Banks identifies three types of calls; these include caller inquiries about (a) normalcy, (b) license to engage in certain sexual acts, and (c) advice about relationship problems. This particular program seems more closely aligned to talk radio because of the anonymity allowed by the call-in format.

Peter Conrad characterizes the talk show hot seat as a "vinyl pillory" in which celebrities as well as private citizens are demeaned and, paradoxically, thereby humanized. He noted the different nature of the "manners" displayed on television by hosts asking highly personal questions: "These intrusions can seem salacious or overbearingly ill-mannered. But they're to be blamed on the medium, not individuals who are its agents. Television has no respect for persons: in surrendering yourself to the camera, you forfeit your privacy."[22] Conrad, like Banks, speculates that the genre may serve a cathartic function for those who step forward to disclose. He suggests that Donahue's appearance and his Catholic upbringing make him well suited for the role of father confessor.

Many writers discussing talk shows generally assume that participants use the genre as a confessional or as a therapy session. Mimi White contends that therapeutic patterns of discourse permeate television programming. She notes the similarities between participants involved in such diverse programs as *Love Connection*, Dr. Ruth's *Good Sex*, and *The 700 Club*: "These are all subjects who are set into televisual representation (sound and/or image) in direct proportion to their willingness to participate in a therapeutic transaction through confession, in a context wherein representation is always commodified, one way or another."[23]

Gloria-Jean Masciarotte, however, in an article jam-packed with novel ideas, compares the declarations on talk shows to the "Protestant activity of testimony or witnessing before the group"[24] rather than to confession or therapy. Linda Alcoff and Laura Gray, in their work on rape and incest survivors' discourse on the media, also eschew the concept of confession: "A witness is not someone who confesses, but someone who knows the truth and has the courage to tell it."[25] Whereas White criticizes the incessant stream of therapeutic talk, arguing that discussion rarely turns to solutions, Masciarotte believes that "resolving the issue is not the function of the talk show, displaying the space for voices is."[26]

Masciarotte notes the gendered nature of the genre and celebrates the forum talk shows provide for women's concerns. Frank Tomasulo, on the other hand, argues that Donahue—usually lauded for being among the first to bring women's issues into televised discussions—actually undermines women's agency. His description of *Donahue* relies primarily on Freudian analysis:

> He [Donahue] represents a surrogate, symbolic Father to his predominant female audience (both in studio and at-home). He therefore functions within a fundamentally incestuous relationship with them . . . [using an] overtly phallic microphone (often shoved into the faces of his female audience members and withdrawn before they've finished speaking).[27]

16

Tomasulo argues that the show appears to be a free-form debate but is in fact controlled by Donahue in numerous ways that strip audience members—a large proportion of whom are women—of their critical abilities to structure their own meanings. He contends that the apparent solutions to the problems discussed on the show are provided in the commercial messages that interrupt the dialogue. His critique of *Donahue* also points to the show's reliance on experts called in to provide advice about what appear to be merely personal, rather than political or class-related, problems.

Many works on talk shows criticize the ubiquitous presence of experts on panels,[28] but Mimi White argues that authority is relativized in the nonhierarchical discussions that ensue. Similarly, Paolo Carpignano, Robin Andersen, Stanley Aronowitz, and William DiFazio describe the studio audience as purveyors of common sense who provide a counterweight to the advice given by experts. However, Susan Bordo decries the particularization that occurs when an audience member's utterance can negate generalizations, detracting from the political nature of the discussions.

Indeed, much of the work pertaining to this genre is critical scholarship that disparages the apolitical nature of the dialogue that unfolds. Sally Steenland, for example, describes a pattern in which issues are discussed at the individual level without acknowledging the political and social forces that underpin the topics: "The largest unit of belonging seems to be that of the family: one's children, parents, sibling. Patterns of abuse, addiction, dependency and low self-esteem [are shown to] stem from these family systems."[29]

Much of the research cited above grapples with the genre's paradoxical workings: participation is potentially empowering and transgressive—while the risks of containment and trivialization are great.[30] Several authors refer to Michel Foucault's work about the power imbalances inherent in confessional practices.[31] Foucault argued that those hearing confessions during psychiatric sessions or religious ceremonies have the power to exonerate, punish, or normalize the speakers' behaviors. Mimi White notes that producers, hosts, and audience members channel participants' stories in various ways that can strip panelists' control over how they tell and defend their life stories. The manifest power differentials on a show such as *Donahue*, in which the host rarely discloses and the audience demands answers to the most intimate of questions, has prompted several writers to voice their concerns about the damaging or limiting potential of the genre when participants attempt to force societal change through public speaking about private issues.

Alcoff and Gray, for example, condemn press treatment of survivors of sexual assault and spousal abuse: "The media often use the presence of survivors for shock value and to pander to a sadistic voyeurism among viewers, focusing on the details of the violations with close-ups of survivors' anguished expressions."[32] Elayne Rapping and Lucretia Knapp believe that the shows hold potential in their ability to heighten the visibility of certain groups who otherwise are not represented on television, but the authors are concerned that the sensational nature of what Knapp refers to as "spectacle" ultimately exploits and subverts the participants' messages.

Rapping argues that the discursive exchanges which occur are neutralized by their placement in daytime. She describes her conflicting feelings about the genre:

> This is as close as television gets to open discourse on serious issues. But it is only possible because the issues discussed are not taken seriously by those in power. And that is why the sensationalism of these shows is double-edged. If they were more respectable in their style and choice of issues, they'd be reined in more.[33]

Knapp contends that the structure and tenor of episodes of *The Oprah Winfrey Show* that pertain to gay issues "insidiously undermine any possibility of a positive response to their lesbian guests."[34]

These authors do not question participants to ascertain their perceptions of the forum or to learn of the outcomes they experienced after the shows aired. Only one small, unpublished study has utilized interviews with talk show guests to provide insight into factors that motivate participation. Rona Feder explored the genre's frequent coverage of white supremacists and found that members of hate groups believed that new converts would be drawn to their organizations as a result of the publicity.[35]

The stance of many of the critical articles generally suggests that participants are "cultural dopes"[36] who are unaware of the potential pitfalls lurking in this contested space. In the chapters that follow, participants speak for themselves, explicating their desire to take part in the pro wrestling-type matches that often occur. They are hardly "cultural dopes," as their interview data reveal; instead, they are savvy contestants ready to join the fray for a variety of strategic purposes.

Mimi White cautions that "it is important to remember that there is little in contemporary American culture that escapes commodification. This cannot be, in itself, automatic terms for absolute critique: the issue instead is negotiating one's position within this context."[37] Issues of differential power and the struggle for self-inscription in this curious genre will surface throughout this text.

Overview of Method

Various exigencies led to an unusual and emergent methodology.[38] The primary target group I interviewed comprised "ordinary" people who had discussed a sensitive topic on *Donahue*. By using the term ordinary—and readers will discover that these folks are hardly ordinary—I mean that celebrities, experts, and people who hid their identity were excluded. Participants who were actively marketing books were not pursued, except for one sample case. Most had appeared on several talk shows.

A rough selection criterion was utilized by primarily seeking disclosers who had discussed topics of a sufficient level of intimacy.[39] In brief, the television disclosures pertained to norm-breaking behavior, sexual topics, and behaviors considered undesirable or embarrassing.[40] One couple who participated in a "best husbands" episode that required very little disclosure was included despite the low intimacy nature of the topic because of their proximity to the researcher.[41] They also provided a useful extension of the range of disclosure for analytic purposes.

At the outset, three components were expected to prove to be important to participants' deliberations to appear: (a) the hosts, perhaps because of perceptions of therapeutic expertise or because of perceived friendships with them; (b) personality and situational characteristics of disclosers, such as various salient goals or the extent of social support networks; and (c) characteristics of the medium and of the genre in particular. These three elements, which interact synergistically, were the focus of the areas discussed during the interviews (see Appendix B for the questionnaire used).

Access to guests who had discussed personal topics on daytime television talk shows proved to be a major obstacle. The executive producers of *The Oprah Winfrey Show, Donahue* and *Sally Jessy Raphael* were unwilling to permit access to their guests or to assist in contacting former guests.[42] The methods of this study were greatly affected by the shows' refusal to cooperate.[43]

When access negotiations with Donahue's staff seemed promising, the *Donahue* show was videotaped and archived daily from January 1 through June 30, 1991. By the time the negotiations fell through, several months of taping had been completed. As a result, *Donahue* became, by default, the target of this investigation. As it turned out, this was fortunate, because more specific information is provided about the panelists during the general course of the program than the other shows generally reveal. These divulgences, although infrequent, facilitated informant contact. The program is also the longest running of the national daytime talk shows, with others in the genre patterned after it.

Thirty-seven people served as the core group whose stories are told in this book. Three others (Bud, "Sam," and Rocki), who had not appeared on *Donahue* but had participated in other major shows, were also interviewed when I happened to come across them as the work progressed. I also spoke informally with several "experts" who had appeared on talk shows to garner their opinions of the genre.

A variety of methods were used to find talk show guests. The process generally worked this way: Taped episodes of *Donahue* were carefully viewed to look for clues for how participants who disclosed on the show might be reached.[44] Labels such as "Dolores French/Arrested for prostitution" provided the correct spelling of the name. The other crucial information required was where the person lived. This was very rarely revealed and severely limited the pool of potential informants. The occasional pairing of location and guest name on *Donahue* permitted the study to be carried out without the staff's participation or approval.

The process of tracking down panelists was very time-consuming, difficult, and often fruitless. Unlisted phone numbers were the most common obstacle; as a result, a diverse mix of access techniques evolved. In some cases, contact was very straightforward. For example, one panelist mentioned the more tolerant social climate in San Francisco. Her name was then in the phone book, and it was a simple matter to contact her by phone. One was reached by sending a letter to the prison where she was incarcerated. Addresses of the more advocacy-based participants were occasionally provided at the show's closing. A directory of organizations was utilized in one case in order to reach two swingers who mentioned the "Lifestyles" organization as a sponsor of conferences for swingers.

Panelists often appear on talk shows with their therapists. A man and his wife identified on *Donahue* as struggling with disparate sexual desires, for example, were easy to track down because a caller asked about the location of the therapists' practice. The couple's phone number was then found through directory assistance for that city. Therapists served as an important bridge to the interviewees in other cases as well. I contacted a couple of people whose numbers were unlisted by calling their therapists and asking if they would forward my request to their clients. I provided therapists with my toll-free number to facilitate contact from patients who chose to call.[45]

I employed unusual means to track down informants whose phone numbers were unlisted or who had not appeared with a therapist. I reached one young woman engaged to a man 40 years her senior by calling McDonald's restaurants near the town where she lived until the one where she worked was located. One man who had been labeled a "heavy drinker" on the show was contacted by writing to him in care of the bar he mentioned frequenting in New York City. He responded to my letter via the toll-free number that had been provided for that purpose. Four people were reached by sending letters addressed to them in care of the program.[46]

I met with all but eight of the study participants.[47] Interviews were conducted in a variety of places, often in respondents' homes. Alternate sites included an office, restaurants, a university student center, a church, and a library. I traveled to Washington, DC; McLean, Virginia; Orlando and Ft. Lauderdale, Florida; Los Angeles, Anaheim, and San Francisco, California; New York City; Bridgeville, Pennsylvania; Atlanta and a medium-sized city in Georgia; and to the small towns of Lyman, Wyoming and Perry, Georgia. The interviewing was carried out between May and November 1991 and intermittently during 1993.

Interviews lasted approximately 2 hours, but many discussions were ongoing, as initial interviews were often supplemented with follow-up phone calls. Informants could contact me at any time via my toll-free number, and many often did to alert me to their appearances on other programs or to fill me in on further fall-out they had experienced from participation. Information about their cases was also procured from items they revealed on *Donahue* and other shows.

I conducted face-to-face interviews whenever possible. Sensitivity to the personal nature of the issues that had been disclosed on the program seemed critical. Although specific questions about the program topic (for example, incest or homosexuality) were not asked, these personal subjects were the core around which the interviewing revolved. In a related vein, the difficult task of asking respondents to self-disclose about disclosure was facilitated somewhat in a personal setting.

I was occasionally pretty leery, certainly, about conducting interviews in people's homes and other places of their choosing. I did so despite possible risks because I felt I could obtain a less varnished picture of respondents' personalities if I could observe their off-camera realities. Quite fortunately, the people I spoke to were not only friendly and articulate but had intriguing stories to tell about intimately disclosing before an audience of millions.

NOTES

1. Erikson, 1989.
2. Carter provided this information about profitability in a June 22, 1992 report in *The New York Times*. Matelski, 1991, asserts that only game shows are less expensive to produce. McClellan, writing for *Broadcasting* magazine, set the overall revenue figure (which includes both license fees and barter receipts) for the talk show genre at about 500 million dollars for 1992.
3. Erikson, 1989. Hofacker, 1979, believes the show's unique style also evolved from Donahue's background as a journalist and the presence of women in key staff positions. Phil Donahue credits the studio audience in his 1979 biography for much of the show's success. Their participation happened rather by accident when Donahue found questions contributed by audience members during commercial breaks to be very astute.
4. Donahue, 1979.
5. The show went national in 1969, and the program is now taped in New York City.

6. Erikson, 1989.
7. Hofacker, 1979. Hofacker also describes two shows in the program's history that were taped but never broadcast in any market. These included a program with guest celebrity Tony Randall, whose enthusiastic plugs for presidential candidate George McGovern were felt to be unbalanced by Fairness Doctrine standards of the day, and an episode featuring an unnamed star who reportedly performed so badly that the staff decided not to release it for distribution.
8. See, for example, Laskas, 1991.
9. Carter described the dentist's crusade in the Feb 22, 1992 issue of *The New York Times*.
10. Oprah mentioned this on a May 19, 1992 episode of *The Oprah Winfrey Show*.
11. Steenland, 1990, provides this figure.
12. Yoo, 1993, discussed this new service.
13. Addresses and contact numbers for these organizations are as follows. *Yearbook of Experts, Authorities, and Spokespersons*: 2233 Wisconsin Ave., N.W., Washington, DC 20007, (202) 333-4904. *Radio-TV Interview Report*: 135 E. Plumstead Ave., Box 1206, Lanstowne, PA 19050-8206, (215) 259-1070. The National Talk Show Registry's address is 6660 Reseda Blvd., No. 111A, Reseda, CA 91335.
14. The phone numbers provided, surprisingly, are only occasionally toll free. *Geraldo's*, for example, is a 900 number that costs $1 to call. Others are sometimes regular numbers with long distance charges for out-of-state calls.
15. Habermas, 1989; Postman, 1985.
16. Meyrowitz, 1985.
17. Munson, 1993, p. 6.
18. Denzin's (1991) definition of postmodernism includes the following elements that aptly describe the talk show phenomenon: "an intense preoccupation with the real and its representation; a pornography of the visible; [and] the commodification of sexuality and desire" (p. vii).
19. Carbaugh, 1989, p. 137.
20. Crow, 1986, p. 479.
21. Banks, 1990, p. 85.

22. Conrad, 1982, p. 54.
23. White, 1992, p. 137.
24. Masciarotte, 1991, pp. 84-85.
25. Alcoff and Gray, 1993, pp. 287-288.
26. Masciarotte, 1991, p. 89.
27. Tomasulo, 1984, p. 7.
28. Alcoff and Gray's (1993) work contains the strongest criticism. They discuss the need for participants to control the conditions in which disclosures occur in order to maximize the transgressive potential: "An important aspect of this autonomy is the disenfranchisement of outside expert authority over our discourse, obstructing the ability of 'experts' to 'police our statements,' to put us in a defensive posture, or to determine the focus and framework of our discourse" (p. 284).
29. Steenland, 1990, p. 7. Steenland does, however, believe that *Donahue* is unique in the breadth of discussion that occurs on the show.
30. Ono's (1991) critical analysis of *The Oprah Winfrey Show* focuses on what he condemns as a watered-down representation of race. He notes that Winfrey's assertion of her color-blindness may facilitate her crossover appeal but asserts that this stance ultimately dilutes the uniqueness of black culture. Ono suggests that the host herself is packaged and appropriated on her own show.
31. Most notably, Alcoff and Gray, 1993, and White, 1992, mention Foucault.
32. Alcoff and Gray, 1993, p. 262.
33. Rapping, 1991, p. 37.
34. Knapp, 1988, p. 4.
35. These interviews were not the focus of Feder's (1993) study.
36. The term comes from Garfinkel, 1967.
37. White, 1992, p. 80.
38. Methodological notes are more extensively described in Appendix A, as are the several stages of analysis.
39. Highly intimate disclosures include revelations of socially undesirable characteristics and inadequacies. Initial criteria were adapted from Berg and Archer's (1982) suggestions for rating the descriptive intimacy of a disclosure.

40. Three parents are included in the selection of informants because the shows' topics concerned intimate subjects their children are grappling with (AIDS, rape, and sexual harassment).

41. It is interesting to note that this couple, the Bryants, were disappointed not to have the chance to disclose on the show. They had hoped to talk about how they managed to have a happy marriage.

42. Raphael's executive producer at that time, Burt Dubrow, agreed to be interviewed but would not consent to any further participation. Donahue's executive producer, Patricia McMillan, initially agreed to permit interviews with her staff and to assist in a minor way in contacting guests who had appeared on the show. However, their participation entailed that an agreement be signed that allowed their staff to review my dissertation and "make any and all factual and/or editorial changes we believe are necessary to preserve the integrity of the program, its employees and guests." Although I stressed that I would make every attempt to present their views fairly and would allow space for a rebuttal if they did not agree with the findings, they would not budge on the issue of "editorial changes." As a result, I reluctantly withdrew from the negotiations.

43. Additional contextual information about television disclosure is needed. An observation of show routines and recruiting methods would provide important information about the setting, but access privileges are difficult to procure. Elements that warrant further examination include the persuasion techniques used by the staffs and information about what percentage of people refuse or ask to be disguised. It would be interesting to delve into the values of the shows' staffs and hosts to learn what topics are considered off limits because of unspoken—or codified—taboos.

    A content analysis of letters and calls to the shows would yield valuable information about what topics people are willing to disclose. Interviews with those who ask to be featured but are turned down would provide insight into the self-concepts of those who are denied access to television.

44. Several informants appeared on shows that did not air within

the 6-month period of taping. These respondents were located in still more ways. Three (Wendy, Sherrol, and Dolores) were located after separate articles about their experiences on talk shows appeared in mainstream print sources. Another informant, Michael, contacted me to suggest that I might be interested in hearing his story when he read an article about my dissertation. Michael put me in contact with the Lykins, who had appeared on *Donahue* on a 1991 program that featured children with AIDS, an episode that had not aired in my market because of inclement weather. I met four informants (Bud, Rocki, Norma Jean, and Ross) when I appeared on *The Jerry Springer Show* in November 1993 to discuss the talk show phenomenon. A magazine writer passed on "Sam's" number. The initial group of 24 informants, who served as subjects for my dissertation research (Priest, 1992), had—with one exception—appeared in the first six months of 1991. The others were added as research for this book progressed.

45. Patient confidentiality was maintained in this way. The therapists seemed intent on probing my intentions before passing on my request.

46. Because the shows quite routinely forward participants' mail, if I were to do this study over, I would simply write a letter to each panelist and send it in care of the program.

47. Time constraints toward the end of the study limited travel, so some of the later interviews were conducted by phone. I believe I came to know several of these informants better than those interviewed in person, because discussions generally spilled over into several sessions. For example, I still occasionally correspond with Sherrol Miller and Mike Elmeer, two people I have never met.

CHAPTER THREE

CAST OF OUTCASTS: WHO ARE THESE PEOPLE?

The cast of characters whose stories are told in this volume are briefly profiled in this chapter to provide a rough sketch of the kinds of people who appear on talk shows. The diversity of the final pool of interview subjects corresponds with the breadth of topics broached on the genre.

I describe each person here briefly in turn.[1] It is interesting to note that only three asked that pseudonyms be used,[2] and one of these ("Rocki") is a stage name by which the participant is widely known. I stress notable facts about their personalities or lifestyles as they are introduced in order to flesh out their portraits.[3] I provide the labels shown on screen in the description if available; these are indicated by the use of quotation marks.

Norma Jean Almodovar, 42, Panorama City, CA: "Cop to call girl." Norma Jean served 18 months in prison for a set-up pandering charge, which she claims was made against her as retribution for a manuscript she was writing about corruption in the Los Angeles Police Department. Simon and Schuster published the book, *Cop to Call Girl*, after her release. She has appeared on *Donahue* four times and has been profiled by *60 Minutes* because of the harsh sentencing she received. Norma Jean ran for Lt. Governor of California on the Libertarian ticket in 1986, garnering 100,000 votes. She heads the Los Angeles chapter of COYOTE, a group that advocates the decriminalization of prostitution. Enrolled briefly in the Philadelphia College of the Bible after she finished high school, she now describes herself as an atheist.

Sabrina Aset (also known as Mary Ellen Tracy), 48, and Will Tracy, 53, Canyon Country, CA: Leaders of the Church of the Most High Goddess. Sabrina, as priestess, "has had sex with 2,686 men." Former Mormons married for 25 years, Will and Sabrina have children but are very reluctant to discuss them. The couple used to raise lions and claim they once had the world's largest chain of karate schools. He was a building inspector prior to their conversion and owned prime real estate in Santa Monica, CA. She has an M.A. in Chemistry and is a former housewife. At the time of the interview, they were in the midst of a legal battle over whether their religious beliefs are protected by the First Amendment. They later served jail terms for prostitution and pandering. This was an awkward interview at first, because I was uneasy in their church, and they distrusted strangers because of ongoing police scrutiny. After some initial wariness on both sides, they were very friendly and open, often jovial.

Carol Austin, 47, McLean, VA: Carol's husband, a board-certified plastic surgeon, also appeared on *Donahue*. His label read "has performed $28,000 worth of plastic surgery on his wife." A housewife who attended but did not finish college, Carol is a frequent volunteer at her children's school. She is a passionate animal rights advocate who devotes time to trapping stray cats and working to find homes for them. She and her husband are philanthropists, giving $100,000 to world hunger causes alone one year. They are self-actualization enthusiasts, attending est and other workshops.

Ralph Paul Bencivenga, 42, Brooklyn, NY: "Would commit murder to avenge his daughter's rape." Ralph, who holds a B.A. in Economics, is a data processing manager who has worked for the same Fortune 500 company for 25 years. He is married and has three children. He admitted on *Donahue* that he is amassing a stockpile of weapons. Although he frequently is criticized by talk show audiences for being obsessed with revenge, he stresses that he has a well-balanced life. He likes to go to the theater, the library, and on outings with his family. A Roman Catholic, he is active in his church. He practices martial arts two or three times each week.

Carl Blandino, 68, and Michelle Mignella, 28, Pittsburgh, PA: "Husband and wife. He is 68, she is 27." Actually only engaged, Carl and Michelle have lived together for six years. They dance several nights each week and love to skate, paint, and lie in the sun. Carl is retired and does the housework, while Michelle works at McDonald's and at a retirement home. Carl, who seems to manage Michelle's life to a large degree, prompted and corrected her throughout the interview. He is a friendly man who likes to talk about his life and virile accomplishments.

Kate Bornstein, 43, San Francisco, CA: "Male to female transsexual in love with a woman." A playwright and actor, Kate also writes a weekly column about gay issues for a San Francisco newspaper. Her most recent play at the time, *Hidden A/gender*, long running in the Bay Area, deals with complex gender issues. She is a celebrity of sorts in the gay community in San Francisco because of the public nature of her work. She has a degree in drama from Yale and also attended one year of graduate school. Kate, who has been married three times, has a 17-year-old daughter who joined a cult and dropped out of contact with her. Kate seemed very pained by this loss. Currently writing a work about freak shows, she spoke quite movingly and richly about issues of marginalization and speaking out. Her spiritual beliefs are "more along the shamanistic tradition."

"Bryan," 29, Atlanta, GA: "Dedicated sperm donor." "Bryan," who is divorced, has a 4-year-old son. He is very active in the Atlanta Men's Center, where he serves on the board and hopes to move the organization toward more community outreach, particularly mentoring. He is an avid photographer who loves to read myths and legends. He describes his spiritual beliefs as "humanistic mystic." Formerly simply a donor, he now works for a sperm bank.

Raymonda and Dennis Bryant, 41 and 37, Perry, GA: Finalists in a best husband video contest. Residents of rural Georgia, Raymonda is a shoe store manager, and Dennis runs the family business, a machine shop. He is a high school graduate; she has her equivalency diploma. Dennis is a gun enthusiast who sometimes lapsed into long tirades against gun control. She is an avid reader who describes books to her husband in detail. Very happily married after previous divorces, they enjoy spending time together, often camping out in the back yard to watch fireflies.

Jim Cobb, 32, Ft. Lauderdale, FL: "Former homosexual." A devout Christian, Jim is involved in a group called Worthy Creations that tries to help gays convert to a heterosexual lifestyle. His wife, who also appeared on the show, was well along in her pregnancy at the time of the taping. Both have traveled abroad for brief missionary training stints. Jim, a high school graduate, is an artist and works in floral design.

Joe C., 45, Van Nuys, CA: "Has had 100 affairs." Joe, who works for an airline, is also a part-time actor who has played bit parts on television. He is divorced and has two children. A transplanted New Yorker who comes from Italian Protestant stock, Joe says he is an "oddball" who does not watch sports. Instead, he likes to sing at karaoke bars.

Craig Dean, 27, and Patrick Gill, 24, Washington, DC: Gay men "suing for a marriage license." Craig, a law school graduate, and Patrick, who has his B.A. in Business and Fine Arts, have been together for five years. They have brought a legal suit against the District of Columbia for the right to marry. They frequently travel the college circuit to speak about gay rights. Craig manages the legal case and visits an alternative lifestyles bookstore weekly to check out the gay news around the country. They seemed to enjoy the flood of publicity that followed the filing of their legal complaint.

Leanne Dees, 29, Bryan Federal Prison, Bryan, TX: "Convicted of adoption fraud." Leanne has given up six of her children for adoption. Two others—one with Down's syndrome—live with her husband while she serves a 30-month prison term for defrauding couples who say she promised her baby to them. Married for 10 years, Leanne has a rocky relationship with her husband, whom she says pressured her to give up each child. A movie of the week has been made about her, and several tabloid programs have covered the topic—always, in Leanne's view, from the other women's vantage points. Leanne's background is fraught with sorrow. Her mother, who was always in and out of mental hospitals, committed suicide when Leanne was 18. Leanne, a recovering alcoholic who has also been homeless, seems determined to turn things around in her life. She says, "I have a great, great dream of working with handicapped children" and, while she admits it sounds crazy, she says she would like to adopt children—especially those with Down's syndrome. Her formal schooling ended at the fifth grade, but she recently received her graduation equivalency diploma.

Mike Elmeer, 27, Ft. Myers, FL: "Former male prostitute" and, on an earlier occasion, "HIV+." Mike holds 2 two-year degrees, one in liberal arts and one in graphic design. His job at an upscale interior furnishings company involves design work. He is an extremely vivacious and likeable person who seemed highly introspective about his motives. His comments during our phone discussions often veered into long digressions about his former partner and about the AIDS epidemic. He serves on a national speaker's list for AIDS education.

Dolores French, 42, Atlanta, GA: "Arrested for prostitution." Dolores, a working prostitute, is an entrepreneur who operates a phone sex business specializing in fetishes. She never finished college because she was "too busy getting an education to get a degree." She enthusiastically attends MENSA conventions every year. Dolores, who is married to a civil rights attorney, has written a graphic autobiography about the sex industry (entitled *Working: My Life as a Prostitute*). Interviewing her was somewhat imposing, because she would often shoot questions right back at me, and she criticized me for faltering over the word pimp during our lunchtime conversation. Yet, she was also funny and high spirited, and extremely straightforward.[4]

Jenny Friend, 37, and Jim Lightner, 36, Anaheim, CA: "Married couple who swing." Jenny, who is working on her second master's degree (in experimental psychology), is the director of education and research for a swingers' organization called "Lifestyles." Jim, who manages the chemistry teaching labs and the chemical stocks for a university, has "most of a Ph.D." and is now working on two additional bachelors' degrees in computer science and electrical engineering. Married for two years at the time of the interview, they said that 99 percent of their friends "are in the lifestyle."

"Reverend" Bud Green (whose real name is Norm Lubow), 32, Los Angeles, CA: "Uses drugs to worship God." Bud has appeared on a variety of shows (*Sally Jessy Raphael, Jane Whitney, Geraldo, Jerry Springer* and others) but never on *Donahue*. He was raised in a Jewish household but developed a new religion which espouses revolution while on an LSD trip in 1982. He earns a living doing telemarketing and is the lead singer in the "real hard rock" band, Just Say Yes. He dropped out of college, where he said he "majored in revolution." He is notorious for his trademark behavior on talk shows: he lights up a joint on stage. His revolutionary ethic is non-violent and humor-filled; his slogans include "Bongs, not bombs" and "Bud, not blood." Bud, who likes to watch sports on TV, lives with his girlfriend and several cats.

Catherine Harrison, 33, San Francisco, CA: "In love with Kate" (the transsexual lesbian described earlier). Born in London and raised in Canada, Catherine does book-keeping and hypnotherapy for her livelihood. She has written and starred in a play about her former occupation as a professional dominatrix in the sex industry. She attended college for two years and has had extensive acting training. Although she wrestles with frequent bouts of chronic fatigue syndrome, she pushes herself to undertake some activities precisely because they scare and challenge her.

Susen and Ken Henningson, 44 and 42, Lyman, Wyoming: This show was billed in *TV Guide* as "Sisters who swap husbands." Ken is married to Susen, his former wife's sister. The ex-wife moved on to marry Ken's brother. Residents of a small town of less than 2,000 residents, Susen does bookkeeping and tax preparation, while Ken works in a shipping department loading soda ash. Ken left school after the eleventh grade; Susen is working on her B.A. in Accounting. Susen was high spirited and verbal, whereas Ken was very reserved, mirroring their behavior on *Donahue*.

Ross Jeffries, 35, Culver City, CA: Author of *How to Get the Woman You Desire into Bed*. Ross bills himself as the "master of speed seduction" and was pleased when *Chic* magazine called him the "sex messiah of the nerds," a phrase he felt was apt. He earns his living schlepping workshops about seduction and through sales of his book. He also runs a mail order business that sells tapes and books. He has a degree in political science from UCLA. In his words, he is "a certified master practitioner of neurolinguistic programming" and of hypnosis. He is a former comedy writer who trained with an improv comedy group in Los Angeles. Ross practices the martial art t'ai chi ch'uan. He is currently single and, as he instructed me to add, dating.

Wendy KruppDespain, 34, a Georgia resident: Rape survivor who successfully prosecuted her rapist, who was an acquaintance. A former flight attendant now attending veterinarian school, Wendy was shy but decisive as she spoke during the interview. Wendy and her husband, an ESPN sportscaster, frequently lecture to groups about acquaintance rape. An avid animal lover, she has eight dogs and a menagerie of other pets, most of which have been rescued from the roadside. Wendy loves to ride motorcycles and is an expert with a .45-caliber handgun.

Bert Lacquement, 36, San Francisco, CA: Gay male who shares parenting responsibilities with a partner from a previous relationship and a lesbian friend. The identity of the biological father has never been revealed. Bert is a former actor who quixotically stated that he was in "forced early retirement" and would now spend his time painting and writing. Currently single, he is actively involved in his 9-year-old daughter's life.

Charlotte and Pete Lumpkins, 43 and 41, Sacramento, CA: "Married but [she] wants to be with a woman." Married for 14 years, Charlotte and Pete are an African-American couple who have eight children. They seem very devoted to each other and are trying to hold their marriage together despite her newfound lesbian identity. Devout Christians, they used to tour the country as a family, singing and speaking out for their faith. She works at Kmart; he worked at a homeless shelter until it closed for lack of funding. He has a high school equivalency diploma, while she has a 2-year degree and is working to finish her B.A. They are both active in the community and in their church, taking the homeless and drug addicts into their home when no other place can be found. Their comments, distilled in print throughout the pages that follow, lack the lovely cadences of their speech.

Marty and Brett Lykins, 41 and 12, Duluth, GA: "Son has AIDS." Marty, a certified surgical technician, works as a receptionist at a medical office to allow flexibility to attend to Brett's medical needs. Marty's husband is a city engineer. Brett, their only child, is a rather shy teenager who was eager for the interview to end so that he could join his friends. Brett is a Nintendo enthusiast who likes to play basketball and watch MTV. He is a big Atlanta Braves fan.

Sherrol Simpson Miller, 44, Louisville, Kentucky: *The Wall Street Journal* dubbed Sherrol the "queen of the talk shows" for her many appearances. Her first flurry of publicity came when she made the rounds to talk about her brief marriage to a gay con-man bigamist. She also appeared on *Donahue* to discuss her boyfriend at that time, a 24-year-old British citizen whom she met when he took a liking to her after seeing her on an earlier episode of the program. Sherrol, a registered nurse, is an incredibly humorous firebrand who is often asked back to appear on shows because of her wit and what she calls her "kick ass" attitude.

Rocki Mountains (her stage name, clearly), mid-30s, Springfield, IL: "Exotic dancer." Rocki has appeared on a variety of shows including *Montel Williams, The Jerry Springer Show*, and *Sally Jessy Raphael*. She has not yet been a guest on *Donahue*. Renowned for the size of her chest, Rocki is a former Illinois Bell employee who decided to quit her job to become a stripper. Rocki, who has also posed for and written a column for "adult magazines," now owns and manages a bar with her husband.

Donna and Dale Potruski, 43 and 39, Orlando, FL: "Treated for sexual desire problem." Dale, who has his B.A. in Radio, Television, and Film studies, is an account executive at a radio station and works part time as a disc jockey. Donna, who attended college but did not graduate, is in the hotel and convention business. Both were previously married; Donna has two teenage daughters. This was a rollicking interview, with a great deal of wise-cracking. They were very personable but were sometimes difficult to pin down on some of the more intimate aspects of the interview.

"Sam," 43, Myrtle Beach, SC: "Sam" and her 24-year-old daughter have appeared on "sexy moms and jealous daughters" episodes of both *Sally Jessy Raphael* and *The Jerry Springer Show*. She and her husband own and manage a busy restaurant. She enjoys beachcombing, but exclaimed, "I have no time for hobbies!" She studied business in college for two years before a near-fatal car accident interrupted her studies. "Sam" says that religion is "something that's been the center of my life." Raised Methodist, she has since converted to Catholicism, her husband's faith.

Joy Schulenburg, 34, San Francisco, CA: Lesbian who shares parenting responsibilities with Bert (described earlier). A freelance writer who studied drama and media in college but did not graduate, Joy traveled the talk show circuit because of a book she had written about gay parenting. She is now in a committed relationship with her lesbian partner. Both are "fairly strong Buddhists." She described herself with a hearty laugh as a "motorcycle riding, leather-wearing, tattooed dyke."

Lorretta Woodbury, 38, south Texas: "Prosecuted her father for rape 30 years later." Lorretta has survived more than incest. She spent time in a state hospital as a teen after accusing her father of molestation; her brother died of AIDS. She has no formal high school education but has taken some college courses. Formerly a developer in the interactive computer industry, she now owns a business in Texas that supplies fly fishing materials. Plans to make a movie of the week about her story reached the script stage but recently fell through. I met with her in her highly secured home, where she was nursing a rescued, abused doberman back to health.

Heather Wright, 16, Mason City, Iowa: "Dropped out of school/Sexually harassed by school mates." Heather is now attending an alternative school after enduring a long spate of cruel sexual harassment. She lives with her mother, Sandi, 46, whom I also interviewed, and a 10-year-old sister. Heather's parents are divorced. Her mother, who is currently unemployed, is an active member of Parents for Title Nine, an advocacy group that fights for safe schools free from sexual harassment. Heather is a very good student who hopes to work for women's rights as an attorney some day. She has done some modeling; a New York City agency has expressed an interest in seeing her portfolio after watching her on *Donahue*.

CHARACTERISTICS OF TELEVISION DISCLOSERS

The wide-ranging diversity of the sample (from a child with AIDS to a "sex priestess") makes it difficult to generalize about the types of people who disclose on the genre. The variety of disclosure topics is merely one facet of the diversity. The heterogeneity of the sample is also reflected in the degree to which the topic of disclosure concerns a chosen lifestyle. For example, active selection is characteristic of informants such as the swingers or the couple who head the unconventional church, whereas the other end of the continuum is represented by the survivors of rape, sexual harassment, and incest. Somewhere in between, perhaps, are those for whom their sexual orientation has determined their lifestyles; the trans-sexual lesbian and her partner are examples. Another difference is the degree to which the respondents are affiliated with their cause; some are leaders in a legal movement (Will and Sabrina, Lorretta, and Craig and Patrick are examples), others make up the rank and file of various causes, and some have no ties to organizations.

What does characterize the bulk of the informants, despite the diversity, is that some feature of their lifestyles, personalities, or life histories is considered abnormal or deviant to varying degrees by society. Indeed, this atypical or marginalized position was what generally earned them an invitation to appear on the show. Many have been confronted with the negative societal response to their outlier status throughout their lives. Kate, the transsexual lesbian, said, "I've just come to expect general ridicule and hostility. It's real interesting. And when I don't get that I'm very surprised. . . . I've learned to assume that everybody looks at me and goes, 'What the fuck is that?'"

Craig, a gay male seeking the legal right to marry his partner, said:

> When you grow up, everyone says, "Faggot this, and faggot that," and you receive so many media images, negative portrayals of gay lifestyles and lesbian lifestyles, and how bad it is to be gay, and you look at that and say, "I'm gay, so I must be bad." You know, "I'm gay, everyone hates me." You take on that hatred. You take on that homophobia, and you hate yourself.

Patrick, his partner, talked on the show about earlier concerns about letting others know he was gay because of not wanting to be "shunned." Lorretta, an incest survivor, said, "I was expecting backlash. I was prepared for it. I expected it because I felt backlash from this thing for years. That's nothing new for me."

Others in this sample are not members of groups considered deviant by the mainstream but face stigmatizing responses to a particular facet of their lives. Carol, whose spouse is a highly successful and wealthy plastic surgeon, said that her husband was careful to represent his medical specialty favorably "because plastic surgeons are already a little on the outside." Rocki, formerly a manager at Illinois Bell, is often the target of catcalls from men and rude comments from women unless she dresses in such a way that her well-endowed figure is camouflaged. Carl, engaged to a woman 40 years his junior, seemed to have a robust self-esteem but grappled with his relatives' and society's harsh evaluation of his relationship with Michelle. Donna and Dale, successful and attractive, are discreditable, to use Erving Goffman's term, when they reveal that they are seeing a therapist for sexual problems.[5]

Talk show participants share this vantage point as outsiders; to a greater or lesser degree, they are situated on the fringes of society or are willing to talk about a portion of their lives that edges them toward the margins. Surprisingly, even Dennis, a finalist in the best husband contest, who would certainly appear to be an exception to this characterization, described his fishing trips with his friends: "They discuss about their wives and all this. I can't do that because I don't have anything to say other than good, and they don't necessarily want to hear that, because 'Oh, yeah, you, yeah, I know you, but us—' so and so. It kind of puts you out, at a distance, and you can feel it, immediately." Although he and his wife are clearly privileged in their social standing compared to most others in the group, even they *felt* left out and, more importantly, believed issues related to working marriages were topics rarely addressed by the media. This feeling that their concerns were marginalized provided the foundation for participants' rationale for television disclosure, as I discuss later in greater detail.

The people I talked to shared other interesting characteristics. Many had seen a therapist or participated in encounter or support groups to work through a difficult period of their lives or to better understand and accept themselves. Those struggling with issues of rape or incest had received help at crisis centers. Marty, whose son has AIDS, visits a therapist sporadically. Donna and Dale appeared on the show with their therapists, whom they had been seeing for a year and a half. Carol, who had had thousands of dollars of plastic surgery, said, "We've done est and mind control, and we've done hours and hours of self-esteem workshops." She also mentioned, "I belong to a woman's group that we've been meeting for years, once a month, 15 of us." "Bryan" is very active in a men's group that explores personal issues. Several others had also received counseling to discuss the central element of their television disclosure or for attendant problems in their lives.[6]

Talk show participants I spoke with seemed to have reached a point of emotional stability after a process of harsh self-examination. Michael said, "I guess I finally came to terms with myself." Both Joe and Sherrol, who had not received counseling, went through a faltering period of grief and withdrawal before shaking off their depression. Jenny, a swinger, related the process nature of her growth:

> When I was a young woman, the whole world tried to convince me that I was—that there was something wrong with me, because I was a sexual being . . . who was more sexual than most of my male partners . . . and it took a lot of working through, a lot of acceptance, a lot of self-exploration, a lot of determination to understand that I am me, and that my level of sexuality doesn't make me wrong . . . that doesn't mean that they are ideal and I am aberrant. It took me a long, long time to accept that. During the course of that period, I went to therapists, yes.

Lorretta described a period three years earlier, in which she grappled with memories of childhood sexual molestation by her father: "I was bro-

37

ken. . . . I was mentally disturbed. And so it took each of those baby steps to get where I got."

This experience of coming to terms with one's special status is an integral part of the rationale to be discussed later; however, it is important to note here that none of the disclosers fit the "fever" model used by William Stiles to describe highly distressed and seemingly inappropriate eruptions of disclosure to strangers.[7] Only Charlotte and Pete, whose marriage is strained by her newfound lesbian lifestyle, and Michael, who disclosed on the show that he had briefly worked as a male escort although HIV positive, are in the midst of a struggle for understanding; the others seem to be well beyond a point of uncertainty about their life choices and predicaments.

Respondents appeared to have social support networks in place that provide them with avenues for self-disclosure. Joy, a gay parent, said, "I've had people I can trust to talk to about it. I came—my mother was somebody I could discuss absolutely anything at all with. You know, and who would hear me out and respect me for my opinions." Raymonda discussed the emotional richness of her marriage to Dennis and spoke warmly of her best friend, "I can definitely talk to her about anything." Carol said, "I have a wonderful network . . . where here every friend that I have in my life are people that I actually have chosen, so that the network of support is unbelievable because otherwise they wouldn't be in my life." The presence of strong social support networks indicates that this group of talk show participants is not turning to a televised forum out of a desperate need for an outlet for self-disclosure.

Most shared an ethic of openness in their dealings with others.[8] Joy, a lesbian parent, said, "I've got a big mouth and I'm pretty much into, you know, let's get skeletons out of the closet." Dale, a panelist whose on-screen label read, "has less sexual desire than his wife," asserted, "I think that the people that really know me know that like, I'll talk about anything at the drop of a hat, you know, and keep very few secrets." Jim Cobb, who once led a gay lifestyle, said, "I've shared my testimony in depth and in detail with a lot of people, and so I was ready to do that." Susen, whose husband was previously married to her sister, said, "We've lived in a small town all our lives, and everybody knows your skeletons. I mean, really, everything's been revealed. Whatever you did, you've already paid for." Wendy, a rape survivor, said, "We don't keep secrets in our family." Carl, a 68-year-old who boasted about his virility on *Sally Jessy Raphael*, said, "I wanted to be open. I'm not ashamed of what I can do."

Similarly, Bert, a gay parent, said, "Most of my secrets are, you know, pretty public, and I don't have—I'm not much in denial about anything." Craig said, "Patrick and I are comfortable with ourselves. You know, we're out to our families, we're out to our friends." Sherrol asserted, " I don't rope off anything." Norma Jean said, "My husband says, you give me five minutes, I tell you my life story." She listed several private aspects of prison life and noted that she would talk about any of them: "I might be embarrassed, but if I thought it would serve a purpose—." The informants also seemed very open in the interview sessions for this work, often revealing unflattering elements about their lives as well as positive ones.

Furthermore, most seemed to have a strong belief that their lives were not lived for or through other people. "Bryan" commented, "I'm a live and let live person. If you don't like the way I live, then don't live the way I live." Charlotte said in response to criticism from the *Donahue* audience: "Nobody's going to jump in the grave with me. I'm doing this of my own choice."9

They seemed, for the most part, absolutely unfazed about appearing in front of the cameras and, by extension, millions of people. Susen responded to a question about whether she had been nervous: "The only thing that scares me is death and going to the dentist. And swimming." Sherrol said, "I'm not scared of anything. I have tackled some rough tasks and emotionally challenging things in my life. Why would I be scared of a talk show?" I think this lack of fear springs from the often difficult circumstances of their lives. For example, Marty's life and death battle with her son's illness threw such things as fear in sharp perspective.

I was also struck during the interviews by the adventurous nature of the group. When I remarked on this fact during an interview with Donna and Dale, who had described many nervy things they had done in their lives, he exclaimed: "If you said, 'Hey, you know, I know it's a little bit like dark out, but there's a tower out, do you want to bungee jump?', I might consider it." Carol described her continuing quest to test herself: "I jumped off a 10-story building, with a thing to catch me, and—I did everything to push myself for 10 years." She said of her husband: "I saw the chance to be with a person that didn't have limitations."

I believe the curiosity and thrill-seeking tendencies were part of the reason they agreed to talk to me and played a role in their willingness to appear on the show. Jim Lightner said of the opportunity to be on *Donahue*: "Here's something new. Let's see what it's like." Similarly, Susen's response was, "Why not? I mean, let's do something different for a change. 'Cause all we do is go hunting and fishing. The same old, same old." Many expressed a hunger for new challenges. Sherrol said, "I make things happen for me. I want to experience lots of things. I'm just not going to sit home and bake cookies and go to work and come home. If I had the humdrum life that most people have, I would just probably just . . . jump in the ocean."

Most saw the call to participate as a rare opportunity. Ken said of the invitation to appear: "Just to do something that many people don't get a chance to do." Rocki said, "I really didn't know what to expect. I wanted to do it because I thought it would be fun. I never thought I'd have a chance to do anything like that."

When the call came from the producers, then, these personality features seemed to predispose them to jump at the chance to do something new, perhaps a little crazy, and definitely an activity most people they knew had not experienced. Several seemed to have a general shorthand for decision making that boiled down, in their words, to "Why not?" rather than a tendency toward hand-wringing and minute examinations of a choice's pros and cons. "Sam" said, "We had no reservations. We thought of it as an adventure. Just something else to add to our memories."

Importantly, many were quite sure of themselves and not embarrassed by their life choices or circumstances. Norma Jean said, "I don't drink, I don't smoke, I don't do drugs. I'm just a whore, that's all." Susen, who drew criticism from the audience for marrying her sister's ex-husband, said, "Really, there's nothing wrong about it; it's just weird, unusual, more or less." Carol, whose disclosures about her many plastic surgeries included a graphic visual dimension, with before and after photographs shown of her in underwear, said: "If someone calls me a Barbie doll, I mean, I know so much I'm not. I'm so okay with myself as a person that there's not anything anybody can really say to me to—disarm me."

Sherrol initially felt terribly humiliated after her brief marriage to a con-man bigamist. She said, "When it finally sunk in that I was a *victim*, that turned the whole thing around for me." Similarly, Heather said, "I didn't do anything wrong. So it's not embarrassing to me—to say what happened to me. It's—I look at it more as an accomplishment, 'cause I made it through that."

Three last commonalities warrant mention because they are notable in their absence. First, only 5 of the 40 informants reported that they had received payment for their television disclosures.[10] Sherrol, Norma Jean, and Dolores were pros at the business and almost always received a fee.[11] Norma Jean and Dolores garnered AFTRA (American Film and Television Recording Artists) earnings, which according to Norma Jean, hovered around the $600 mark.[12] Sherrol, who has appeared three times on *Donahue*, never requested a fee but was such a popular guest that she received payment each time she was asked back. Kate and Joy occasionally asked to be reimbursed for work missed. The majority of participants received no material remuneration from the show staff for television disclosure. A few did, however, stipulate that their address be shown in a chyron, or still frame, at some point during the show taping, in what was essentially a free advertisement for their causes.

Secondly, respondents stated that they were almost totally unaware of the camera and monitors during the show taping. Most found the give-and-take character of the discussion so engrossing that the televised nature of the event was overshadowed by the demands of the conversational interplay that unfolded. Wendy said, "I don't even remember a camera being there." Raymonda said, "I never looked. I was so busy watching the audience." Sandi said, "Once you start talking, you—we're just all so passionate about this issue, you even have a tendency to just sort of even block out the audience." Many reported that the studio audience's heavy involvement made them feel like only one of many participants. Donna, for example, said, "I have to admit that I became a little bit mesmerized with the audience. . . . I relaxed almost immediately on the show because I felt like I was the audience and that they were the guests." Although most had planned their disclosures to varying degrees well aware of the national audience, it appears that the saliency of the camera and monitor receded during the real-time experience.

A third area of surprising commonality for this group is that there was no evidence of a parasocial relationship, a term coined by Donald Horton and R. Richard Wohl to describe the deeply felt but unreciprocated tie that some viewers express toward favored celebrities. Although many were rather excited to meet Phil Donahue and liked him, none were intense fans. Raymonda, for example, said, "He was just a dude. He was just a guy who had an hour show on television. He started it all and then all these other people started cropping up." Ken commented, "It had nothing to do with [being] fans or nothin'—you know, that we really liked him." Only Carol and Sandi expressed any degree of prior affinity, linked largely to Donahue's long tenure on daytime television. Carol said, "I felt like I've always known him, because, you know, Donahue's been on the air for 20 years." However, she and the others knew very little about Donahue except that he was married to Marlo Thomas.

The prior assessment for most informants of Donahue's expertise or character was limited to a belief that he would be fair. Jenny said:

> And I thought Donahue would be the most fair, would be the most open. [Why?] Well, I—just the few times that I've watched Donahue, I've—I've felt that the treatment of his panel was um, to incite controversy, yes, but not to be derogatory to members of the panel themselves, as opposed to um, Geraldo, who I had seen be derogatory.

Her husband, Jim Lightner, added, "More of a good debate forum." An expanded treatment of the informant's beliefs about Phil Donahue and the genre of daytime talk shows will be presented in Chapter Six.

In short, and as will be expanded on in later chapters, these were very lively, articulate people unafraid—in fact, eager—to step into a contested forum to discuss their lifestyles. They believed in openness and risk, and they were self-confident, unwavering, in their belief that there was much to be gained by self-disclosing on television.

NOTES

1. Respondents are described in pairs in those cases where both informants were interviewed simultaneously. Importantly, information provided in this section—items such as age and occupation—are from the date of the interview.
2. People chose to use their real names primarily because they felt they had nothing to hide. Furthermore, they had already come out nationally about the topic on *Donahue* and other shows. Some, like Sandi, purposefully shouldered the public role so

that people whose children were being sexually harassed at school could contact her for information and support.

3. Two of the respondents are African American; the others are of European-American ancestry.

4. Unfortunately, because of a mistake on my part, the tape recorder malfunctioned during my interview with Dolores. I gleaned several direct quotes peppered throughout this book from her autobiography, *Working: My Life as a Prostitute*.

5. Goffman, 1963.

6. Susen and Ken were among a handful who had not received counseling. She said, "People are different out here [in Wyoming]. Guys, even if you have a problem, wouldn't go to a counselor." Later, she added, talking about the complex marriage ties within her family, "Really, why would you want to talk to somebody about it? There's really nothing wrong with it."

7. Stiles, 1987.

8. McCroskey and Richmond, 1990, call this the willingness to communicate. The authors note that there are cultural differences in this trait.

9. February 22, 1991 episode of *Donahue*.

10. Although many show staffs deny that they pay guests but blame others for doing so, the bottom line is that talk show guests very much in demand are often paid. Cunningham reported in *Glamour* magazine in 1993 that some members of the "Spur Posse" made $2,500 dollars for their appearances on a variety of shows, which included *The Jenny Jones Show* and *The Jane Whitney Show*.

11. Those who had received money did not ask to be paid for every media appearance. Dolores, for example, did not charge CNN or MENSA when she was asked to speak publicly, because she was a fan of both organizations. Norma Jean recounted how she charged Geraldo a hefty fee for her appearances, because she found him "sleazy": "There's no forum for me there at all. So if he wants me as a guest on his show, and he did, then he has to pay us a lot of money."

12. Dolores noted that she also received AFTRA earnings when repeat broadcasts were aired.

CHAPTER FOUR

THE CONTESTANTS: EVANGELICALS, MOTHS, PLAINTIFFS, AND MARKETERS

Again and again, people ask me, "Yes, why *do* people go on talk shows?" To delve into issues of motivation, I asked talk show guests questions about what drew them to disclose, what factors figured into any weighing of whether to participate, and what conceptions of the genre, the hosts, and the potential audience they held. This chapter and the three that follow examine these and related questions organized according to Lynn Miller and Stephen Read's goal-based model of self-disclosure which takes the discloser's goals, resources, beliefs and strategies into account.

Apparently, self-disclosing on talk shows is very useful on many levels, as each respondent generally mentioned several reasons for agreeing to participate. For example, although it was not the driving force behind their decision, many mentioned that they had never been to New York or wished to return. The invitation to appear seemed like a great opportunity because the plane ticket and lodging were free. Susen, who had never flown and had rarely traveled far afield, described the allure: "Going somewhere I'd never been. 'Cause I'd never afford to go." Marty said: "I was as excited to go to the big city, the big apple, as I was to be on the show. And they were putting us up in the Drake Hotel, which, you know, I've seen on TV. That was going to be nice, I knew."

I have roughly categorized participants into a four-part typology that groups respondents according to the galvanizing factor that drove participation.[1] This typology is useful as a shorthand descriptor of the primary purpose participants were hoping to achieve, but, as with most typologies, the story is undertold by such categorizations. In fact, multiple strains ran throughout each interview.[2]

The driving motivation expressed by most informants, especially for those who represented severely marginalized groups, was a desire to remedy stereotypes and educate a national audience about discrimination and alternative lifestyles.[3] Participants hoped both to educate the mainstream audience and—equally as important—to communicate to others that they are not alone in struggling with a similar dilemma or stigma. I refer to this two-part rationale for discussing intimate details on television as *evangelical disclosure*. The concept was explicitly expressed by Pete, who said, "Even though we started preaching from the pulpit on the street corner, I do see this as the bigger message . . . the tolerance that we all need toward one another. . . . It's still evangelism, really." "Reverend" Bud, constantly seeking venues from which to urge the public to overthrow the government, said, "It gives me a chance to preach to the nation."[4]

This underlying theme of crusading evangelicalism (which I discuss in greater detail in the next chapter) ran throughout almost every interview session, despite the diversity of the informants. This calling to address injustices and remedy stereotypes engulfed other considerations such that any hesitancy about disclosure was outweighed by the perceived benefits to society and to the standing of each one's marginalized group.

The relative emphasis of this factor for each informant differed widely, however, such that the remaining informants fall into three groups.[5] Those whose primary, overriding rationale might be summarized as a yearning for "15 minutes of fame"[6] represent a group I call *moths*. They said the imagined razzle dazzle of the television business beckoned to them like a siren. Several stepped forward primarily as *plaintiffs* to plead their cases against people who had victimized them. Lastly, the *marketers* are those who eagerly seized the chance to hawk a book or business venture. Like the core group of informants who are solidly evangelical in their intent, the members of these three groups also often expressed a desire to provide encouragement to beleaguered others and to educate the public, but evangelicalism was not the determining factor in their decisions to participate.

MOTHS

This category comprises a small set of participants whose primary rationale revolved around the opportunity to be on television, often fulfilling a life-long dream. Lured by the flickering light of the screen, Bert's rationale places him squarely in the moth category. He said:

> What propels you? Um, that old Andy Warhol, for me that Andy Warhol thing, 15 minutes of fame—yeah, that. If I'm on TV, I'm worthy of something, because there's a lot of people watching me. You know, it is ah, grand self-affirmation. . . . So that's one of the reasons I did it for, you know, that fame stuff.

Carl, "Sam," Donna and Dale, and Susen and Ken also fit this category. Susen said:

> I always wanted to be [on television]. My little sister—my dad was in uranium, and she was on TV when she was like a year old. Her and dad and our dumb dog, and we've got this picture of her that went on national television cause he was really making the bucks in uranium. . . . Well, I was kind of jealous that she was picked to be on TV because it was the "Little Susen" mine that had made the money, not the "Donna Jean." And I thought that was unfair, that she should get on TV.

This early incident seemed to play a formative, if lightly examined, role in her desire to take her rightful place in the TV netherworld. Later in the interview, Susen elaborated on her desire to appear:

> You know, to be able to say, "I'm on television." 'Cause we had a blast telling everybody we was gonna be on television. . . . So I think it had something to do with it, yeah. And I was kind of curious to see what it would look like on television, 'cause you look in the mirror everyday, but it's still different.

Sixty-eight-year-old Carl, engaged to a 28-year-old, had similar yearnings. He had written to *Sally Jessy Raphael, The Oprah Winfrey Show*, and *Donahue* to suggest that his relationship with Michelle would be a good topic for their show. He commented:

It's something I always—I've wanted to be in show business and this—since I come out of the service, my wife would not go to California. . . . I was ready to start out as a dancer. I told her, "If you'da taken me out, you never would have heard of Fred Astaire and—and Gene Kelly." 'Cause that's how good I was. . . . And I wanted to go on stage and do that. Well, this is the closest I can come to being on stage.

Dale, who appeared with his wife to discuss their dissimilar sexual desires, said that as a child, he had often told people he was going to be a game show host when he grew up:

In my circumstance when I heard like that uh, there was an option to be on *Donahue*, my thought was like, you know, not like, "Why me?" but like, "Why did it take 'em so long?". . . . I never paid attention in class 'cause I was too busy practicing my autograph. I was going to be a rock hero or something.

"Sam's" yearnings seemed less overtly conscious. She described watching talk shows on various topics such as chronic fatigue syndrome and thinking, "I wish I were on that panel, I could really tell 'em.'" When asked if she literally thought of appearing on a show, she replied: "I never thought of ever, you know, being on TV." Yet, when *The Sally Jessy Raphael Show* broadcast an appeal for daughters to call in if they felt their mothers were too sexy, she herself called in pretending to be her daughter. This seemed out of character, so I asked, "What did it mean to you, the chance to call the line?" She responded:

It's really strange, because it was just like I was—I was supposed to call at that *moment*, I guess—I don't know, and I'm not a celebrity type person . . . and I'm not one of these that wants to be seen and heard all the time, that's not me at all, but um, like I said, for some reason, it just sort of grabbed me, and I thought . . . somebody needs to know about, you know, about what it's like [when mother and daughter look very much alike]. 'Cause there's like, we've—I've seen shows before, they've had mothers and daughters, but [my daughter] and I really had a good story to tell, really a good story to tell.

The allure of stepping into the spotlight was the driving force behind these seven participants' rationale for participation. They jumped at the chance to step in, and, in fact, some had long been waiting for the spotlight of attention to spin around.

PLAINTIFFS

The plaintiffs' rationale often echoed of an opportunity to be on the *People's Court,* as participants hoped to receive a sanction for their behavior and a censure of the other party's actions.[7] Donahue, in fact, often refers to the audience as a jury, heightening the sense of his program as an extrajudicial court of opinion. Michael had petitioned the talk shows for the opportunity to tell how he had been betrayed by his former partner, who had slept with him without revealing he was HIV positive. Michael had talked to a lawyer but was told at the time that there was no legal recourse for such cases. Similarly, Ralph found the police could not help him secure justice for his daughter, whose rapists had not been caught.

Many found that the judicial system had failed them and felt the talk show genre offered another opportunity to court favor or seek redress in the court of public opinion. Leanne said:

> I felt like I was the only one that could stop the cycle—from years and years ago, I had been taken advantage of. I've been used; I've been hurt. And I was allowing it to continue in my life by allowing Debbie [her chief accuser] to slander me, and I was still allowing this abuse to go on . . . and I had to draw the line, I had to stop it, and wasn't no one going to tell my side of the story except me. And I had to let people know that I'm not a bad person.

Talk shows occasionally feature men and women from prison who are trying to influence the outcome of their appeals. Leanne, however, did not seem to be participating with an eye toward the appeals board, because people had told her that the Board of Prisons frowned on such publicity seeking. Instead, she wanted to clear her name, and she reminded the *Donahue* audience that not everybody who is in prison is guilty. She said of deciding to appear on *Donahue* despite the risks to her clemency hearing:

As I said my prayers, before I went, you know, before I set down in that chair, I said, you know, "Lord, if I lose that appeal, that's OK, because I just want people to know that I'm not a bad person, regardless of what happens, if I end up serving the full three years, and never get my two kids back, I just want people to know that I love all of my kids, that I would never use my kids for financial gain."

Although plaintiffs do not make up a large portion of the respondents I spoke to, I believe they constitute a growing proportion of talk show participants as the genre moves to more squabble-type shows pitting mothers against their daughters and other pairs willing to disclose about each other's habits. A September 10, 1991 episode of *Donahue*, for example, featured a "deadbeat father" who owed tens of thousands of dollars in child support. When asked by an audience member why he agreed to appear on the show, he replied, "I didn't expect a lot of sympathy; I just wanted people to basically hear my side of the story and let people know that I'm—I'm human. I'm not a monster." Similarly, a convicted rapist who appeared on an April 4, 1991 episode of *Donahue* responded to a similar question during the program: "So everybody knows I'm not so bad after all."

When persuading potential guests to appear, the show staff fosters a sense that the real story will finally be told. Leanne was concerned about appearing on *Donahue* because her chief defendant, who tirelessly had worked to put Leanne in jail, would be there on stage as well. Leanne described how the producer said, "We're doing this for you. We are not, you know, doing this for her and then having you come on to defend yourself." Later, she continued: "It's real hard to resist. . . . 'We want to help you' is the big sales pitch." Groups other than the plaintiffs were rarely prodded with a hard-sell campaign; they did not generally need to be talked into appearing.[8]

Ralph, Michael, and Leanne each spent a lot of time during interviews with me talking about the particular people who had wronged them. For example, when I asked Michael about who he envisioned in the audience, he replied wistfully:

I guess I always wanted [his former partner] to see it. I mean, I hate to say that, but you always—I think the person you're victimized by, you fantasize is out there watching you. I'm sure you've heard this from others. You want to show them, because there's no communication between he and I—I think you want to show him, or that person, you know, whether it's the rapist who raped the woman— it's a lot of that—I think it's your way of showing that person that I'm going to do whatever it takes to survive what you did to me.

Michael is an interesting case study of a plaintiff, because his tumultuous emotional state at the time of his first of two appearances on *Donahue* made him very vulnerable to the genre's potentially negative forces. Michael admitted, "I think I gave them the ammunition they need to use against me" because, in an effort to get on, he had revealed the fact that he had briefly worked as a male prostitute. He related that bit of information in letters to various show staffs because he knew that it would be likely to hook producers, and because he felt the behavior was an indication of how low he had sunk after being victimized by his partner.

Crucially, however, the three-week stint at an escort service was not a defining feature of Michael's self-concept, and whereas he was willing to admit to past mistakes, that subject was not what he wanted to get on the show to discuss. Instead, as a plaintiff, he wanted to relate the story of how his former partner had placed him at great risk. The *Donahue* show, naturally, focused on the prostitution angle. Before the show, Michael had been thrilled that he was asked on, despite the fact that his parents would learn about his job as an escort at the same time *Donahue's* audience did. He said: "I felt like I had finally succeeded in— in the cause that I was fighting for, and that's that I had been victimized. So I was still living in this sort of euphoria about the *Donahue* producers want to talk to me because of my victimization."

Plaintiffs often participate while in a state of highly charged emotion, still feeling wronged, and they believe evidence that the other person is the true culprit is amassed on their side. The range of disclosure Michael volunteered to share for the privilege to appear as a plaintiff on *Donahue* caused both episodes to spin out of his control. He bemoaned the fact that he ended up looking like the villain as a result.

Ralph's willingness to be on any and all talk shows sprang from his rather single-minded pursuit of his daughter's rapists. He said, "I feel like this is the only way I can fight." He took every opportunity to reach the public with the story of his daughter's rape and abduction on the slim chance that the perpetrators would be apprehended by a tip from an audience member who might recognize the men from a composite drawing he exhibited when permitted. In fact, the police did get "an enormous amount" of calls, and viewers donated reward money. Ralph sorrowfully described appearing even on local shows in the New York City area that did recreations, a production element his family found very painful. His decision process was simple: "If I can present my case. And seek justice. I can reach out to more people. . . . I know that the media can get me that kind of profile, that kind of exposure."

MARKETERS

An appearance on a talk show serves as a free commercial in a national venue with advertising rates that most small and mid-sized companies find prohibitive.[9] Rocki, who at the height of her talk show spate of appearances was an exotic dancer touring Canada and the United States, said, "I went on the show really more or less for publicity for my new career."

Carol's lovely appearance essentially functioned as a mannequin for her husband's board-certified expertise, as he had shaped her face and body in a series of plastic surgeries.[10] She said:

> Plastic surgery is more like a—of course, my husband would die if he heard me say this, but it's true, it is more like a business. . . . There is a part of it that you want to be known. And you merchandise yourself, and you become known, and so, I've always done that, and so I make a good team-mate for him because I've been a very good asset for him in business.

Discussing the graphic before and after photographs shown on the show, she admitted, "It's embarrassing—[but] it's part of the game."

Marketing on talk shows is a very common reason for appearing. I generally excluded talk show participants who were clearly stumping to sell their books or other merchandise, but did choose one, Ross Jeffries, to profile this strategic use of the medium.

Ross is a man the audience loves to hate, and his mock confrontational manner has earned him billing on countless talk shows. He uses his appearances to plug his book and taped series about seduction, and he definitely ratchets the spectacle into high gear to gain attention. Ross compared the talk show format to pro wrestling:

> I play the bad wrestler. I'm the guy who throws salt in the eye, pulls the hair, and gouges when the referee isn't looking. . . . I always liked the bad wrestler, the guy who hit the guy before the bell even started, pulled a little piece of metal out of his trunks and gouged the guy in the face.

He said his decision to appear boils down to "Will it make me money?" The marketing link is indirect, because the women who make up a large portion of talk show audiences hate him. "But," he says, "it gets recognition."

Ross's talk show career began when he placed an ad in *Radio/TV Interview Report,* a trade publication targeted to talk show producers. He paid $400 for an ad that read, "'Women hate nice guys,' says sex book author." When invited to appear, he always asks that his address and number be exhibited on-screen, so that he can market his catalog via this free commercial. He declared, "I am essentially a marketer." He continued wryly: "I come from a family of bullshitters. I mean, my father's father, my grandfather, was a con man on the streets of New York. . . . My father saw me on TV, and he said, you know, 'Your grandpa Abel is looking out from heaven and smiling.'"

"Sam" told me about a mother and daughter team she met on *The Jerry Springer Show* who appeared solely to further their careers. "Sam" recounted how the mother turned to her moments before the taping began and said:

> I hope you understand . . . but we have an ulterior motive for being here. We're from California, and my daughter's an aspiring actress, and I'm an aspiring talk show host, and so we are going to get as much in for as long a period of time as we can. So please don't be offended, you know, if we don't give you time to say anything.

Marketers tended to be the least evangelical; the forum simply represented an excellent opportunity for promotion. Furthermore, they tended to be less disclosing; they were there to talk about the product.

CRISS-CROSSING STRAINS

The nonevangelicals were not wholly self-serving in their reasons for appearing; most, like the evangelicals, also expressed a desire to provide more positive depictions of their group or to help others. For example, Donna and Dale, who were moth-like in their attraction to the medium, also expressed an evangelical intent. Dale said:

> I mean, I was really anxious and eager to be involved and have the opportunity to like maybe shed some light on like a problem that evidently, as stated in the opening part of the tape, is ah, you know, a situation that affects a major percentage of, like, men or couples . . . how did they deal with it, this is how I dealt with it.

Moths, marketers, and plaintiffs were, however, far less evangelical and were more likely to comment that the trip's perks were an additional incentive. Bert said that what cinched the deal was "more for the trip and the food." Susen, who lived in a Wyoming town of less than 2,000 residents, said, "And besides, it was a free vacation."

The various strains in the typology are present for many evangelicals as well. For example, although Sherrol is best characterized as an evangelical because of her passionate desire to warn people about con artists, she was also excited to have the chance to expose her former husband:

> I wanted to get even with this guy. Listen, this guy had ripped off, he had married 10 women, had hurt many children and women and ruined many lives. And he would just go from place to place and relocate, and set his life up and just live a happy, happy life. And I wanted to expose him. I would have liked to put him in prison, but he just always acted within the arm of the law.

Evangelicals, who seemed earnest in their desire to transform society, also admitted that there were ego-related reasons for going on the show, such as the perks, the excitement, and the opportunity to be seen on television. These elements, however, were the icing on the cake; what mattered most was access to a televised pulpit from which they could reach millions.

Respondents frequently used terms such as *opening, gift, doorway, window*, and *avenue* to express their belief that the shows presented a valued means to connect with others. The strategic nature of the act of television disclosure across this typology of disclosure rationale was striking. Participation stemmed from a desire to strategically correct stereotypes, to step in the limelight, to tell one's side of a story, or to sell.

These strains can usefully if somewhat awkwardly be addressed all at once because of the broad reach of the medium. Plaintiffs capitalized on the wide sweep of the broadcast wave to pick up in its path their victimizers, whereas others sought to reach the millions listening in that day.

NOTES

1. Derlega and Grzelak, 1979, identified five functions of self-disclosure for nonmediated interactions which include: (a) expression or catharsis, (b) self-clarification, (c) social feedback, (d) relationship development and maintenance, and (e) control over others. They stressed that research needs to be done that illuminates why people self-disclose and what value the act holds for participants.
2. Some participants' rationale changed as experience with the talk show format altered their views about the power of the medium. After receiving repeated thanks from people who felt their outgroup had been well represented, disclosers often came to be more evangelical. On the other hand, participants like Sherrol, originally primarily an evangelical, learned that appearing on shows was fun and easy, and she would accept the opportunity to speak on any topic that producers came up with for her.
3. Parasocial interaction may underpin the rationale for participation more prominently for panelists on other shows, and further differences may be discovered as well. However, many informants had disclosed on a variety of programs. Other studies will be needed, however, to learn more about individuals who appear more selectively.
4. Bud said this on *The Jerry Springer Show* on November 22, 1993 and in conversations with me.
5. Fourteen informants are classified as nonevangelical in their primary intent. One of them, Michelle, merely appeared because of Carl's moth-like drive to garner attention for their relationship and for himself. Other moths are Bert, Susen and Ken, Donna and Dale, and "Sam." The marketers are Carol, Ross, and Rocki. Plaintiffs include Leanne, Ralph, and Michael, although both men showed strong traces of evangelicalism as well.

6. This well-known phrase comes from Andy Warhol, 1969.

7. Plaintiffs sometimes appear with their lawyers, although none of this group did. Participants often are conscribed in what details they can tell so that they are not at risk for being sued for slander. For example, Sherrol could only use the first name of the con artist who cheated her, and Michael never used his former partner's name on the show. Nor did they show pictures, although several would have liked to.

8. Most people jumped at the chance to appear because of the goals they hoped to fulfill there. However, another common pitch participants reported was that the producer would say, "This will help other people."

9. I interviewed Ross after I met him at a taping of *The Jerry Springer Show*, although it was clear that he was hawking a book and other merchandise. A handful of the evangelicals also had books to sell, but the books often came later in their talk show careers, as was the case with Norma Jean and Dolores. Joy had also written a book, but was not pushing it; in fact, she mentioned during the interview that it was generally not in stock during the first round of appearances because of a problem with the publisher. I first saw Joy on a repeat show that occurred long after she had written her book, which she did not mention on the show.

   People's stories are saleable in the current crush of attention given to reality-based dramas. Some who seek to get on talk shows hope to get the attention of a producer who will give them a movie-of-the-week deal, for which the earnings can be great. Leanne's main nemesis garnered $67,000 from selling her story rights; Leanne earned $7,000, every dollar of which was immediately remanded over to the judge. A young family who had been lost in rural Nevada in a snow storm for 8 days who appeared on *Donahue* in 1994 sold their story rights to be made into a movie of the week for an astounding $600,000.

10. Carol was an extremely nice and well-rounded person who was hardly simply a mannequin, although that was the gist of the function she fulfilled on the show. She would have liked to talk about other issues important to her, such as her animal rescue work.

CHAPTER FIVE

PULP PULPITS: EVANGELICAL DISCLOSURE

Access to a valued medium—attaining a pulpit—was key for evangelicals with a message for America. The two-pronged nature of the evangelical rationale includes a broadcasting and a narrowcasting component.[1] Both involve a desire to address questions and alter stereotypes. The broadcasting component of television disclosure refers to the talk show genre's ability to deliver a mainstream audience. The televised revelations are made during an attempt to humanize and broaden the representation of the outgroup, whether they are swingers, gay parents, intergenerational couples, transsexuals, or other groups considered deviant by society.

The prime target of these counterstereotypical messages is the public at large. Craig said: "I think in order to achieve civil rights, people have to see you in a positive light. Visualization, humanization—of us as gay people. You know, as opposed to what the jokes are, and the image of queer, the image of dyke, to say, 'Oh, gee, well, those are real people.'" Craig's partner, Patrick, said: "And I think that this is a situation where they were able to personalize us more to the people that my parents were dealing with on a daily basis and kind of, maybe they could empathize more with me rather than sympathize with my parents having a gay son."

Joy described the desire to communicate with mainstream viewers about gay parenting:

> To try to get that message across, that we are competent, so that maybe when they run across somebody else, again in Iowa and then you know in small town South, is gonna . . . think twice and say, "Well, maybe that's not automatically a liability." Because there's a lot of people getting their kids taken away from them.

Catherine, the gay partner of a transsexual, said:

> I thought it was actually a real gift to be given the opportunity to be
> able to reach millions of people and perhaps change some con-
> sciousness around lesbianism, around transsexuality . . . a positive
> view of something, of our lifestyle, of us, that it could make life a
> lot easier for other people, perhaps those people who've known
> someone else who's going through a transition.

Although most informants were conscious of society's view of
them as deviants, they were striving to demonstrate their normalcy.
Erving Goffman wrote of the stigmatized group member's desire to cast
off labels of deviancy:[2]

> The stigmatized individual can come to feel that he should be above
> passing, that if he accepts himself and respects himself he will feel
> no need to conceal his failing. . . . It is here that voluntary disclosure
> fits into the moral career, a sign of one of its phases.[3]

Stigma management was a driving force in television disclosure, because
participants were aware that stereotypes need to be addressed before
society's boundaries of normalcy might be adapted to let their groups in
under the wire. Television talk shows serve as an available forum for the
"voluntary disclosure" Goffman mentioned.

Several respondents viewed people in the studio audience as sur-
rogates for neighbors and family members who might be hesitant to
inquire about things they found puzzling. One woman, for example, who
appeared with Jenny and Jim on a *Donahue* episode about swinging said
the show was a "great way" for her parents to learn of her lifestyle.
When Donahue and the audience laughed, she continued: "The way we
looked at it is, they're going to have a lot of questions, the same questions that these people have."[4]

"Bryan," who felt that sperm donors were unfairly stigmatized and
therefore used a pseudonym both in this study and on *Donahue*,[5] felt that by
appearing he could remedy negative impressions held by the public:

> If everybody in the world has this perception that sperm banks are
> nothing, you know, but just peep shows run by doctors, and sperm
> donors are nothing but dirty old men in raincoats whacking off for

50 bucks, then the actual usage of the services is actually going to
be sullied. And the children who are the result from that are going to
be stigmatized. And that's just not acceptable to me.[6]

Many hoped to inform the public through their television disclosure about the need for tolerance and understanding. Brett, a 12-year-old
boy stricken with AIDS, said:

I want to try to get people educated—lots of people educated, so
that when people come out, come forward, that they have, um, the
AIDS virus, nobody will be afraid of them, because they'll all be
educated. . . . I think there's still a need for me to go—me or others—to go out and talk about the virus, because someday everybody
is going to know a relative or somebody with AIDS.

Brett was well aware of the persecution experienced by Ryan White and
others who had revealed their HIV status and had been forced out of their
communities. The risks are very real, yet he and his family felt compelled to step forward.

Heather's mother, Sandi, felt their reasons for appearing on television were different from others whom she believed used the genre for
self-aggrandizement. She said: "It's not for the personal publicity or to
make our name famous or to—to go on TV and air the—the dirty details
of our horrendous story, but our purpose is for people to know what is
happening in our schools all across the country."

Wendy, who had talked freely with her co-workers in an effort to
educate them about acquaintance rape, said:

And through that, too, I was realizing the level of ignorance about
this crime, and I started realizing that we needed an educational side
here. . . . I think part of it, too, was uh, I had a tremendous amount
of anger at my—my employer, at the legal system, and this was a
way of getting information out, uh, [about] the injustices as well.

Sherrol, too, was frustrated by the limitations of the judicial system, and she stepped forward in a different kind of contested arena: the
talk show. An evangelical thrust is evident in her drive for protection for
both men and women tricked by con artists. She said:

The courts just angered me so badly. They wouldn't do a thing. . . . If you tell 'em you're married to a bigamist, they'll laugh at you. And I thought, okay, if the courts won't help you, and the law enforcement people won't help you, what is next? I thought, one to one. What's wrong with getting together and telling one person, or a group of people, what happened to you and then, just kind of spreading the gospel.

Lorretta hoped to educate the public about the prevalence and pain of incest. She felt the studio audience would be most affected by her testimony. She said, "That's 210 people that'll always have that awareness. That was what it was about for me." Craig said of his choice to seek publicity after their filing of a discrimination suit against the District of Columbia, "And I figured at the very least, if we lost, we could raise some consciousness about oppression, discrimination."

Also of paramount importance was the chance to use the broadband medium to pinpoint a small subgroup of viewers for whom the topic would resonate, people in the viewing audience who were struggling with a similar dilemma. Wendy described her intent: "I think my being out there and talking to people is gonna tell them that they can—if I can get through this, then they can get through this. You can survive this. Just being there tells that." Donna said, "Dale and I needed to get a message across to couples who are in a quandary—and didn't need to be."

Participants valued the opportunity to address others similarly ostracized who might tune in when the day's topic concerned them. Kate, a transsexual, said:

I don't think there was ever really a question of not doing it. I uh— for so many years, I thought I was the only one in the entire world who felt like I felt up until around age 11, I thought I was, and then I heard about Christine Jorgensen. And then even after that, there was no one to talk with about this and there was no transsexuals walking around, "Well, sure, kid, I'll talk to you," and uh, I kind of made a deal with myself, that um, if I was asked to do something, if I had an opportunity to do something like that, I would do it. And so that's why.

Expressions of the desire to target other members of one's marginalized group and assure them they are not alone surface rather frequently on talk shows. For example, a former battered wife said on

Donahue, "We thought we were alone. That's why we're living examples here trying to encourage everybody, anybody in that type of situation, just leave."[7] An episode of *Donahue* on the men's movement showed a group of men in a huddle in the green room prior to the show. The leader solemnly spoke to the others in a warm-up that was a cross between a pep talk and a prayer, saying: "This is for the men out there who need this desperately."[8]

Jenny believed that coming out as a swinger would help others who might be interested in the lifestyle:

> If you see somebody else who is in a situation or who is doing something that you yourself have wanted to do or have doubts about your own self about—to see somebody else who has the courage or the—the basic foundational belief, to get out there and say, "Ah, it's OK," then I think it has the ability for people to accept themselves more. And I think, in that way, that these kind of shows can be beneficial to society.

Respondents had often worked through a period of self-doubt and wanted to ease that painful process for others by providing positive role models and evidence that others like them exist. Joy, a gay parent, admitted she was "addicted" to radio talk shows as a teen and recalled the positive feedback she received after phoning in her thoughts on alternative lifestyles. She said:

> [It] raised my self-esteem tremendously. . . . It made me realize I wasn't alone in some of the thoughts that I didn't know anyone else was thinking. So I'm hoping that, you know, that this will also affect other people who may be isolated and think they're the only ones.

Another common theme was the desire to let others know that untraditional pairings can be successful, rewarding relationships. The opportunity to present and embody working relationships that do not fit the standard heterosexual/same race/same age standard prompted many to appear. Carl said, "Like she [Michelle] said [on the show], 'Love hath no age.'. . . I want people to know that two people, one person older than the other, can make it." Catherine said:

It could make people who are transsexuals themselves not feel alone like I think that perhaps the transsexuals who, when they're going through the change, wonder if they're ever going to have a lover again, uh, to be able to show that, these—regardless of how different one can be, that there's hope for relationships, that there is love there.

Craig and Patrick were partly targeting gay adolescents who might be watching, because they believed that many teen suicides can be linked to the despair of gay teens who feel they face a future of loneliness. Craig discussed the "hundreds and hundreds" of letters he had received as a result of their appearances on talk shows. He summarized the responses, most of which had come from young gay males: "They all say something to the effect that, 'I was feeling hopeless, but you've given me—. . . . I see that one day it's possible that I too may have a loving relationship.'" Craig and Patrick hoped to counter the negative messages about being gay generally communicated by society, and the letters fueled their desire to continue their crusade.

Heather was leery about appearing because she did not know whether the harassment directed toward her in her community would become more intense. She said, "I decided I didn't want this to happen to other people, and if I could help, you know, just one person by saying what I had to say, I'd do it." Many felt a responsibility to speak out on behalf of others who were weak and vulnerable. Joy, for example, said:

I was in a position of um, being, you know, in a really safe situation. I had family support. . . . I was self-employed at the time, and I lived in San Francisco. Most of the people, most of the gay parents that I knew did not have that measure of safety. They risked everything. Somebody has to go out there and speak for them. And speak for the—you know, the people who are really in danger, the people who are living in small towns in Iowa, in a closet, and in danger of losing their kids if they open their mouths. Somebody's gotta be out there and talk. . . . There's an incredible amount of gay-bashing going on. . . . I'm also, you know, in terms of somebody's seeing me on the street and decides to bash because they've seen this is unlikely. I mean, I'm six foot tall and 250 pounds. . . . People don't mess with me, but there is, for a lot of people, there is a significant risk in being public.

Similarly, Lorretta said, "Did you ever go to one of these incest meetings? These are some really groping people; they need the 10 percent like me to be examples for the 90 percent of the others." Brett's parents kept his HIV status secret for two years. His mom recalled that period: "It just tore us up not to be able to feel like we were helping, you know, and speaking out. . . . We feel like now that we're public, we can speak for those who still can't."

Dolores, too, described how she knew she was speaking for many prostitutes, a group she had found to be powerless, spoken for and about:

> At the time I remember thinking, this is going to lift the burden off of everyone. I knew I would be doing it for hundreds of thousands of women. I would be sitting on camera proving that a prostitute does not necessarily wear hotpants or Tammy Faye mascara or have 5-inch nails. I wanted to show them that someone could be mature, intelligent, and pretty and still could say, I'm proud to be a prostitute.[9]

A handful of respondents reported that they hoped to forge connections with fellow outgroup members. Pete, who was trying to adapt to his wife's new lesbian identity, said, "It was like firing up a flare; Hey, it was like shooting up and somebody will see it and recognize each other—coming to the rescue." Sabrina, a high priestess, said: "We feel it might be some kind of universal mind or some vibrations or whatever psychic thing you want to even think of, but people that feel in tune with us will then be able to know, oh, yes, they're out there, and they will try to contact us."

Will, her husband, said, "When you saw the lower thirds [an area of the screen that provided their names and the day's topic] . . . were our names spelled correctly? In other words, we don't care what you say, just so you spell the name right." Unlike more mainstream groups, Will and Sabrina were not allowed to provide their church's address, but they felt people could contact them nonetheless if their names were provided. Will and Sabrina were confident that their message would strike a chord with some members of the audience.

Many felt their message was suitable not only for their particular marginalized group, but for others who are excluded from the mainstream. When asked whom their target audience was, Charlotte replied:

Pat, I want to use the word in a broad sense, it's community, it's people who find themselves different. Or whether they're Oriental, black, Hispanic—got the jokes, heard the jokes. To me, it's lifestyles. . . . So my idea is if you broaden, Pat, if we broaden the door, we could get more people in. Instead of narrowing it. And excluding people. Those that are holding that door open or have charged, so-called, the guard has to change. And as they change that guard, people like Pete and I are willing to broaden that door. To get more people in. [Not just gays?] Whatever they are, you can't exclude them.

Several felt that they represented a more palatable subgroup of a marginalized sector and therefore could sometimes serve more effectively as spokespeople. Marty, when asked what she hoped to do by speaking out, said:

I think to change attitudes, hopefully, and open people's eyes. And, unfortunately, a lot of people still are ignorant and think this is a gay disease and they deserve it. . . . They don't have any sympathy or compassion for maybe a gay man who has it, but a child, they do, and it shouldn't be that way.

Informants reported that both the broadcasting and narrowcasting elements of the opportunity were important to them. When asked which group she was most trying to reach, Joy responded:

A combination. It was equally much so, and I probably, even if I'd only reach one or the other of audience, these two audiences, I would have done it. As it turns out, from the feedback I got, I reached both. One is the public at large who had an opinion and would interact with gay and lesbian parents. The other one were the gay and lesbian parents who were isolated.

Lorretta said: "I most wanted two things: It was twofold, and one's no more important than the other. I wanted to reach other survivors of incest. And I also wanted to reach people. I wanted it to quit being the 'i' word that nobody could talk about." Respondents were addressing both groups simultaneously, just as evangelists preach both to the converted and to those not yet won over to their message.

The term *evangelical disclosure* was purposefully chosen over a more neutral term that might have indicated the disclosers' intent to merely inform. *Evangelical* was selected as a core category partly because it sprang from Pete's use of the word. The term is generally used to indicate members of a conservative Protestant faith who believe fervently in Christ and the authority of the Bible and who feel compelled to spread their faith to others despite any derision or persecution they might face.[10] The connotative weight of the word, if not the religious aspects, largely fits for this group of informants. Like religious evangelicals, the talk show participants I talked to often were ardent believers in the critical importance of their message as a way to foster understanding and thereby affect personal and political transformation.

Sometimes the driving force behind participation was explicitly related to religious beliefs. Craig, campaigning for the legal rights of gays to marry, said, "When you believe how much you're doing—you know, when you have faith—that—I mean, my—my own life experience has taught me that as long as I do what I believe is right, you know, God is going to take care of me." Lorretta, who was trying to advance the legal protection available to incest survivors, said, "Part of spirituality for me is about being supportive of others . . . of being each other's keeper. . . . That's why I went." Sabrina, whose television disclosure included information about the sexual rituals that are integral to her church's spiritual beliefs, said, "We want to get people to realize that the religion exists, that they do have a heavenly mother, and that what their purpose is in life—the basic things that all religions deal with."

Some felt that they had been chosen by God to appear on *Donahue*. Jim Cobb, an active member of a Christian organization that tries to help former gays, said:

> We're not the only people who are ex-gay and married. There are a lot of people. Probably a lot of people have more knowledge than I do, but, you know, we were the ones that were chosen to be on the show, and we felt that was kind of special from God, you know, that God allowed that to happen to us. You know, not so much that Phil Donahue allowed it, because, you know, we believe that God had control over him, too.

Pete and Charlotte had spent much of their lives devoted to Christian evangelism. They believed that the show represented another opportunity to preach of understanding and commitment to marriage. Pete, whose wife now identifies herself as a lesbian, said, "And I do believe in my heart of hearts that all these things, in fact that when I called they were gonna do a show . . . coming along a line of uh, you know, God's will." Charlotte talked about their work as missionaries in their community and said of the opportunity to appear on talk shows: "This was next; this was Providence. This was Providence."

Others also used words imbued with religious connotations when describing the driven nature of their appearances. Sherrol, as noted earlier, used the phrase "spreading the gospel." Michael, a young HIV positive male who had told very few people about his disease before his national debut on *Donahue*, said, "I truly think that when the *Donahue* show came into my life . . . it was like a message from God or something, or a message, saying that you have a story to tell, and it's up to you to get—to be involved and stay involved [in AIDS causes]."

Several who were not members of mainstream American religious groups also asserted that spirituality had infused their disclosure decision. When Kate was asked, for example, if her belief in shamanism intersected with her decision to appear on the show, she replied by first describing her gender alteration experience:

> I think what happens is, there's a death of this one facet of one's self, then there's this revert, but somewhere in between the two, there's a moment of timelessness, there's an inkling or part of the truth, this is what they say, that the shaman . . . is given a portion of the truth. The shaman then returns to the culture and hah! is reborn . . . and has this little bit of the truth. But there's a catch, the—the—catch is that if the shaman doesn't talk and share that, the shaman goes mad.

Kate laughed at the close of this description, but seemed earnest throughout the interview about the obligation to speak out.

Another major similarity between religious evangelicals and television disclosers is that both groups often face a tough crowd of nonbelievers who may be hostile and jeering. Both Ross and Dolores compared the studio audience's response to a public stoning. Included in the audience, however, are those who may be receptive to the message. Norma Jean, when asked about the kinds of people who would "throw stones," a phrase that surfaced on a show she appeared on, said: "There's nothing you're going to be able to do about them in any case. I'm not appealing to them. I could care less. I want to appeal to the persons who have an open mind, who can listen and hear what I have to say, and . . . get past the titillation."

Participants were not overly concerned about being denigrated, because they believed that some viewers would be won over to their message. Jim Cobb, billed on the show as a "former homosexual," said:

> What we had thought about when we thought about doing a show was not about so much a studio audience, 'cause being in New York City we knew it was going to be probably very liberal, but we figured that the people across, you know, the country, who saw it and who were like us, who had, were from middle America, and uh, had been hurt and abused and hadn't found yet, and that's the kind of people we really felt the show was gonna touch—those kinds of people more than these other liberal people who were—probably wanted nothing to do with what we were talking about.

Jim also believed that some listeners might respond to the message much later in their lives. He related how he had seen the leader of Worthy Creations, the parent organization for his evangelical group, on *Donahue* 10 years earlier:

> But my mother was there, so I didn't want to show any interest, like I was really paying attention. . . . So anyways, I had seen him, and I look back to that and say, "I saw him, you know, I heard about it, and I went on and I was searching," you know. And I feel there are a good many people out there today who saw that show, they may have laughed at [it], they may have said it was ridiculous. But later on, they'll hear about something else, and something else, and then, you know, it will touch their lives.

The term *evangelicalism* here has been largely stripped of its Christian connotations (although the Christian emphasis certainly applies to informants like Jim Cobb and Charlotte and Pete). The analogy also breaks down if strictly applied, because participants were generally not explicitly attempting to convert members of the audience;[11] instead, they hoped their presence would serve as an impetus for further thought and, in a best case scenario, for social change. However, the idea of a religious fervor to expose others to ideas—despite the possible risks—is the component of the concept that is most apt and strikingly similar.

Dolores said that the chilling prospect of her parents discovering she worked as a prostitute was outweighed by thoughts "of how so many prostitutes feel—ashamed, alone, frightened, stigmatized."[12] Michael had begun a new job at a prestigious firm which he felt might be jeopardized if further publicity "branded" him unfairly as a prostitute, as he believed his *Donahue* appearances had. He felt compelled nevertheless to continue his crusade for AIDS awareness because of the urgency of the task. He said, "The whole bottom line is that we're talking about an issue that's killing a lot of people."

Ralph detailed several risks, among them that tapes of his various talk show appearances could be used in court some day against him to establish premeditation if he ever apprehends and murders his daughter's rapists. His response was, "So be it." He continued:

> Maybe by stating my case and being uh, thought of as a vigilante, maybe I knock down some of my possibilities of um, promotions and or standing in the community—and friends, but, you know, when you do that, you know, you pay a price. And I guess that's the price I pay. Is it high? Well, I feel good about what I did. I don't feel negative. Um, and I have no other area in which I can fight. They gave me an arena to fight, and I took it.

Sabrina, for example, who is clearly evangelistic in her desire to let people know about their religion, said, "The greater good was to get instruction out to the rest of the world. My own personal disaster had to be really, you know, suppressed." Jim Lightner, a swinger, said: "By ending up appearing on the show like this, uh, we may end up catching a little flak for it, but we're pushing the boundaries of society a little bit so that the next individual who comes along doesn't have as much hassle."

Evangelicals, who generally represented highly stigmatized groups, stepped from the farthest reaches of the margins of society. Moth-like informants, plaintiffs, and marketers might best be described as discreditable; they can "pass," to use Erving Goffman's term. They have not experienced the legacy of discrimination that propels the evangelicals to step up to the televised pulpit at any cost. The evangelicals are already discredited, or they can pass without detection but are angry about the injustices that members of their group suffer. Charlotte, a lesbian who remains married to her husband, said:

We [as African Americans] are constantly reminded of where we can and cannot go. In the lesbian community we are constantly reminded of where we are not and where we are accepted. As long as I patch onto him, I can grow my hair and keep my lipstick, and Pat, I can fit. But—that's a but. The reasoning to step aside is for those that cannot fit.

Many who held fairly privileged positions in society also felt compelled to speak on stigmatizing topics which, for a variety of reasons, had become central to their lives. For example, Joe spoke with great sorrow during the interview about his many infidelities and how they had hurt his former wife. He had been absolutely certain that many in the studio audience would skewer him and treat him with scorn. Nonetheless, he was determined to appear because he felt driven to talk to as many people as he could about the pain infidelity causes. He said:

The hurt is over now, although the memory of it is still there in back of the mind. But, like I say, I can't undo it, but I feel better about myself, and I'm bettering my life by trying to help others, you know, learn from my experiences. And what better way, you know, to do that, than on TV? You can really hit a lot of people that way. You're never gonna stop it, you know, that's not gonna happen. Let's face reality here; it's never gonna stop, but if you can get just a couple of people to think about the subject you're talking about, something you know about, and get 'em to stop and think, "Wow, is what I'm doing . . . right?"

In summary, although nonevangelical reasons often played a role in participants' decisions to appear on talk shows, an evangelical refrain ran throughout the interviews and was often passionately expressed. Many wanted to use the opportunity to confront the public's questions pertaining to their stigma so that stereotypes could be broken and replaced through a process Craig called "humanization." Additionally, some were using the broadband medium to empower or forge connections with other members of their fringe groups. This desire to reach both the populace and minority group members was underscored by participants' beliefs, strategic tactics, and the scarcity of resources available to them, as I discuss in the chapters that follow.

NOTES

1. The evangelical rationale is treated here in far more depth than others in the typology because of the deep-seated and insightful nature of the comments pertaining to it. Responses were often articulated in the context of long-term discrimination toward the stigmatizing feature participants appeared on the show to discuss, such that the story evangelicals tell about their rationale is well defined and rich with details about living in the margins.

2. Kate brought Goffman's work on stigma management to my attention. She described how television disclosure afforded a way to make her world easier to get around in. She said, "One of the big problems I have is—are you familiar with Erving Goffman's work? Okay, great. The book on stigma. And, um, you know, he calls it the management of a spoiled identity. . . . When do I come out, and when I first meet you, when do I say, 'Um, I need to tell you something?' And so this saves me a whole lot of trouble." Most respondents spoke more generally about stigma management for their groups, as did Kate in the rest of the interview.

3. Goffman, 1963, p. 101.

4. The show aired on February 5, 1991.

5. "Bryan" chose to use a pseudonym on the show partly out of respect for his family, whom he felt might be slightly embarrassed, particularly as his father shared the same name. Furthermore, however, he read portions of his donor biography on the air, and he did not want to be recognized by people who had used his specimen and might remember those details of his biography. "Bryan" explained that confidentiality is of very great concern to parties involved in sperm transfer. The audience, however, seemed to view his unwillingness to reveal his name as rather cowardly. His goal to end public perceptions that attach an element of shame to sperm banks was somewhat muddled by his secrecy.

6. There is also a marketing component embedded in his rationale, however, as he now works at a sperm bank and has a

professional interest in drumming up business.

7. This was a two-part series on battered women broadcast on March 7 and 8, 1991.

8. This show on "new warriors" aired on August 21, 1992.

9. French and Lee, 1988, pp. 170-171.

10. Hunter, 1983, wrote, "Behaviorally, Evangelicals are typically characterized by an individuated and experiential orientation toward spiritual salvation and religiosity in general and by the conviction of the necessity of actively attempting to proselytize all nonbelievers to the tenets of the Evangelical belief system" (p. 7).

11. The potential to win converts to their cause was of great value to some of the participants. This was clearly true for Jim Cobb, whose revelations on the program included a passionate testimony for his Christian faith. The leaders of the Most High Goddess were also hoping to swell the ranks of their church membership.

12. French and Lee, 1988, p. 170.

CHAPTER SIX

TELEVISION AS A "NATURAL" RESOURCE

Members of stigmatized groups have few resources to draw on in their quests to circulate new meanings about topics important to them—whether swinging, step parenting, or surviving rape. There is a particular dearth of legitimate forums for reaching the mainstream audience. A power imbalance exists in issues of access to the influential medium of television. The participants' only currency is their uniqueness, their stigma, which, in fact, enabled them to appear. Respondents saw daytime television talk shows as one of few arenas open to them.

Most were keenly aware that other forums were sealed off. Bud said:

> I always tried to interest like *20/20* and uh, *60 Minutes* and these type of shows, to do a story on me, for what I'm doing. You know, I went their-the route. I talked to somebody one time who said "I would never book you, because I don't believe in what you're saying—to give you the chance to go on TV." So that's what—that's why the talk shows are so important. They don't care, and that's the way it should be, actually.

As mentioned earlier, thousands petition the talk shows each week for the chance to appear, and many do so because they feel barred from other channels of communication. Eric Sherling, an intern at *Sally Jessy Raphael,* told me of a native American fighting for better conditions at his reservation whose letter said, "Sally is our last hope."[1]

Sabrina, whose religious practices landed her in jail, had her own cable access program, but the viewership of access shows is traditionally

73

minimal because of poor channel positioning, time slots, and production quality. She hoped to expand this via satellite to other locales; however, she and Will were finding the cost prohibitive. Charlotte said she was taking a class offered by the local cable operator so that she might one day have her own cable access show in which she could showcase gay and lesbian issues. Kate has a weekly column in a gay newspaper. Both she and Catherine are writers who use their craft to write plays that foster a dialogue on issues important to the gay and lesbian community. These forums afford limited potential for exposure to mainstream audiences.

On an interpersonal level, some members of marginalized groups have resources such as support groups and crisis centers that they can turn to for fellowship. Brett had many friends among the children who participated in drug trials at the National Institute for Health. His mom said they knew a network of people around the country because of these monthly trips to Washington, DC. She also often sought advice about dealing with the media from AID Atlanta, an advocacy group.

However, two respondents reported that they were marginalized even from these marginalized groups. Kate, for example, was ousted from a transsexual support group because she is a lesbian. Charlotte described the response she received at a lesbian support group meeting when she revealed to the women that she intended to stay with her husband: "They pulled me out, they cut me out. . . . 'You're out of here.' I didn't go back."

Talk shows are even more important resources for those excluded from marginalized groups, who saw the programs as opportunities to pinpoint a narrower, invisible audience. Pete contacted the *Donahue* show as well as other talk shows in his search for resources to help him and his wife through the crisis that Charlotte's newly discovered lesbian identity presented to their relationship. He initiated the contact with the *Donahue* staff when he could not find help in bookstores or in gay support groups.

In summary, the disclosers had few alternatives for reaching the large audiences that shows such as *Donahue* deliver and found it harder still to connect with fellow group members who are largely invisible and not easily contacted through support groups already in place. A few informants had communication outlets with limited circulation potential available to them, such as a cable access show or a column in a gay paper. The chance to appear on a talk show presented them with a resource too valued and rare to refuse.

THE PERIPHERAL ROLE OF TELEVISION

The minimal role the medium played in the lives of the majority of the respondents is striking. Most believed they could easily do without their set if it were taken away. In fact, Jim Cobb, a devout Christian, returned his new television within a week because he was appalled by the violent content. Susen, whose husband Ken was one of the few avid viewers in the group, said, "If he's not home, that TV's off. I hate that TV; it drives me crazy."

Will told me about his wife Sabrina's lack of knowledge about television: "If you were to ask her uh, who Sally Jessy Raphael was two years ago, she would have said, 'Who?' Uh, I mean, . . . she knew who Johnny Carson was, but other than that . . . she never watches television." Joy said:

> We watch maybe an hour a week. . . . We're *Star Trek* freaks. The new one primarily, but yeah, that's like our little ritual every Saturday night. And occasionally you know, we'll pull out a video or if something interesting is on—the news, occasionally if something's going on. We're not—we're readers, we're very heavy readers. . . . I mean I think the TV gets used more for Nintendo.

Mike said he watched very little television, and he explained how his AIDS status figured in to his detachment: "I'm always trying to educate myself, and . . . looking at a television set is just doing nothing, to me, it's just a waste of time, especially living with this, I guess. You know, I always think about exercising or running 'cause that's like living to me." Norma Jean said, "I don't watch much television. I have no use—I have a life! I have things to do."

Similarly, Rocki said:

> I never really watched a lot of television; we were always so busy doing other things. And I really didn't watch a lot of talk shows, and I still don't. The only reason I even watched any at all really after that [her string of appearances] was if there was absolutely nothing else to do in a hotel room or if one of the other girls that I knew was going to be on there.

75

Rocki and her husband live out in the country, where they are not served by a cable company. The wind blew over their satellite dish, and they have never had it fixed.

Kate also exhibited the groups' basement-level affinity for the medium:

> Um, I was married to my third wife, we, neither of us really wanted to watch television, we wanted to get to know each—uh, so we didn't watch much television. . . . And then when I began living by myself, it was like, I really wanted to get to know me. The television I would watch would be something like *Star Trek* at 11 o'clock at night, you know, before I would go to bed. It would be like to totally zone out from the day. I would use it like a drug. Literally. I—I would measure it out to myself, uh, to get to sleep at night. But uh, I don't watch much television.

When asked how television fits into his life, Jim Lightner responded, "For the most part, it doesn't. . . . A lot of stuff on the television that's on there for entertainment value doesn't have anything for us." Many voiced this latter point, that they did not find anything on the dial that spoke to their concerns or interests. Susen said that television programming "doesn't apply to anything I want to use." Kate said:

> I'm even getting fed up with NPR news. Uh, because even like the MacNeil/Lehrer report when I—it dawns on me that, you know, how many white middle-aged men they have being interviewed all the time. . . . When their special is, "What to do with your money because of the savings and loan crunch." Money? I've got $29 in the bank. . . . You know, all of the sudden it got me, who are they really putting this show on for? And I went, "They're not talking to me. They don't care about me." I'm very sensitive to that now.

Much of this disaffection stemmed from a belief that the medium does not mirror their realities as members of marginalized groups.

Crucially, many complained, as did Kate, "Television decidedly did not fit into my—it never had me on there. I could never see myself reflected in anything that television ever did." Furthermore, she said she only liked to tune in when she felt it offered some glimpse at truth: "That's why I watch television—I don't watch it for *Alf*, I don't watch it for even *Star Trek* anymore, which I'm sad to say, I gave up, because that's not true—for me."

In addition to the degree of evangelical intent, the moths, plaintiffs, marketers and evangelicals were differentiated by the degree of influence television exerted. The less evangelical groups' affinity for the television medium was much more in line with the average American viewer's, particularly in contrast with the meager levels of viewing reported by the evangelicals. Leanne admitted she was a "couch potato," explaining, "You gotta remember I was pregnant all the time." Susen reported her husband Ken's viewing habits when he was reluctant to admit to them: "He really, really watches a lot of TV. . . . In the wintertime, he's been known to sit there for 8 hours in one day. . . . My sister makes this joke, his ex-wife, says, 'If you ever leave him, take the television; otherwise, he'll never know you're gone.'"

Carl, too, is an avid viewer. He confessed, "I've been watching too much" and admitted he had occasionally burned dinner while absorbed in a show. He described his special devotion to television talk shows:

> Before I was on there? Oh, I used to watch them almost every day. I made sure I got up and watched *Sally*. And *Regis,* and I would flip back and forth. . . . [Later in the day] I'd watch *Donahue*. I'd watch him everyday. And *Oprah Winfrey*, four and five. I'd watch them both. *Sally* I flipped. It depended what was on. Anything interesting on, I'd watch her for a full hour. And then *Geraldo*.

Later, when asked why he watched the talk shows so faithfully, he responded: "I want to see—I want—to hear about people. I'm always interested in people's problems. . . . Some of the people brought me to tears. . . . I learned every time I watched the shows. . . . TV helped me psychoanalyze these people that I meet everyday."[2]

Bert, grouped with the moths because of his desire for fame, is not currently a heavy viewer, but he reported that he was a television enthusiast while growing up in Illinois: "But, yeah, I do remember out of high school when I wasn't employed and I wasn't in school and watching *Donahue* at 12 o'clock every afternoon. . . . Why I watched them? 'Cause it's a part of TV."

In general, however, television did not play a vital role in participants' lives. The only exceptions to this characterization were Carl, Ken, and Leanne, who were heavy television users. The others expressed low affinity for the medium in terms of viewing levels and the peripheral rather than central place it occupied in their lives. Many cited the violent content, the general negativity, and their belief that the medium was oriented toward white males as other reasons for not tuning in. They did, however, sense television's influential role in society in presenting images—particularly images of their marginalized groups—to mainstream America.

People knew about television's power to inform the public. Norma Jean said: "I always knew—and I still think—that, obviously, the media is very influential, for most people. I mean, it can change people's minds. It can educate them. It brings to their attention things they may not have known anything about. And I think it's a very important tool." Sabrina, a priestess, said, "I am aware of using it as a vehicle to reach people and instruct people, but I don't find anything in the local shows other than the news that I want instruction in."

Ralph, who monitored his children's TV use because of his concerns about the medium's steady diet of violence, felt certain of television's lasting influence. He recalled powerful images of John F. Kennedy: "Those things stick in my mind for years and years, and I'm saying, you know, when these things happen, if I can get that publicity, to get something done, not for any kind of material gain, but just for my own method of—of—getting these people."

Participants were also aware of television's influence through the important impact certain people in the forefront of their causes had had on educating them. Several people noted heroes they held in high esteem, people who had become accomplished spokespeople for their causes or lifestyles in various public forums. Marty, for example, spoke highly of Elizabeth Glaser and Jeannie White, both of whom were outspoken champions for AIDS awareness. She was essentially stepping forward to emulate their behavior by participating, yet she insisted that she was not in their league by any means.

Importantly, many resented the media's narrow and/or negative representations of their groups, and several explicitly linked their television disclosures to their outrage about harmful stereotyping. Craig pointed out that much of what is reported about homosexuals is related to AIDS and death. He decried the negative depictions of gay and lesbian lifestyles, which he felt often lead to internalized homophobia as well as gay bashing. Norma Jean said:

As long as prostitutes remain a mystery to the general society, and all they—all they see is what the television shows on the news when they bust the hookers on the street, and they continue to think that that's all there is, they don't have a lot of sympathy for the women, and they could care less whether the law is fair or not. But if they start to see us as human beings, with lives . . . then they begin to respond a little bit better to us.

Catherine said of her decision to self-disclose on television, "It can be positive, that there's a—a positive role model there . . . 'cause the media presents transsexual or gay people most of the time as being psycho killers." She continued:

I think the whole thing is usually we are completely invisible. . . . If you look at television land . . . there are a few gay people, but usually . . . you see them independently, you don't see them together. So I think what that projects out there is that lesbians or gay men are alone.

Later in the interview, she picked up the thread of this comment, discussing a gay character introduced on *L. A. Law*:

One of the characters is like I guess is discovering her lesbianism. . . . But I thought to myself, "Yeah, what's gonna happen though, is, of course, this is not going to last, that they're putting it in because it's cool to put it in; it's not going to last" . . . so media—it can be . . . almost a subversive in a way, almost in some ways worse presenting it. . . . It will just say, "Well, this is not feasible."

I found this desire to strategically insert viewpoints into the national consciousness striking because it was expressed by a diverse array of participants, whose topics ranged from the mundane to profane. Raymonda, who had entered her husband in the show's video contest that spotlighted exemplary husbands, said: "I felt good about going on TV for this purpose—to let people out there know that there are people who love their husbands, and husbands love their wives, instead of all this stuff that Geraldo and Phil and all of 'em drag out of the gutter." Marty said, "You heard about people dying with AIDS. You never heard about people surviving." She went on to say, "We had a positive story to tell."

79

Susen said her appearance was partly a reaction to common depictions of stepparent families on talk shows. When asked why she wrote a three-page letter to *Donahue* describing her family's unusual situation, she replied:

> Just to show 'em that it's no big deal that an ex-wife and a wife gets along for the kids' sake. . . . I think that makes a worse problem, being related. . . . Most of his programs are like that, people fighting and screaming and arguing, and I thought, that's really dumb, let's do something different.

Television disclosure is often prompted by participants' perceptions that current television portrayals of one's group need balancing and correction. Kate, one of the few respondents who had also appeared on *Geraldo*, a forum many I talked to considered illegitimate, said:

> The only reason I agreed to do *Geraldo* was because the therapist that they had . . . suggested me to balance it out, because their show just sounded so awful, always like, "The terrible fears of dread—" So I was going on there, you know, with much more of an agenda.

Jim Lightner also stressed his desire to present depictions that would not engender the public's fear or loathing:

> Hopefully, I think beforehand we can end up getting some information across to people. . . . We can end up showing them that . . . there are other people who uh, engage in alternative lifestyles, and no, they're not the prejudicial idea that they might have of these people if they end up knowing anything about it to start with. In other words, not all swingers are out there ready to jump in with any person who comes along on the street.

Talk shows are one of the few places where a seam in the solid shield of television's surface is evident—a rupture that allows gutsy participants to slip through to contest the barrage of prevailing depictions floated by television.

Informants were generally neither enthusiasts of television nor of daytime television talk shows. Only a handful were fans of the genre. Sixteen-year-old Heather admitted she was a talk show fanatic because she found them interesting. "Sam" had gone through a period several years ago when she watched a string of three talk shows in a row daily. She said, "We had heard of course that talk shows were somewhat similar to the tabloids that you see in grocery stores, but no, no, not to [my daughter] and I, you know, they were very, very serious topics." She added, "I was diagnosed with chronic fatigue syndrome, years ago. Those were the ones I really enjoyed watching, because I could relate."

Others were highly critical of the genre. Raymonda, for example, said that her neighbor watched so many talk shows that she became depressed. Raymonda advised her friend, "Turn that damn TV off." Her husband Dennis characterized talk show panelists as "homosexuals, every darn thing. It's the worst." Sandi said: "I was offended, you know, at some of the shows that they would have, I mean when they would have their transsexuals on, and 'I slept with my husband's brother' . . .— to me that's trash, that belongs in the *National Enquirer*." She conceded, however, "It depends on the topic. I think there's a lot of things out there people need to be educated about."

I talked briefly to an educational consultant, Therese Keegan, who had appeared on an episode of *The Oprah Winfrey Show* about organ donors. She was skeptical about bringing such a private topic into an arena where "they like to pull out the weirdest thing about something and examine it under a microscope." She also felt that public accolades for freely given gifts were rather inappropriate and wondered what purpose the show could serve. Both her husband and the kidney recipient, however, convinced her that the program could bring attention to the urgent needs of people awaiting organ transplants. Nonetheless, she remained uneasy about the forum, saying, "Because so much of what is displayed, if not lauded, on these kind of shows is of such questionable value, it sort of puts it in that category in a way that is uncomfortable to me."

Ralph, describing the mix of topics from transsexualism to mate swapping, said, "That's just like you're scraping the bottom of the barrel and every kind of deviant that's around here, and that to me is just like tabloid-type stuff." He described his frustration that he was treated by the studio audience at *Donahue* as the most irresponsible because he espoused vigilantism—despite the fact that the panelists included a prostitute who had chosen her profession to better support her children. He lamented, "Prostitution is almost acceptable." He continued, "It's the exception that's almost becoming the rule nowadays. It's ridiculous. It's gotten out of hand." As had others, however, he had seen shows he found highly affecting and acknowledged their power.

Ken, married to his former wife's sister, said, "Sometimes the talk shows get boring because they're all the same thing. . . . All it is is queers and homos and lesbians." Marty said she and her husband watched *Geraldo* occasionally in the morning as they dressed for work and thought, "Where does he get these people?"[3]

Two knew very little about talk shows. Susen thought the studio audience was hired to appear daily and that the panelists were supplied with cue cards. Michelle, engaged to a man 40 years her senior, said, "Like I said, a lot of them shows, I just thought they were fake. I didn't think they were the real people's lives." She said she had been shocked when she learned that the shows were reality-based: "Too many of them are like gay—gay people."

Participants who were most critical of the genre tended to be those who held only slightly marginalized positions in society. They saw themselves as distinctly different from the usual parade of characters on the show, believing that their day's topic was a legitimate one in the mix of subjects the show covers. In fact, panelists sometimes expressed bemusement at the nuttiness of the other guests who had shared the stage with them. When I interviewed several panelists from a *Jerry Springer* episode that featured people who had capitalized on riding the talk show circuit, each one lamented his or her decision to participate, because they believed the other guests had been freaks.

Those most solidly on the outskirts of society, however, frankly and wryly acknowledged the sensational nature of the show through the use of terms such as *freak show* or *circus* and recognized their roles as the *freaks*. Kate said: "The way I see the talk shows is they are the electronic 20th century version of the 19th century medicine shows. You know, bring on the freaks and we'll get the crowds to watch the freaks and then we'll hawk our wares." Similarly, Bert said, "Well, they wanted the freaks. . . . These shows are like Barnum and Bailey freak shows; the way I see them, they impart information to the masses, but they also sensationalize."

Generally, the more marginalized group members' evaluation of the genre was less harsh because they saw the shows as opportunities to address the *freak* label while they reached others who felt like freaks. Kate said:

> So, I mean, frankly, truly, but I think that I know that if ever I saw the word *transsexual* before I made my decisions, if ever I saw the word *transsexual*, I would be there, so I know who is watching that television set. It's like when you're little and you look up the word *homosexual* in the dictionary, or you look up the word *intercourse* in the dictionary, 'cause you gotta know what it is. . . . People who are transsexual don't have models, they don't have role models, and ah, so they're gonna watch. I know who was watching my show.

Kate felt daytime talk shows could be worthwhile, even exciting, television. She cited a particular *Donahue* episode that concerned ugly people:

> And I could watch that. Because I feel ugly. . . . I think people who're doing that also have gone through this death/rebirth thing and also have a little bit of the truth. If I can hear it right from their mouth then I can add it to my bit of the truth and then it starts to add up.

A handful of the participants had a vague sense that the norms of the genre would work in their favor. Rocki said: "From being on so many shows that I have been, and from even watching the shows it seems like before 90 percent of the shows are over, the audience is—whoever's on the panel—the audience is saying, 'Yeah, whatever you want to do, that's okay.'" This echoes Donal Carbaugh's work identifying norms of individual choice on *Donahue* and as an ethic valued by Americans.[4] Several saw the genre as one of few opportunities to naturalize their outgroups and make their lifestyles one of many choices; talk shows thus served as a "natural" resource for this goal. Charlotte said, "One thing about talk shows is showing the world, raising the consciousness, that there's lifestyles out there . . . [other] than what you read in the newspaper."

Some participants' views of the show had changed over time,[5] especially those who now grappled with a facet of their lives that gave them a new understanding of the program's potential. Joe's views had changed dramatically. Before his wife left him abruptly, he had hardly been aware of the genre. After his separation, however, he began to listen with great interest to talk radio and, later, to talk television shows because he had become acutely aware of his deficiencies in relationship maintenance. Now, he regularly reviews *TV Guide* to determine whether any of the shows are highlighting relationship issues, and he tapes those episodes to watch when he gets off work. He repeatedly used the phrase "a light bulb went off" to describe the life-altering experience of his divorce. He then discovered that the talk genre provided the very education he needed and that he could inform others via that channel as well.

Charlotte's opinions, too, had changed drastically. She said, "No, in fact, to tell you the truth, some of the stuff that used to come on, years ago, before I came out, it was, 'No, no, no. Those are sinners, and they are living bad lives. And this show is propagating that kind of lifestyle.'" Charlotte and Pete had come to view programs in the genre as significant opportunities because of the program's reach. Pete said:

> [I was] initially just calling around. . . . Afterwards I began to kind of see the sense of it. Because . . . it's seen as . . . not really that—that serious a format to work with, but yet it's still—it still gets out there. It's almost like, you know, people use puppets and clowns sometimes to get a message across, but still you're trying to get the message in because that's the way you can get the message in.

Although some had only recently discovered the genre's usefulness, many others knew the shows could serve as a cultural resource because they had seen a program that had been meaningful at some point in their lives. Because of *Donahue's* longevity, the particular show cited was often Phil Donahue's. For example, a 16-year-old bisexual described his struggles with anorexia and depression on a 1993 episode of *Donahue*.[6] He admitted that he had tried to cut his wrists after being institutionalized by his mother. He talked about an earlier period when he felt "unnatural." He turned to Donahue during the show and said: "Then in eighth grade I watched your show with two lovers that were married on it, and then I said that, you know, 'I wasn't a leper, and I wasn't unusual, and was just like other people.' So, um, then I came out to myself."

Marty had squirreled away talk show episodes about AIDS, hiding them above the microwave so that Brett would not come across them, so that she and her husband could watch them after their son went to bed. She saved a *Donahue* episode featuring Ryan White for Brett to watch after she broke the news to him about his disease. Brett now felt he would take advantage of every opportunity to go on any show (and he has been on *Donahue* twice) because of the opportunity to enlighten people, as Ryan White had educated him.

Sandi had seen a family on *Faith Daniels* struggling with sexual harassment; she then began corresponding with the mother, who later became "her mainstay," a source of information and support. Sandi said she knew about Title Nine legislation but had no idea how she might use the laws to help Heather until she saw the episode. Later, her appearances served a similar function for several families throughout the midwest who have reached out to Sandi as a source of information about securing the safe schools the law mandates.

Pete, as mentioned earlier, had contacted the various shows' staffs in the hope that they might serve as a sort of clearinghouse of information about others who were successfully dealing with similar challenges because the shows traffic in various subcultures. The programs also supply people with news of their outgroups, providing linkages with formerly invisible others profiled in an episode.

Marty described the process:

> I look through *TV Guide* and if I see, like the other day, *Sally Jessy Raphael* had a show on, it was women—women who were infected by their lovers—or something. . . . If I see something's going to be on, I'll tape it. It's a habit. And my mother-in-law says the same thing, you just go through the newspaper and just look for that one four-letter word, AIDS. She says, I don't care if it's Contra Aid or what kind of Aid—you get tuned in to looking for that word. . . . I'm always hoping to hear, you know, about the breakthrough, or something new.

Participants were clear in their understanding that talk shows could touch a lot of people as they had been touched, but they were also aware that such forums were not ideal. Will said, "I have never seen any of them interview a Nobel Prize winner. Right? They have what is—I refer to as a bumper sticker mentality." Respondents agreed to appear nonetheless because they felt that their message needed to be heard, and they believed they had the capability to withstand the gauntlet of ridicule and interrogation. Dale, who warned his wife that they would be portrayed as "limp dick" and a "whore," said, "I've got enough backbone that I think I could like, you know, given, you know, given an opportunity, I think I could state my case and still like, you know, come out standing even."

Ross used the analogy of a trojan horse to describe his view of the theatrics and guile necessary to market his ideas and book. He said:

> The vehicle—is the TV talk show. But hidden within it is things that are really true, but if I just presented those without any hype, directly to people, I wouldn't get any attention. It doesn't necessarily have to be a freak show, as long as it can get people's attention. If you get their attention by pissing them off, which is what I do, that's fine, too. Anything to—the whole thing is—anything that will grab people and make them continue to watch and not change the channel. Whether it's freak show, you know, a woman with 90-inch breasts.

The most startling case of strategically utilizing this forum is Norma Jean's, whose fame as a "cop to call girl" has been fodder for a decade's worth of appearances on talk shows. She said she became so sickened by the corruption at the Los Angeles police department that she finally felt compelled to blow the whistle. She explained her surprising strategy to garner a hearing for her account of the graft and criminal behavior she had witnessed:

> One of the reasons that I chose prostitution was because I knew it would give me a forum—um, because sex sells—and, you know, having watched the talk shows often enough, I knew that there was a very good possibility, since there was a shortage of women who were willing to go public and talk about their lives as prostitutes, that I would probably be able to get on a talk show and talk about the corruption.

She lamented on *The Jerry Springer Show* in November 1993: "Who's going to listen to Norma Jean the traffic officer and doll maker? 'Cause I'm a doll maker, and I make jewelry. But nobody cares! No talk show has ever called me because I'm a doll maker. But as a call girl, here I am still after 10 years."

The general attitude toward television might be best character-ized as pragmatic. Most were not fans of the medium, but they were cog-nizant of its powerful role in society. Will said, "Television is a vehicle by which we see what the rest of the world is thinking." Jim Cobb said:

> And, uh, I feel there's a lot of good educational things on TV. Even if it's not according to my viewpoint of what should be done, I think it's kind of good for people to see, you know, even for Christians to see, this is how the world thinks, because they can get into their lit-tle shell and they don't even know what's going on in the world anymore. Or how to relate to these people.

The pragmatism describes Charlotte as well, who said flatly, "The type of people we want to reach watch those type of shows." Pete said:

> I kind of see it as viable. Getting something across, even though you're gonna look like. . . . If you've got a message, you'll look like no different than the, you know, the nude dancer that was on the show before you . . . but . . . all in all, you're gonna get, and I told Charlotte this just before we left, that I look at, you know, even though I don't agree nothing with David Duke, and his whole thing, but I really look at the fact that . . . he ran his campaign, that he found out there was 6,000 people in Louisiana that agreed with what he said, so all is not lost. So I said, in the same way, even though what you do may seem negative to a lot, if you get a connection point there, then it's still worth the—worth the risk. You know, his political career's not over, I mean even though nobody's agreeing with what he's saying, look at what he found out still in the process. I think that's the same way that—that even though everything is gonna be looked at as just another, you know, sensationalized thing, it's just another talk show . . . those phones stayed lit up, every one . . . and I want to tap into that interest.

In summary, the informants were not fans of television but were instead critics of a medium that they felt neglected their interests or broadcast stereotypical images of their groups. Virtually all of the infor-mants were critical of the daytime television talk show genre because of its sensational nature. The less stigmatized members of the sample felt that they were disclosing about a legitimate topic on what was normally a forum for deviants. Others, however, were firmly aware of the freakish nature of their portrayal and felt the audience's exposure to the topic was worth the risks.

PRIOR VIEWS OF PHIL DONAHUE
AND THE PROGRAM, *DONAHUE*

To investigate the role of the hosts in squeezing out disclosure, I asked participants their perceptions of the various ringmasters who direct and headline the shows. The primary focus of the questioning was on Phil Donahue, as all but three respondents had appeared on his program. Most held fairly tepid opinions of Donahue prior to their appearances. Charlotte said, "I couldn't say I'm a fan. Susen said, "Just didn't really have an opinion." No one exhibited a deeply parasocial relationship with him, and most knew very little about him. Dale said: "I know, you know, like Geraldo had a little bit of journalistic background; I know Oprah like lost weight, gained weight; Phil, I don't know anything about. He's white haired, he's married to Marlo; that's all I know." Lorretta mistakenly believed that Donahue was a psychologist because she recollected that she had been paid $50 several years ago to evaluate a program featuring "psychologist Phil Donahue." At the other extreme, everyone knew a lot about Oprah Winfrey and often responded excitedly to questioning about her with the phrase, "Oh, I love Oprah!"

A few held negative prior opinions of Donahue because of their perceptions that he could be confrontational. Jim Cobb said, "Everyone who knows Phil Donahue knows he could have torn us apart, and everyone warned us." Jim's friends cautioned him that Donahue was "really awful to Christians." Dennis, whose prior view of Donahue was that he was a "jerk," said: "The reason I didn't like him? Oh, was more so the way that he would put the other people down on the show; I felt he was putting 'em down, he'd cut 'em short, he would antagonize 'em, push 'em into a view that he wanted to hear."

It is interesting to note that the informants who expressed negative opinions of Donahue before their appearance were, relatively speaking, on the inside of society's margins. Carl, who generally liked Donahue but believed he could be "vicious," felt that he catered to "men who go for men." He continued, "He sort of apologizes for them. . . . And so he rides a straight man like me."

The informants in the sample with sharply alternative lifestyles perceived—and appreciated—a bias toward gay and humanist issues. Craig and Patrick felt they detected a pro-gay stance. Craig said,

"Pushing . . . more than positive. More than a supporter, an active—
'This is where I stand, and will you stand with me?'" Pete, who had
become sensitized to society's discrimination against gays since his
wife's coming out, described a *Donahue* episode about a sting operation
in Michigan, where gay men had been videotaped having sex in a park:

> I've seen Donahue totally come out of himself in defense of the gay
> community, I mean to the point that he kind of lost it, you know, the
> only time, and I'm starting to really say, "What is this guy's, what is
> it, you know, his connection?" Not that I think anything personal.

Bert said, "I definitely think he's a humanist. And—and I think Oprah is
that also, but . . . [the] gay and lesbian thing fall into more of the freak
category for her."

Marty appreciated Donahue's advocacy for AIDS-related causes. She said, "We always admired him because he had that connection
with Ryan White, and, um, you know, went to the funeral."

Importantly, whether they held positive or negative views of
Donahue, most respondents simply felt that he would be fair. This was
perceived as an important advantage because they were seeking an
avenue to get a message across. "Bryan" believed Donahue was nonpar-
tisan: "I've seen him attack both liberals and conservatives." Kate said,
"He's always seemed to give a fair shake." Jim Cobb said:

> Well, I don't think he particularly is trying to help. He has an agen-
> da which is more liberal and—and anything goes and—you can't
> tell anybody what they should do with their life because it's their
> choice, and uh, I knew that basically that's where he was going to
> be coming from. The only thing I felt was positive was that he
> didn't mind having other people on who didn't share his viewpoint.
> You know, and which is, that's good.

Catherine knew little about Donahue except what others had told her,
which included a belief that he "treats things more fairly than others."

Most respondents believed that the mood would not be as antag-
onistic on *Donahue* or on *The Oprah Winfrey Show* as it could be on
other talk show stages. This was a major concern for virtually everyone.
Jim Lightner said, "If we knew there was somebody with a very strong
bias, then we probably would have [been concerned], because we wanted

to be able to talk, not be ridiculed." Kate said of Donahue, "I've seen him be courteous, and um, and I think that's a lot of it. I haven't seen others be courteous."

Several felt that Donahue was less sensational than other daytime talk show hosts in carrying out his duties. Wendy said, "He just seemed to handle the topics real well. He seemed to bring out good information and handle it seriously." Jim Lightner said, "I think Donahue has a tendency to go for a bit higher level with respect to the audience's capabilities." When discussing the heightened sense of spectacle on talk shows, Bert said, "That's the nature of the business. And I think the *Donahue* show tries to side-step that as much as possible and still cater to what the *Hard Copy* sensationalism ah, requires, but a minimum of that, a minimum."

In a related vein, most of the informants considered *Donahue* to be a more legitimate forum than the others in the genre. Joy said:

> Actually that it had more integrity than your average daytime viewing and that it actually might be worth something. . . . I mean, there was just a handful I've seen, for example, as a gay person, I'm real aware that they do have some fairly positive ones on alternative sexual orientations.

The perceived respectability was partly linked to the longevity of the show and its more frequent coverage of political issues. Jim Lightner said, "I remember Donahue from back in the '60s when he used to do the good stuff, where he'd end up interviewing Kissinger or somebody." Bert remarked:

> When . . . Phil Donahue started in the '70s, it was about uh, the audience interviewing the person or the personality, and getting information across that you would not normally get in a—in perhaps a newspaper, or um, whatever kind of uh, media was used, and it wasn't so sensationalized.

Only three informants expressed a perception of *Donahue* as a highly esteemed forum. Marty noted the international scope of its distribution. Carol remarked to her husband after their appearance on the show: "You've made it. There's nothing else to work for as far as you don't have to get any more well known now, you can relax, you've done it."

Bert, who had completed a whirlwind talk show circuit, stated that *Donahue* was the program he had most desired to appear on. He said, "That was like the pinnacle."

Note that two who held a high regard for Donahue were characterized earlier as "moths." Most, however, felt fairly neutral about the show. The legitimacy of the program was largely expressed in comparison to other shows in the genre. Both *Donahue* and *Oprah* were considered the most legitimate of the "freak shows." This was especially true in comparison to *Geraldo*, which was frequently cited as a worst-case example.[7] Craig said, "Some people have said stuff like, 'I'm glad you didn't do *Geraldo*.'"

Attitudes toward *Donahue*, as with the respondents' views of television, were generally pragmatic rather than fan-oriented. Charlotte said of Pete's efforts to contact several forums: "So it was closed, closed, open. We went to what was open." Later, she added, "It would have been anybody who opened the door. Donahue opened the door." Similarly, when Craig had to make a choice about which show to appear on because all the offers initially demanded exclusivity, he decided to appear on *The Oprah Winfrey Show* because he knew that her show had the highest ratings, and because Patrick was a fan of hers.

To summarize, many of the television disclosers were responding to the negative or missing representations of their group on television and were seeking to sketch themselves in to the imperfect television landscape. The chance to clear up misconceptions and present alternate depictions on the very medium that often propagates damaging stereotypes galvanized many to agree to appear. Most respondents held a critical stance toward daytime talk shows and thought of them as "freak shows." Many felt that *Donahue*, however, was more legitimate than other shows in the genre because of their perceptions of Donahue's more even-handed and less sensational treatment of issues. Overall, respondents were pragmatic in their choice to appear on *Donahue*, viewing it simply as an available forum. The disclosure is strategic, entailing the use of a currency the otherwise powerless participants trade to gain access to a significant contested site.

NOTES

1. Eric tried to pitch the man's story to producers, who dismissed the idea of doing a show on the topic, saying simply that it would not "rate."
2. Carl's description fits neatly with Rubin et al.'s (1985) characterizations of people with high affinity for the television medium: He is emotionally involved, considers the information to be reality-based, and watches faithfully.
3. I think respondents were partly interested in participating in my research because they, too, found the talk show phenomenon puzzling. I very often had to hold off their questions about my findings until I had a chance to hear their cases.
4. Carbaugh, 1989.
5. For example, Rocki's views changed as she began to glimpse the power of the genre to break the stereotypes people held of big-busted blondes. She said: "I didn't realize until I did the first show, and I talked quite a bit more then; I didn't realize how much of a reaction people would have after that. You know, not that I'm any genius . . . but a lot of people assume you're just a real dingbat, and I got a chance to express my opinions, and I think they realize there's something more up there than you know, just a blonde head and, you know, and a body walking across the stage."
6. The episode aired on December 23, 1993.
7. Many could not explain exactly why they believed *Geraldo* to be the worst; when pressed, several said they had simply heard that about the show. Susen and Leanne expressed positive views. Leanne was a big fan: "I'm just madly in love with him . . . he seems to be real sympathetic to the underdog." Susen liked him but said she would feel intimidated if she went on his show because of his "big, fancy" vocabulary. I believe his vocabulary is exactly what makes the show most sensational. For example, on a show in 1994 on relationships involving middle-aged men and teenaged girls, he repeatedly intoned the show's focus at the cut-away for commercials: "Dirty dogs or puppy love?"

CHAPTER SEVEN

STRATEGIC SELF-DISCLOSURE

The decision to speak about private issues in public was an easy choice for almost everyone; concerns were focused instead on issues of self-presentation. The freak show nature of the forum prompted an active planning phase so that the negative potential could be neutralized as much as possible. Participants' emphasis during interview sessions on their prior planning points to the tactical nature of the intimate disclosures offered up to the public.

A critical concern for many was what to wear. This choice was more difficult than rather mundane considerations about how to dress for an important social occasion. Instead, this decision involved meticulous impression management.[1] Charlotte, grappling with her new identity as a married lesbian, summarized this concern by saying, "I thought about what did I want to go as." Wendy also gave careful thought to her attire, finally deciding on "a very plain dress." She explained her decision: "I didn't want to help perpetuate any myths, what we wear and how we look, and what's a typical rape victim look like."

Bud's friends convinced him that he should cut his hair in order to present a better image on *Sally Jessy Raphael,* his first big national appearance. Later, he was angry with himself for giving in not once but twice to considerations of appealing to the mainstream and has not altered his radical image since for his various appearances. Kate said, "Really, I mean I spent more time wondering what to wear than whether or not to do the show. . . . I let a couple of friends talk me into, 'Well, you want to be respectable . . . you don't want people to get turned off by your appearance.'" Jenny felt that her demeanor and clothing on

Donahue contributed to a successful experience. She said, "I presented such a—um—conservative appearance that Donahue even commented on it. And so . . . being the swinger that nobody would identify as a swinger was like saying, 'See, we don't have S's embroidered—.'"

Several carefully studied the shows' routines in order to be better prepared. Kate said, "I watched *Geraldo* for weeks to just get kind of a sense of his rhythms and his techniques and his tactics." Similarly, Catherine said, "I would watch the show . . . the audience interaction with the panelists and what worked and who I liked and why I liked them—watched more than anything else . . . how Donahue handled it and handled the people on the panel."

Almost everyone held brainstorming sessions to determine what kinds of questions might be asked and to rehearse answers. Women incarcerated with Leanne role played the *Donahue* setup so that she could practice her responses. Patrick discussed his preparation for his first national television exposure:

> In knowing Oprah's show and her audiences and what they're like, who they expect, I think we both thought through some questions that we would expect them to ask. Not with each other, but I think in our heads and how we were gonna answer them, so we were well prepared. Jump up on the soap box.

Joy, who had more experience on talk shows than her co-parenting partners, said:

> So what I did is sit down and prime everybody. . . . I said, "Okay, these are the 15 most common questions you're probably going to be asked out of my experience. Think about 'em, remember to have short, snappy answers." You know, so I sort of coached Jeff and Bert.

Carl also instructed his young fiancée Michelle about what kinds of questions would be asked and how she might answer them because she had little familiarity with the show.

Several participants devised strategies for dealing with or evading certain questions. Craig described his tactics:

> Whatever the question's involving personally, if of a personal nature, you can talk about the issue. And people want to know, . . .

"Oh, do you guys have AIDS?" You can say, "Well, I think what's important here is to encourage groups will be tested.". . . . So you can avoid getting real personal.

Susen reported her brother-in-law's plan: "Cecil says if they ask him something that was too personal, he would just say, 'Are we getting paid for this?'"

In practice sessions, most developed approaches for dealing with the most difficult questions they could imagine so that they would be ready to face them gracefully. Brett, who, at 12, has been interviewed repeatedly about living with AIDS, said he sometimes liked to ask interviewers beforehand about the kinds of questions they would ask so that he could avoid answering with a long "uh—" if they "asked a hard question." Many were concerned about how well they would field the tough questions, because they felt that any hesitancy would undermine their positions. Joy said, "I had to look at what issues for me I was afraid of. Because they might, someone might ask me about them, and it really wouldn't be a good thing if I went "Uh—." Jenny felt that "if you let them see that there's something that maybe bothers you, then that's what they're going to focus on. . . . If you're angry, automatically people think that you're hiding something or you feel guilty about it."

Appearing irresolute was of particular concern to Jenny: "I didn't want them to see any weakness. . . . It is something that is a common belief in society, is that the male pushes the female into it [swinging] . . . and that's absolutely untrue." The visual component was also important to Jim Cobb, a fundamentalist Christian, who said:

And the first 20 minutes of the show, we were so discouraged because they're talking about sex, and they're being very graphic, and we were both kind of nauseated with what was going on and thinking— we're both praying. . . . I felt, you know, I am not gonna laugh and I'm not gonna smile; I'm not showing any kind of approval for what's going on. In any way, I didn't want to be like condemning them, but I didn't want to show that I was in on it for fun.

Bert felt it was critical not to get into an argument. He said, "It doesn't look good on TV. . . . Let them look like a fool, uh, by them condemning you, and you just accept it and say what you have to say and be as calm as possible about it."

Many felt they were able to avoid making certain mistakes from watching talk shows prior to their appearances to see the audience's responses to certain disclosure styles. Respondents cited negative examples of guests whom they believed had presented their cases poorly. Kate discussed a *Sally Jessy Raphael* show featuring a person without gender named Toby: "But I think as a spokesperson, and especially with Sally Jessy, Toby came across as very sullen, very sullen, very petulant, very um, combative, very defensive, and I watched that and I thought, 'um, um, um.'" Pete mentioned *Donahue* episodes in which the panelists had "come off fanatical" or tended to "argue and browbeat." He felt the audience was then likely to "write you off."

Many sensed that a light-hearted approach would be an effective tool to disarm the audience. Erving Goffman suggests the use of humor for managing stigmatized interactions. He wrote, "In addition to matter-of-factness, levity is also recommended."[2] Will said:

> If you can come back with a bumper sticker response, it's going to impress them a lot more. They won't remember what you said, but they'll at least remember you said something important. . . . The way to diffuse hostility is to have people laughing.

Carol was worried that her husband, a physician, would be too serious to come across well. She said: "He's more rigid, and to me, I mean the show's fun part of it was that it was light. But he wanted to present kind of the fact that it was serious, it wasn't like going to a beauty parlor. . . . I guess we played our roles well."

In addition to plans that maximized the stylistic presentation of the disclosure, respondents also considered which elements to withhold to optimize their stigma management efforts. In this way, they retained some control over the direction of the conversation. This was especially true for Lorretta and Joy. Lorretta, an incest survivor, chose not to reveal on the program that she is a lesbian. She explained her decision: "I did not want to confuse issues on this show. I was there on incest; I didn't want them to say, 'Oh, she's gay because,' or 'Oh, she's just a lesbian.' I just wanted to stay real focused on—my lifestyle wasn't the issue." Joy said, "I identify, as I said, in black leather and chains, but basically, I didn't want that to come up because it really does, it's a separate world from my parenting. But people will confuse it."[3]

Both planned similar strategies for dealing with questions pertaining to their sex lives. Lorretta said, "'Cause I was gonna say, 'I don't know what if—what my sexual orientation has to do with the issues here'. . . . I would have laughed, probably; I'd have done it to where I never really said, but you think whatever you wanted." Joy said, "So it's once or twice I've had to say, 'That is irrelevant. We're talking about how my kid is doing.'"

Marty, who is agnostic, felt uncomfortable whenever the audience asked questions about God's role in their lives. She discussed an incident in which the question came up on a local show in Florida:

> I said, "I get a lot of my strength from Brett, cause he's dealing with this [AIDS] head on." And I really do. He's a trooper. . . . If I believed in God, I think I'd be really mad at Him, and I don't understand why this happened to this kid. Why did He allow me to get pregnant to have kids, to have one die, and then this other one have this? I don't understand it, so that—that would be my response if I didn't feel like I'd probably be getting letters in the mail.

Others did not want to disclose certain facts because of the potential negative impact on family members. One informant did not want to name who had initially involved him in the gay lifestyle. Although he generally believed in openness, he felt that this disclosure could hurt his family. As did others, he determined in advance which things to hold back.

However, most stressed that their major concern was not what to withhold but how to best get their messages across. Joy felt she "had to somehow find the right words so we could communicate." She described her view of the audience:

> People with somewhat limited range of personal experience of alternative lifestyles. People from middle America. I saw them as challenging more than threatening. Challenging to communicate with. I wasn't sure we were really speaking the same language, the same dialect, and I really had to look, and I realized that I might be their first time contact with somebody like me.

Respondents emphasized rhetoric familiar and valued by Americans. These included explicit appeals during the show about love, family, civil rights and individual choice, among others. Jenny and Jim, for example, stressed the consensual nature of their involvement in the swinging lifestyle. Joy responded to an audience member's criticism of her gay parenting partnership by stressing the outpouring of love her daughter receives. She said later of her remarks on the show: "And who can argue with people loving their kid? That's usually what I kind of summarize with, 'What counts is the love.'"

Others felt these rhetorical attempts were less important than the concrete representation of their pairing, which stayed intact even if the desired focus of discussion strayed. Catherine believed her close relationship with Kate came across pure and simple:

> The feedback that I've got from people [was] that Kate and I—it was clear that we really love each other a lot. And I think a lot of times people tend to think it's just a sexual thing—they think it's just like, "Oh, these deviants, you know, they just like to have perverted sex." Whereas actually, there's a very caring, loving relationship, and I think that when people see the love, then they kind of accept it.

Bert said, "I don't think we came off so sensational because we presented ourselves as a family. . . . And, uh, that's what we were trying to get across ultimately."

Patrick spoke to the *Donahue* audience about the very real economic and legal impact resulting from society's denial of marriage rights to gays and argued that he should be granted the same citizenship rights as other Americans. Pete's comments on the show included a comparison of his wife's lesbian identity to the immutable character of his race and stocky size. These attempts at issue framing were one method of control available to television disclosers. Craig told me that he began his disclosure on *The Oprah Winfrey Show* with the declaration: "Well, the bottom line here is Patrick and I love each other." Craig earnestly believed that "everyone can relate to the couple and the traditions around marriage."

Bert may have applied this strategy of utilizing mainstream-oriented themes to excess. When asked whether he would have preferred to leave undisclosed that all three co-partners got in bed together to conceive a child, Bert explained his rationale for the revelation: "Letting them know that it was not any turkey-basted thing, that it was done, uh, the way that you are supposed to conceive children, you know . . . love and affection and family and caring." This did not seem to draw the intended response of recognition from the members of the studio audience.

Somewhat similarly, because Sabrina wanted to stress that sex is not evil, she purposefully revealed on the show that she had acted in an erotic movie. However, the studio audience's reaction indicated that they believed this disclosure undermined her claims of sincerity about her religious beliefs. Much to Michael's dismay, his honest revelation about his brief stint as a prostitute, which he offered up as evidence of the utter degradation of his emotional state after his partner left him infected with the AIDS virus, caused him to unwittingly assist in the show's portrayal of him as an irresponsible villain. Some panelists were simply better at impression management than others.

Those with the most media savvy used additional control strategies to increase the chances that the television disclosure would be successful. Craig, for example, negotiated with the *Donahue* staff. He described his intent:

> Well, I think it's important for what we're doing to be in control and to be able to know exactly what we're getting into. . . . Like for instance with *Donahue*, we told them the first show we wanted to do was in order for us to come up, do his show, we said for the first segment, we want him to sit down and talk with us. We don't want him to go into the audience. 'Cause we felt a very real need to humanize us.

Will and Sabrina made certain stipulations as well, including the restriction that no long string of questions be asked without an opportunity to address each question in turn. Will also demanded that no fundamentalist Christians be allowed on the panel, because, in his view, "They have the opportunity to present themselves everyday." He and Sabrina also tried to secure the participation of religious experts who would speak to the veracity of their claims that the history of their sect pre-dated Christianity, but none agreed to appear.

Craig was a talented negotiator with producers because his ground-breaking legal suit was a story that staffs sought to secure for their shows. Others, however, did not feel they held any power and therefore did not push to include items about themselves that they had intently hoped to introduce into the dialogue. Carol, for example, who is remarkable in the depth of her involvement in philanthropic activities, said, "I actually was hoping in all this [her appearances on talk shows focusing on plastic surgery] that they mentioned it, only because otherwise it just looks like these dippy people that only want to look good." Carl and Michelle wanted to show a tape on *Sally Jessy Raphael* of their dancing. Carl said, "We want to dance for them, to show them that a 68-year-old man can move." They believed that the visual presentation of their compatibility would balance the discussion, but their request to show the video was not approved. Instead, much to their dismay, the show centered on their sexual relationship, and the audience hit Carl hard for being what one caller termed a "dirty old man."[4]

People were especially cautious when shows they were unfamiliar with asked them to appear. Joy said:

> I would have to call somebody and say, "What's this show like?" You know, "What's their style? Are they going to give me an opportunity to actually present this in a positive light or am I going to be a sitting duck?". . . Unless . . . there was some hope for some communication to take place, I wasn't going to waste my time and energy doing it.

Although aware of the risks, they noted a variety of factors that made them feel less vulnerable. Dale said his therapist assured him, "We will intervene if at any, any circumstance where maybe we see you appear to be uncomfortable or if Phil maybe turns vicious." Similarly, Lorretta felt protected by the presence of both her therapist and her attorney. Her lawyer, the prominent feminist Gloria Allred, has appeared on countless talk shows. Lorretta recounted that Gloria assured her before the show taping that "I could be sweet and she would be the heavy."

Lorretta was also not too concerned about being asked to tell some of the details of her achingly sad history of childhood sexual assault, because she felt "they couldn't get too personal 'cause they would be in violation of their federal communication codes." Both Norma Jean and Dolores noted that they were accustomed in their profession to speaking carefully so that there were no suggestions of solicitation.

Several developed strategies for feeling less afraid. Brett thought of the experience as just talking to one person. Donna said, "If you don't think about them, they're not there." Carol was glad she had not worn her glasses so that she was unable to clearly see the audience and the intimate photos of her liposuction surgery.

Everyone had become increasingly savvy in their dealings with the media. Marty and her husband had carefully mapped out their strategy for telling their community that Brett had AIDS, gingerly testing community reactions before taking each successive step. When Brett came out to the children in his class during show and tell as the child in the school with AIDS, his mom recalled thinking that "the phones are going to be hot tonight in Duluth." They then called AID Atlanta for advice on bringing in the media. They spoke to a reporter the next day from the *Atlanta Journal*, because their plan was simple: "Let's get this out like we want to get it out." Although not originally conceived as a tool for stigma management, the talk show genre came to be seen by many outgroup members as a particularly useful avenue for getting out their agenda.

Television disclosure is a controlled process for many, not a hotheaded or impetuous one. The disclosures are therefore instrumental but nonetheless risky. Among other risks, the circle of people who know of the stigma is dramatically widened.

Several were warned or asked by third parties not to appear. Wendy's employer asked her not to participate because, they argued, they did not want her to be recognized. She said, "I took that as a slap in the face. I felt like that was very insulting to me. We decided it was worth the risk." In most cases, participants immediately jumped at the opportunity when the call came from producers and began to think about how to minimize the fall-out by preparing parents and others.

While participants conduct strategy sessions, the staffs carry out fairly lengthy interviews on the phone with potential panelists to determine who is a good storyteller, who will give over the goods. The disclosure stream, then, begins early on, with producers as gatekeepers. Information gleaned from these preinterviews is often brought out by the host during the show to flesh out or stoke the story when needed.

Once on the scene, however, the staffs at the better shows did not work to squeeze further disclosure from participants. Carol described the warmup given prior to both *Donahue* and *The Oprah Winfrey Show*: "They said to us ahead of time, 'Say anything you want to say. Say *anything* you want to say.' I was surprised—I somehow thought we'd have a list of things we couldn't say but I think they like that. . . . I love the freedom of that."

At the other extreme, two young women who had been on *Ricki Lake* told me that producers prodded them again and again—right up until air time—to practice their responses to the scripted question Ricki would ask. Furthermore, they were cast, essentially, according to their willingness and ability to heighten their fury at a male roommate for one of many variations of a common *Ricki Lake* theme: "Men are dogs." One of them described the producers' refrain, from the initial contact onward: "They kept telling you that you had to get real mean and vicious when you came on the show, and if you couldn't do that, then you couldn't go on."[5] I never heard about this kind of incitement to theatrics from anyone else. Sherrol, for example, said emphatically, "I have *never* been told what to say. I have never been coached."

At *Sally Jessy Raphael* the spectacle nature of the show was often exaggerated by a variety of tactics that sometimes made participants uncomfortable. In "Sam's" case, for example, producers asked her to wear a bathing suit or a slinky dress that the staff provided so that, visually, the case for her as a "sexy mom" was better told. She refused, saying, "This just is not me!"

Clearly, there were risks, particularly for those who might be vulnerable to the shaping of the story by producers, hosts, other panelists, and the audience. However, participants knew that other forums had their own limitations. Norma Jean said, "On a news story, oftentimes, you get edited, and on a talk show, you don't." Leanne, who had been the subject of many a tabloid edition, found the highly edited pieces had represented her as someone that even she would not like. The give and take nature of the talk show forum allows strong participants to seize the unfolding story and tell it their way. The genre, however, is fraught with perils, which participants tried to navigate as carefully as possible.

In summary, almost everyone had prepared and sometimes rehearsed their disclosures beforehand with an eye toward a national audience. They described the use of various impression management tactics chosen to present an image of themselves or their marginalized groups that the audience would find palatable. Preparation included thinking through what elements of one's story should not be revealed and what themes should be used so that the mainstream would be more accepting of those outside the margins.

NOTES

1. Goffman, 1959, provides the metaphor of everyday life as a stage, with individuals as actors engaged in the presentation of various guises of self. He stresses that people actively work at impression management, the effort to convey to others one's intent, character, and preferred definitions of situations.
2. Goffman, 1963, p. 116.
3. Both Lorretta and Joy gave me permission to reveal this information here.
4. Carl had a good comeback to this; he reminded the woman that she probably did not think of her father in such a derisive way.
5. I spoke with these women close to press time and therefore did not have time to integrate their reports about their experiences into this work. Furthermore, although they described their frustrations about the staged nature of the show during the interview in some detail, they were a little leery about these views being published, because they had signed papers which mandated that they could not talk badly about the show to anyone. I was also shocked when the women told me that producers suddenly stated at a certain point in a stream of phone calls that they could not back out—that they had essentially committed to participation because of these continued conversations. The women felt the producers treated them like children, and they were extremely disgruntled about the experience. They have since stopped watching the show, which had been a favorite.

CHAPTER EIGHT

DISCLOSURE AS A SOCIAL MOVEMENT TACTIC

Talk show panelists' willingness to self-disclose on television situates them in the vanguard of citizens striving for social change. The use of personal testimony to advance a cause has deep roots in the history of American evangelicalism. The well-known abolitionist Sojourner Truth, a powerfully effective Christian evangelist of the 19th century, often self-disclosed during her speeches. Her most famous remarks about women's suffrage were contained in a response to a man in the audience who asserted that women were too delicate to vote. Her reply included these words:

> I could work as much and eat as much as a man when I could get it—and bear de lash as well. And ain't I a woman? I have borne children, and seen 'em mos' all sold off to slavery, and when I cried out with my mother's grief, none but Jesus heard me—And ain't I a woman?[1]

The women's movement and gay rights advocacy groups also have traditionally used self-disclosure to highlight the connections between private realities and politics.[2] In addition to consciousness-raising sessions, an increasingly common tactic of social activism is the act of *coming out*. The term, primarily used by the gay community, concerns the behavior of individuals who can "pass" but choose to proclaim their inclusion in a marginalized group's ranks.[3] Outing pronouncements have also been used more recently by incest survivors and others who choose to come forward to force the public to confront a topic and to realize the numbers of people who are involved in what was formerly hidden and stigmatized.

Loralee MacPike, in an edited volume consisting of homosexuals' stories about coming out to their children, explains: "Every time we come out—to our children or others—we alter the balance of homophobia in American culture. . . . But every tiny piece of the truth about lesbian and gay people adds to the visibility and reality of lesbian and gay lives."[4] Relatives and friends of stigmatized group members also share in the discrimination. *Beyond Acceptance*, a book about parents accepting their gay offspring, urges relatives to step forward to dispel myths about homosexuality. Authors Carolyn Griffin, Marian Wirth, and Arthur Wirth proclaim:

> We speak because we question the fairness of the stigma. We properly want justice for our children and ourselves. Finally we speak because we want to work to change the prejudice of society. We have learned that our negative inner messages are merely antiquated judgements based on lack of truth. We have a deep desire to correct a misinformed society. This is how human society has been changed throughout history.[5]

bell hooks asserts that speaking out is important for the empowerment of marginalized groups:

> Moving from silence to speech is for the oppressed, the colonized, the exploited, and those who stand and struggle side by side, a gesture of defiance that heals, that makes new life, and new growth possible. It is that act of speech, of "talking back," that is no mere gesture of empty words, that is the expression of moving from object to subject, that is the liberated voice.[6]

Kerran Sanger calls this course of action "definitional protest," which she describes as "a symbolic redefinition, or reclaiming, of the self from others more powerful who would seek to impose limiting definitions."[7]

THE LABELING THEORY OF DEVIANCY

Within sociology, proponents of the labeling theory of deviance argue that the parameters of what is considered deviant are socially negotiated.[8] Howard Becker argues:

> Social groups create deviance by making rules whose infraction
> constitutes deviance, by applying those rules to particular people
> and labeling them outsiders. From this point of view, deviance is not
> a quality of the act the person commits, but rather a consequence of
> the application by others of rules and sanctions to an offender.[9]

Theorists who hold this view of deviancy as socially defined also suggest
that individuals who rank low in society's hierarchy are most likely to be
labeled, whereas the wealthy and powerful are less susceptible.[10]

Edward Jones and his co-authors list six facets of a discrediting
feature (such as a physical disability or an addiction) that have important
ramifications on the probability of acceptance by others.[11] The dimensions include: the extent to which the feature can be hidden, the pattern of
development and expected outcome, how much it infringes on daily routines, the aesthetic nature, the cause, and the danger presented to others.

Jones and his colleagues have described the process by which an
individual is marginalized because of a discrediting characteristic of his
or her personality, lifestyle, or appearance:

> Stigmatization is an extreme form of categorical inference, whereby
> some clue regarding membership . . . gives rise to drastic attribu-
> tional outcomes . . . [which sometimes] "engulf" the identity of the
> individual; they become the filter through which his or her other
> characteristics are seen. They are also imbued with strong affect,
> primarily negative in tone.[12]

Importantly, Erving Goffman argues that stigmatized individuals see
themselves as normal. Among the tactics he suggests for stigma management is to forthrightly address the questions and misconceptions held by
others. Goffman believes that individuals considered deviant are more
adept at impression management because of years of practice at passing
(avoiding detection), covering (minimizing the saliency of the disability),
and tactfully assisting "normals" in their awkward responses.[13]

Fred Davis identifies several phases in a process of deviance disavowal in which those who are handicapped or exhibit other negatively
evaluated characteristics try to move others from fictional to true acceptance of the stigmatizing feature. Davis describes the potential for normalization, a process that occurs when a nonstigmatized individual
"comes to view as normal and morally acceptable that which initially

strikes him as odd, unnatural, 'crazy,' deviant, etc."[14] Ronald Farrell and Thomas Morrione argue that forums are needed in which members of stigmatized groups can directly address "normals":

> There is a relative absence of reciprocated communication directed toward accurate as well as sensitive mutual definition. Such curtailed interaction does not allow one to test his conception or definition of the other via interactional feedback, thus the process of redefinition or reconceptualization is severely, if not completely, restricted.[15]

This suggests that television talk shows may provide important venues for such interaction to take place. They provide a soapbox—imperfect but available—from which stigmatized group members can confront mainstream stereotypes.[16]

COUNTERHEGEMONY

The talk show participants I interviewed felt an imperative to provide a countervailing force against the images beamed by television and society in general. bell hooks has written of disenfranchised groups finding their voices: "Speaking becomes both a way to engage in active self-transformation and a rite of passage where one moves from being object to being subject. As objects, we remain voiceless—our being defined and interpreted by others."[17] hooks calls this process of self-transformation "counter hegemonic discourse."[18] The risk of "talking back" entails public knowledge of one's discrediting features, but the potential to gain ground in political terms drives many to engage in this form of social activism that defies conventional propriety.[19]

Taking an active role in self-definition is an act of resistance to society's definitions of one's group and to demarcations pertaining to the boundary lines that separate normalcy from deviancy. Raymond Williams's definition of hegemony emphasizes this idea of limits:

> [The] saturation of the whole process of living—to such a depth that the pressures and limits of what can ultimately be seen as a specific economic, political and cultural system seem to most of us the pressures and limits of simple experience and common sense.[20]

Antonio Gramsci argues that the resulting view of normalcy as derived by simple common sense is the crux of the power that makes hegemony difficult to resist and forceful in its consequences. Russell Ferguson has described hegemony's invisible yet potent force:

> We know that the phantom center, elusive as it is, exerts a real, undeniable power over the whole social framework of our culture. . . . It defines the tacit standards from which specific others can then be declared to deviate, and while that myth is perpetuated by those whose interests it serves, it can also be internalized by those who are oppressed by it.[21]

The media, of course, are primary purveyors of hegemonic messages.[22] Although broadcasters claim they objectively report reality, it is this very posturing of objectivity that gives credence to certain depictions of normalcy and not others. Gaye Tuchman, for example, describes journalistic routines by which television news mirrors current power relations in society: Reporters highlight certain topics at the expense of others, choose certain sources, and frame the story and key players in particular ways.

Certain values are naturalized by media practices and are therefore difficult to counter by groups whose beliefs fall outside of an area Stuart Hall calls media consensus. Hall refers to two regions beyond the area of consensus: toleration (in which differing definitions of reality overlap to a degree) and dis-sensus or conflict (in which sharply divergent definitions are put into effect). Groups that defy cultural norms are generally situated by journalists on the hinterlands of the ideological map, with their viewpoints presented in terms of harsh contrast to the status quo. Jock Young feels this positioning of fringe groups "as wild beasts . . . existing at the edge of the social universe" can dangerously imperil outgroup members if biased treatment by the press magnifies public feelings of suspicion or fear.[23]

Members of marginalized groups are generally left out of the shaping of the depictions broadcast to society about their groups. John Fiske and John Hartley addressed what they called television's sociocentrality in this way:

> The bardic mediator tends to articulate the negotiated central concerns of its culture, with only limited and often over-mediated refer-

ences to the ideologies, beliefs, habits of thought and definitions of the situation which obtain in groups which are for one reason or another peripheral.[24]

Edward Herman and Noam Chomsky identify economic inequalities as a primary filter in the dissemination of news, pointing out that media outlets with considerable reach have been prohibitively expensive for all but the wealthiest citizens for more than a century. Despite what appears to be an ever-increasing panoply of viewing choices on cable, only public access programs occasionally provide alternative paradigms or ways of organizing reality. The notoriously small audience for such programs, however, afford the potential only to dent the polished armor of hegemony.

The resulting "reality" packaged unobtrusively in mainstream media products teaches viewers what is important, acceptable, and of concern. All else is marginalized. Marcia Tucker has described the process: "Through shifts in position, any given group can be ignored, trivialized, rendered invisible and unheard, perceived as inconsequential, de-authorized, 'other' or threatening, while others are valorized."[25] Talk show panelists, concerned about the negative or missing representations of their groups, were taking an active role in the production of messages pertaining to them. The counterhegemonic struggle concerns important rewards for the winners, because hegemony marks out the boundaries of society, determining who and what is acceptable and, importantly, which groups are protected under the law and granted certain rights.

As noted in the previous section describing the paucity of resources available to them, out-groups are almost powerless players in the "reality" shaping that goes on, in large measure, on television. Elayne Rapping wrote, "Hegemony is the terrain upon which those of us who work for change must move, but it is not our home turf. We do not have the material resources for the battle that those in charge have."[26] However uneven the terrain, the cultural resource held by participants, however, is their stigmatizing feature and their willingness to display and speak of it.

John Fiske has noted:

There is a power in resisting power, there is a power in maintaining one's social identity in opposition to that proposed by the dominant ideology, there is a power in asserting one's own subcultural values against the dominant ones. There is, in short, a power in being different.[27]

Fiske is speaking here of audience members' contested readings of cultural forms; but the quote is perhaps more applicable when discussing talk show guests whose differentness is the source of their power that affords them the opportunity to represent themselves on the medium.

Talk show participants were acutely aware of television's power, perhaps because their marginality had been greatly shaped by it. Stanley Cohen and Jock Young recognized television's role in plying refracted images of outgroups back to them:

The deviant's own knowledge of how "most" others perceive him derives from this mass media portrayal; indeed in the case of the isolated deviant, even his knowledge of others involved in the same form of action might derive from this source. This makes each social problem group feel more marginal when facing, what they often presume, is a monolith of agreement.[28]

Although daytime talk shows are derided by the mainstream public, members of marginalized groups look to the programs pragmatically as forums for stigma management. Their "reading" of the show, to use John Fiske and John Hartley's conception of "reading television," is vastly different than those reading from society's center.[29] This is due in part to the lack of alternative forums, as discussed earlier, such that outgroup adherents make the best of their limited choices for access. The different attitudes toward the genre also speak to the negotiated and sometimes oppositional view[30] taken by members of marginalized groups resisting society's depictions of them. This is not felt by the mainstream, who, because they are already "in," generally do not sense the same longing for representation. As a consequence, the general public seems to view the noisy voices on talk shows as further evidence of the panelists' deviancy.

The voices of resistance on talk shows may be an example of the minority identified by Elisabeth Noelle-Neumann who continue to speak out despite the pressures in society toward conformity and silence. Noelle-Neumann's theory about the "spiral of silence" identifies the powerful "motive of not wanting to be isolated, to be on the fringes."[31] Members of marginalized groups, however, are already outside the boundaries of society. They recognize the risk of losing ground by appearing on talk shows but hope to strategically gain space in the shifting boundary demarcations. Charles Stewart, Craig Smith and Robert Denton have noted that social movements are "criticized for not handling the controversy through normal, proper channels and procedures—even when the channels and procedures are denied to the movement."[32] This lack of assets prompts participants to trade their sole resource—personal disclosures—to gain access to the public airwaves.

REARTICULATING DEVIANCY

An integral part of the definitions that television disclosers are resisting are the often pejorative labels that society bestows on members of marginalized groups. Howard Becker, utilizing Everett Hughes's distinction between "master and auxiliary status traits," found that deviant labels come to be seen by "normals" as *the* defining feature, taking precedence over other characteristics a marginalized group member may have.[33] Becker demonstrated a stigmatized individual's longing to overcome this engulfment by quoting a character in a Dorris Lessing novel who said she "didn't mind being thought schizophrenic but didn't like people to think that was *all* she was."[34]

By agreeing to appear, panelists are accepting the label; in fact, they are identified on the program with phrases such as "former homosexual." This is part of a paradoxical process occurring on these programs: Participants hope to disavow or delabel their marginalized status while simultaneously declaring themselves members of marginalized groups. Some felt their labels were unnecessarily hyped on various shows but played along with the exaggerated characterizations given them because, again, it facilitated access.

For example, Ralph originally was asked to appear on a number of shows because his daughter's rape was a racially motivated attack, and hate crimes were eagerly covered by the press when the incident first occurred. His "vigilante dad" twist developed over time, as producers took great interest in the revenge elements of his outcry for justice. He admitted: "If I didn't make it known that it was a bias-related crime, and I didn't make it known that I would attempt to take the law into my own hands . . . what would television want me for?"

112

Somewhat similarly, Joe (whose on-screen label read "has had 100 affairs") admitted he had no idea about the number, and he did not think it mattered. He knew that the more affairs the shows claimed he had, the more people would listen. The labels, then, like the disclosures, were vehicles to garner attention so that the messages could be delivered. Donahue himself frequently talks about the need to get people in under the tent. The hosts lure viewers to sell them in bulk to advertisers, and participants, meanwhile, piggyback their messages along with the ads.

It is critical, however, for participants to be willing to shoulder the label the show will inevitably affix on each guest. Michael was ardent about his wish to warn people to protect themselves from the AIDS virus and not rely on the honesty of others. However, as he observed ruefully, "The whole purpose was all canceled out by the label 'prostitute.'"

A few grappled with the one-dimensional nature of the labeling. In line with the character's lament that her schizophrenia engulfed others' views of her, Therese Keegan, an organ donor who had appeared on *The Oprah Winfrey Show*, told me, "I don't want to be known in life as the woman who gave a kidney!" She continued rather playfully:

> I had something different in mind for why I would get recognition in life, and I thought, "Oh, my God, this is what my fifteen minutes is going to be about? Come on! Giving an organ? Get outta here!" So I was really pleased we were only on for two minutes, 'cause I figured, I have thirteen left.

Clearly, Therese recognized the importance of organ transplants, but she felt the act was completely natural, something anyone would do. She noted that she would rather have the attention for accomplishments that were more difficult, such as "a book I had written or a law I got changed." She seemed to feel diminished somewhat by being portrayed so narrowly, when her life was teeming with interesting challenges and accomplishments.

Most participants, however, particularly those situated on the far margins of society, found that the public already fully characterized them by their distinguishing feature. Talk show guests hoped to recode these labels' meanings to include more expansive and less negative elements. They did this in part, as mentioned earlier, by stressing commonalities the group shared with the mainstream such as the ethic of family, love, and other abiding themes in American life. The sought-after results are a recoding of the marginalized features and a focus on essential similarities that warrant equal treatment.

Harrison Trice and Paul Roman identify three possible delabeling mechanisms available to members of groups considered deviant by society:

> First, organizations of deviants may develop which have the primary goal of changing the norms of the community or society, such that their originally offending behavior becomes acceptable. . . . Secondly, it is possible that the mandated professionals . . . may create highly visible and explicit "delabeling" or "status return" ceremonies which constitute legitimized public pronouncements that the offending deviance has ceased. . . . A third means is through the development of mutual aid organizations which encourage a return to strict conformity to the norms of the community.[35]

Television talk shows have components of the first two processes in that they provide highly visible delabeling opportunities to alter norms; however, panelists are not repentant nor declaring a return to community standards. Instead, they are trying to include their outgroups within the boundaries of those standards. Appearing on talk shows is a ritualistic sloughing off of stigma for members of marginalized groups willing to run the gauntlet and able to carry off the stigma management. Although the primary rationale for participation may be different for various shows in the genre, self-disclosure on *Donahue* appears to be instrumental, a manifestation of personal empowerment, not dysfunction.

Norma Jean directly addressed the notion of deviancy when discussing a newspaper article written about her after both *Geraldo* and *Donahue* episodes featuring her aired the same day. The article said that the shows had been reduced to sharing the "same deviant." I asked how she felt about that term being used to describe her. She responded:

> It depends on how you want to define deviant. Is it a person that deviates from the so-called normal? Is that what you call deviant? Well, then, yes, I am a deviant. Is it a person that has a bad or suspect lifestyle? No, I don't. So, in that sense, no, if that's how you want to define deviant.

Norma Jean and other talk show participants strike me as scrappy contenders engaged in a tug of war over the lines that delimit deviancy.

THE DEBATE ABOUT CO-OPTATION

It is paradoxical, but the only place available for members of stigmatized groups to confront society's negative conceptions is at the "freak show." In a discussion of black feminist discourse, bell hooks warned of the risks of co-optation:

> Here [in the United States] the idea of finding a voice risks being trivialized or romanticized. . . . Such rhetoric often turns the voices and beings of non-white women into commodity, spectacle. In a white supremacist, capitalist, patriarchal state where the mechanisms of cooptation are so advanced, much that is potentially radical is undermined, turned into commodity.[36]

Both Bert and Kate acknowledged that they were being used as a commodity. Bert said, "And so I always figure that it's just, you know, another way for them to sell their soap by having uh, two queers and a dyke that had a baby." One of Kate's main concerns when deciding whether to appear was the knowledge that her story would be used to sell products. Dolores said that calls from producers were especially numerous during sweeps months. She wryly commented, "Here were TV and radio stations making money off prostitution, while it was illegal for me to make money off prostitution."[37] Michael said, "They're going to do whatever they can to get those ultimate ratings. They treat you like gold, but you're there for a purpose."

Several people criticized daytime talk show producers and hosts whom they felt had treated them more like an object than a subject. Joy, for example, said, "Some of them like *Sally Jessy* really treat people like things . . . that sense of 'Okay,' you know, 'You're a thing now. We're done with you. You're used up.'"

Virtually everyone was keenly aware of the loaded nature of the contest. The emphasis on impression management strategies is evidence of the cautious resistance. Repeatedly, respondents voiced their initial concerns about how a show would frame them. Kate's first response to the call from the *Donahue* staff was to ask about the working title of the show.[38] She then commented to the staff member, "It's sweeps month, right?" Kate went on to describe her emotional response to the sensational tone: "I was a little angry, uh, that uh, oh, it's sweeps month, trot out the transsexuals. . . . But I figure, fine, you know. . . . The other edge to that sword is that, in sweeps month, more people are gonna watch and get what I have to say." Craig exhibited a similar wariness:

> I mean, I just turned down Jesse Jackson last week, to be on his show. I didn't like the format. You know, they wanted uh—me to appear with Jerry Falwell, and Gary Bowers. He's head of the Family Research Council. And . . . they wanted to mike me in the audience and have them up, up on the set—so it would be confrontational that way, and I said, "No." I said, "All you want me to do is appear as a—a radical fag, and that's not . . . what I'm about."

Craig said he "practically produced" the first episode of *Donahue* that he and Patrick appeared on by playing an active role in determining who else was asked on the show, how much time they received to talk alone with Donahue, and other features of the program. He could exert some influence because the nationwide discussion of their legal suit made them highly sought after guests. Craig said, "I realize who has the media power. They want us. We give them ratings." Craig was confident in his ability to draw an audience; he asserted that he and Patrick precipitated a jump in the ratings whenever they appeared.

The tension of resistance is evident in Craig's recounting of his involvement in the second *Donahue* show they appeared on, an episode that featured the in-studio wedding of two gay men. Craig said:

> We were going up there to talk. And talk about issues—ah, you know, and I knew the show was a freak show to begin with because of what they were doing. . . . Not only was it a gay black couple, but it was a short black man—It was a freak show. And they wanted us to come on to lend a legitimacy to what they were doing. They wanted to use us. You know . . . and I felt for the good of the ah— gay rights movement, that we were needed there to present uh something a little more palatable to the American public. And I also felt there was another opportunity for us to get our message out.

Craig discussed some of the reasons he and Patrick were dissatisfied with the representation of gays when they appeared on *Donahue* the second time:

> What we did on the second show, was these guys came up, vroom, they got married. There was no humanization—and people reacted like "You faggots, look at this shit you're putting in our face . . ." as opposed to "We love each other and . . . we're going to express our commitment to each other." Yeah, there's a really big difference so I'm pissed at what happened.

He criticized the tone of the second show: "It seems like they wanted a real fluff show. . . . This is what gay is about, we've got the Flirtations singing . . ." Craig's frustration evokes Cornel West's claim that "critics of culture" are "simultaneously progressive and coopted."[39]

Elayne Rapping has expressed her concern that the reverberating voices on talk shows simply echo dully within the glassed-in arena rather than pierce the defenses that deflect social change:

> It is, in the grand scheme of things as they are, a good thing to have these arenas of ideological interaction and open-endedness. But, finally, these shows are a dead end. . . . They are all talk and no action. Unless someone yells something from the floor (as a feminist did during the eating discussion), there will be no hint that there is a world of political action, or of politics at all.[40]

However, television disclosers are becoming more savvy in their resistance techniques. William Gamson and Andre Modigliani use the term *interpretive packages* to describe the easily grasped frames developed by the media, corporations, and social movement groups to get messages across to the public.[41] Talk show participants serve as individual interpretive packages, self-fashioned and part of an effort to further their groups' social momentum. Several, most notably Lorretta, Craig, and Patrick, were carefully attempting to widen the discussion to political concerns during show tapings.

Lucretia Knapp has criticized talk shows for taking advantage of panelists: "As feminists have come to understand, continuing to portray women as victims only perpetuates their victimization."[42] However, Lorretta, an incest survivor, believes her appearances on talk shows sound a clarion call to other survivors. She said, "That's another reason I'm out there—is get people riled up enough. It's part of being political . . . to do something for themselves. They don't have to be a victim anymore if they don't want to."

Both Sandi and Heather admitted that there is an element of sensationalism when show hosts ask Heather to detail the phrases used to harass and humiliate her. Sandi said:

> It's not that it doesn't bother her [to recount the terms] . . . but in a case like this, for the number of kids that it's happening to, the kids even almost need to hear that somebody else is being called the exact same kind of names that they are for them to be able to relate and understand that hey, this isn't right, and there are people that are fighting it. And I don't think that people get the message as much when you circumvent the question, than when you answer it directly.

An imperfect forum was considered better than none. Dolores reported that the studio audience was very hostile toward the topic of prostitution but believed "there was a kernel of understanding, that maybe something we had said may have penetrated a few minds."[43] Jenny, a swinger, argued:

> Having an opportunity to bring up a taboo subject is a—no matter what the reaction is—is a step toward opening the dialogue, and I approached it in that way. Even if we as people were made to, I mean, I was hoping that we could present ourselves in such a way that we wouldn't look like uh, the most terrible people walking the face of the earth, but even if we were made to look bad as people, as human beings, just the mere fact that we could walk out on a stage in front of a television camera and talk about our sexuality, talk about our lifestyle, opened a door. And that—allowing people to talk about it . . . breaking the taboo about talking about this kind of a personal thing in a public arena allows other people to have that same kind of a thing.

Most knew that they would be portrayed in an extreme fashion. As mentioned earlier, Dale warned his wife that they would be portrayed as a "limp dick" and a "whore." At the risk of being co-opted and ridiculed, respondents were willing to step up to the electronic soap box, because without information and new depictions, the potential for change, in their eyes, was dismal. Kate said:

What's different about this particular thing is that, in the old freak shows in the 19th century, the—the freaks that they would take around . . . the freaks would be real live Negroes, or real live Indians, um, they could talk, if they could talk at all, they were scripted. Otherwise, the medicine person, you know, the hawker, would stand up there and tell the story. The difference in this particular century is that I can say my own words. Within reason, within television code reasons, reason . . . and that's why I figured, "Okay."

In this 20th century version of the freak show, audience members, the hawker, and the freaks jostle each other for space in the spotlight.

NOTES

1. Quoted in Bass, 1972, p. 57.
2. Contesting society's entrenched practices and conceptions through speech characterizes expressive movements, which Herbert Blumer described in the following way: "Cultural drifts [have] only a general direction, toward which they move in a slow, halting, yet persistent fashion; [they] stand for a general shifting in the ideas of people, particularly along the lines of the ideas people have of themselves, and of their rights and privileges" (Blumer, 1939; quoted in Simons et al., 1984, p. 793). Some sociologists do not consider such "cultural drifts" to be full social movements because of their amorphous quality. Simons et al. define a social movement as a "sustained effort by noninstitutionalized collectivities to mobilize resources, resist counterpressures, and exert external influence on behalf of a cause" (p. 794). Simons et al.'s article is an excellent overview of the social movement literature. Morris and Mueller's (1992) edited volume, *Frontiers in Social Movement Theory*, is also a useful collection that stresses the struggles faced by movement groups trying to wrest control of competing interpretations of issues important to them.
3. Gross's (1991) work describes the newer and more controversial tactic of strategically "outing" others who may have wished to keep their membership in an outgroup secret.

4. MacPike, 1989, p. 246.
5. Griffin et al., 1986, p. 106.
6. hooks, 1990, p. 340.
7. Sanger, 1992, p. 37. Lipsky, 1972, has noted that members of disadvantaged groups use protest as one of few resources available to them.
8. The labeling theory of deviancy, also called the societal reaction theory, has been criticized for being too deterministic and for implying that no behavior is deviant until it is so defined. However, the view that the parameters of deviancy definitions can be negotiated is the germ of labeling theory that is of special value here.
9. Becker, 1963, p. 9.
10. See, for example, Farrell and Morrione, 1979.
11. Jones et al., 1984, also note that these dimensions greatly impact the person's self-concept and the range of impression management techniques that can be utilized.
12. Jones et al., 1984, pp. 295-296.
13. Goffman, 1963.
14. Davis, 1979, p. 154.
15. Farrell and Morrione, 1979, p. 134.
16. This active but rather limited participation in social issues may be an example of a 1991 Kettering Foundation Report finding that citizens generally feel impotent but do "engage in specific areas of public life when they believe they can make a difference" (p. 4).
17. hooks, 1989, p. 12.
18. hooks, 1990.
19. See Gusfield's (1986) work pertaining to status politics.
20. Williams, 1977, p. 110.
21. Ferguson, 1990, p. 9.
22. See Althusser, 1971.
23. Young, 1981, p. 402.
24. Fiske and Hartley, 1978, p. 89.
25. Tucker, 1990, p. 7.
26. Rapping, 1987, p. 15.
27. Fiske, 1987, p. 19.
28. Cohen and Young, 1973, p. 342.

29. Fiske and Hartley, 1978. See also Fiske, 1987.
30. See Parkin's (1972) paradigm of different "meaning systems."
31. Noelle-Neumann, 1984, p. ix.
32. Stewart, Smith, and Denton, 1989, p. 7.
33. Becker, 1963, cited race, certain occupations such as the medical profession, and stigmatizing characteristics such as physical handicap or homosexuality as examples of master status determining traits that will override all others.
34. Italics in Becker's citation. Becker, 1986, p. 143.
35. Trice and Roman, 1981, p. 473. It is interesting to note that while avenues that allow a normalizing process to occur are rare, the flip side is relatively formalized. Kai Erikson, 1962, described the ritualized nature of according deviant status on individuals in a series of "ceremonies":

> They provide a formal confrontation between the deviant suspect and representatives of his community (as in the criminal trial or psychiatric case conference); they announce some judgement about the nature of his deviancy (a verdict or diagnosis, for example,) and they perform an act of social placement, assigning him to a special role (like that of a prisoner or patient) which redefines his position in society. (p. 311)

Trice and Roman argue that ritualized delabeling of deviant status occurs less frequently partly due to beliefs that deviancy is irreversible.
36. hooks, 1989, p. 14.
37. French and Lee, 1988, page 179.
38. Kate recalled that the title was something like "People who change sex to have sex with the opposite sex."
39. West, 1990, p. 20. Italics in the original. This inevitable churning through or absorption of marginalized groups is a defining feature of hegemony and is a cooptive process that normally strengthens the dominant ideology. Rapping, 1987, described the slippery workings of hegemony: "Sometimes it allows for new, divergent attitudes to become legitimate and for limited changes in social practice and belief to occur. More often, it persuades us, disingenuously, that our feelings of dissatisfac-

tion can be assuaged within the limits of existing social practice" (p. 14). See Gitlin, 1987, and Rachlin, 1988, for further
comments on this topic.
40. Rapping, 1991, p. 38.
41. Gamson and Modigliani, 1989, p. 3.
42. Knapp, 1988, p. 4.
43. French and Lee, 1988, p. 173.

CHAPTER NINE

SELF-DISCLOSURE AS CURRENCY

Self-disclosure is deployed from talk show participants' meager stock-pile of tactics in a struggle against the public's complacency, hate, ignorance, and inattention. The strategic nature of television disclosure is apparent from the amount of planning that occurs and the driven quality of the behavior that sweeps aside concerns for risk. The tactical and public characteristics call into question whether these are "real" and authentic self-disclosures that are exhibited on talk shows.[1]

THE SELF-DISCLOSURE LITERATURE

Numerous definitions of self-disclosure exist within the literature.[2] I prefer D.V. Fisher's: Self-disclosure is "verbal behavior through which individuals truthfully, sincerely and intentionally communicate novel, ordinarily private information about themselves to one or more addressees".[3] Fisher makes a distinction, however, between self-disclosure and self-*presentation* that I find troublesome. He classifies truthful and heartfelt revelations used strategically as self-presentation, because he considers such utterances insincere. I'll return to this thorny notion of sincerity in a moment.

Work done in the self-disclosure field almost entirely involves experimental manipulations of paired individuals, one of whom is usually a confederate disclosing at a predetermined level of intimacy. Findings in the literature are quite mixed, partially due to the use of varied definitions and measures. Two consistent patterns, however, have emerged. The foremost of these is that disclosure tends to be reciprocal.[4] This is interesting to consider in light of the characteristics of shows such as *Donahue*, because the disclosures exhibited there are generally directed toward the host and the audience and not to the other guest disclosers. However, there may be a sort of delayed reciprocity or patterning modeled on hearing so many disclosures over the years spewing from the screen by celebrities and other talk show panelists.

Donahue himself rarely reciprocates disclosure, although he and his wife, Marlo Thomas, are occasionally featured in magazines or prime-time interview programs. He has written a fairly revealing autobiography in which he discusses, among other topics, his divorce and his disaffection with the Catholic church. Other talk show hosts, particularly the women, occasionally reveal sensitive information.[5] However, the power imbalance teeters sharply in favor of the host, such that neither the audience nor the guests seem to expect reciprocal revelations. More important, as described earlier, informants felt driven to participate because of their evangelical fervor, and they were fully aware that the expected disclosure of details granted the privilege of an invitation.[6]

Irwin Altman and Dalmas Taylor's theory of social penetration is often used to explain the role of reciprocal self-disclosure in relationship formation. The authors point out that intimacy levels of topics discussed increase as relationships become closer in a spiraling process of deepening intimacy they call social penetration.[7] This, too, seems interesting to consider in terms of mass-mediated discussions on talk shows.

The concept of parasocial interaction, first discussed by Donald Horton and R. Richard Wohl in 1956, may explain the perception of a relationship with the show host that some guests—particularly of hosts such as Sally or Oprah—may feel they have. Several features of the genre (such as the daily scheduling and the opportunity to serve as audience member or guest) would suggest that tendencies toward parasocial relationships would be strong. For some viewers, this facsimile of an abiding relationship might facilitate feelings of closeness, which might then lead to high levels of initial disclosure, particularly for plaintiff types who petition the shows to air their grievances.

Sally Jessy Raphael, for example, tells an interesting story in her 1990 autobiography about a rape survivor from Connecticut, Stephie Berezowskyj, who had never told anyone about a violent sexual assault that occurred when she was 15. Berezowskyj—after much cajoling and sympathetic listening by a staff member—disclosed on *Sally Jessy*

Raphael about the heartache of the rape and subsequent abortion. She had grown to feel she could trust Raphael after listening to her radio program for years. Steve Lowery, in an account of this case in the Raleigh *News and Observer*, described how Berezowskyj said she pushed aside thoughts of the audience: "It was like just me and Sally. I really believed if I talked to Sally she could solve this."[8] An article in the magazine *For Women First* also mentioned Berezowskyj, who is quoted as saying, "I could never have done this on *Donahue* or *Oprah*."[9] This suggests that a fifth category in the typology for disclosure rationale may be necessary to include those seeking a sort of therapeutic release linked to feelings for or expectations about particular hosts.

A second fairly consistent finding from the literature is that disclosers tend to be liked by the individuals they have opened up to, often because the revelation is seen as an indication of trust and positive regard.[10] This finding may help to explain the positive outcomes reported by talk show guests that I detail in the next chapter. However, a key element of television disclosure makes it different from the context in which correlations of liking and disclosure have been identified. The broadcast nature of the televised act rules out an attribution that the disclosure is personalized; a person is unlikely to feel special and trustworthy when millions of others are also listening in. Furthermore, the early timing of the disclosure, paired with what is often a topic with negative valence, suggests that disliking would result,[11] so the finding of liking—or some emotion indicated by enthusiastic greetings—in this televised context is remarkable.

Gender differences are another common but far less consistent finding in the field. Women typically disclose more than men, although situational factors and questions about gender definitions muddy this effect.[12] A myriad of studies provide a general portrait of high disclosers as likely to have feminine characteristics and to be extroverted, white, American, and situated late in the family birth order.[13] The context of the disclosure situation is critical. Researchers have identified the following as factors affecting disclosure levels: the gender,[14] proximity,[15] status,[16] and eliciting behaviors[17] of the person who is disclosed to; the stage of the relationship;[18] and the prospect for future interaction.[19]

Several researchers have posited theories about high levels of early disclosure, the very element that makes television disclosure so puzzling. Karen Prager discovered that subjects who did not have an intimate primary relationship disclosed at high levels to friends as well as strangers. Joseph Stokes presents a model that illuminates a different relationship between loneliness and disclosure. He argues, first, that openness is a trait. Second, he defines the receptivity of the person fielding the disclosure as a key component in a cycle that leads either to less disclosure and resulting loneliness or more disclosure and heightened feelings of intimacy.[20]

William Stiles provides a model of self-disclosure processes that he compares to immune system functioning. He argues that high disclosure levels can be indicative of an individual's healing process and can result in increased self-understanding and cathartic release. He stresses the importance of available disclosure targets during the feverish period when the need for the disclosure is most salient.[21] Dan Coates and Tina Winston discuss the dilemmas individuals face during this period that they call distress disclosure; these include the tendency to wear down social support systems and the need to modulate the disclosure so that it is not utterly depressing or stressful for others. Both works cite the need for responsive targets for self-disclosure, arguing that disclosure can result in increased physical and mental health.

Other studies have investigated the link between self-disclosure and health. Sidney Jourard, the first to use the term *self-disclosure*, wrote, "Real self-disclosure is both a symptom of personality health and at the same time a means of ultimately achieving healthy personality."[22] He believed the relationship between disclosure and mental health is curvilinear; too little or too much disclosure results in poor relationships and emotional disturbance. Jourard also felt that people who do not have at least one target for disclosure are at risk for mental and physical health problems. James Pennebaker has found that what he terms confession can have positive psychological and physical benefits, particularly when the affective components of a painful revelation are released during the telling.

As mentioned earlier, respondents for this study appeared to have social support networks firmly in place. Furthermore, most had passed through a cathartic stage. Many expressed a sense of well-being about their lives. Television disclosure was not a distressed revelation laden with affect. Instead of a cathartic rush of emotional testimony, the televised disclosure is better characterized by a model of planned, descriptive relating of facts.

In summary, the most consistent findings in the self-disclosure field are that disclosure is generally reciprocated in dyadic situations and that increasingly intimate disclosures characterize developing relationships. A complex interplay between dispositional and contextual factors influences self-disclosure levels. Findings reported in previous chapters reveal that participants' studied awareness of the context as well as personality traits of openness, among others, combined to influence participation in a forum that requires personal revelations. Television disclosure to millions appears to be different from the standard dyadic model most notably in the lack of reciprocity.[23] Yet, social penetration in a true social sense may be operating, as participants strive to develop links between communities of people rather than between individuals.

SELF-DISCLOSURE OR SELF-PRESENTATION?

Participants' use of varied tactics to ameliorate the potential negative effects of the genre suggests that the phenomenon of television disclosure might be more precisely classified as self-presentation according to Fisher's definition of self-disclosure that excludes divulgences that contain strategic elements. In fact, Fisher believes that laboratory experiments, which make up the bulk of the self-disclosure studies, tend to elicit self-presentation as well.

His particular demarcation does not seem to be gaining acceptance in the literature, however, perhaps because of the inherent difficulties in assessing sincerity.[24] More importantly, postmodern works theorizing concepts of self have scrapped the sincerity/insincerity dichotomy. Modernist notions of an essential self papered over with various strategic guises have been replaced with the analogy of a pastiche of selves—varied aspects of each individual played out in a range of relationships and situations, with no single version most "authentic."[25]

The disclosures on daytime talk shows generally are both extremely earnest and personal, and for this reason I believe the term self-disclosure is fitting, despite the fact that the self-presentational elements of the behavior are patently clear. I contend that a concern for impression management does not necessarily rule out sincerity, and participants seemed to be very sincerely trying to communicate their differentness.

An individual's self-disclosure can be characterized on several dimensions. The three most commonly measured are the intimacy level of the information content, the amount of expressiveness, and the extent of

127

imitation or touching on the content of the other's disclosure.[26] Arthur Bochner lists three additional dimensions: the breadth of topics discussed, the time spent disclosing, and the positive or negative valence of what is revealed. The lack of expressiveness on the show is most notable. Instead, the emphasis (largely because of demands by the studio audience and the host) is on a wide sweep of disclosure topics and on the depth of intimacy.

Although certain items were sometimes strategically suppressed such that the impression management was maximized, many respondents expressed a willingness to reveal even those areas of their private lives if full disclosure became necessary. Furthermore, the valence of the disclosures on talk shows often encompasses negative elements, such that the resulting impression is not wholly crafted for positive effect. Despite the impression management that accompanies participation, there is a declaration of self, of identity, that I believe makes the revelations very authentic or true-to-self. Indeed, there is a sort of "take it or leave it" tone permeating remarks made on talk shows that does not usually characterize tactics used for self-enhancement.

It is also interesting to note that many often expressed a skepticism about the sincerity of others who utilized the genre as they had. Rocki was somewhat suspicious because she noted, "Never once on any of the shows that I was on did they do anything to verify that what I had to say was true." Similarly, "Sam," who had been a fan of the genre, became disaffected after her appearances, because she no longer believed that the participants' stories were always genuine after she heard producers at one show prompt a participant to cry on cue.[27] Also, as mentioned earlier, two women who appeared on *Ricki Lake* related stories about the coaching they received from producers to play-act that they were furious at their roommate. The experience soured their previous enthusiasm for the show, because the veracity of others' stories now seemed suspect.

However, everyone else I talked to seemed genuine. Even Ross, who did a lot of macho posturing and always kept discussions at a fairly low level of disclosure, said, "I'll tell you one thing. Despite all the hype, and everything else, I do believe in everything I'm saying."

Issues of authenticity confound our postmodern era characterized largely by its profusion of simulated images. Richard Dyer's markers of authenticity ("lack of control, lack of premeditation, and privacy")[28] would again seem to indicate inauthenticity in this case. Participants give over all but the barest shred of privacy when they enter, and there is a great deal of premeditated preparation involving strategies to control unfolding events. However, Dyer is describing stars, whose commodified images are even more highly constructed. Talk show participants, although commodified and perhaps used as images by others, are fully representing themselves, not characters, when appearing. Joe, an actor, stressed that he was not acting, that he had appeared as himself. The sincerity issues are more toward authenticity on a continuum of sincerity than the medium usually affords.

Clearly, however, not all talk show panelists are on the level; show staffs—and audience members—have been duped in the past. A 1988 *Newsweek* article detailed the fraudulent posturing of two actors who posed as impotent and aversive to sex on several major shows.[29] A recent article in *The Baltimore Sun* described a hoax on *The Montel Williams Show* in which a man with AIDS claimed to have raped 90 prostitutes. The man admitted his confession was faked soon after he left the stage, but producers ran the two-part episode later without a disclaimer. The *Sun's* reporters condemned the producers of the show for not being more skeptical and attributed their credulity to the fierce battle for ratings.[30] My respondents felt that other guests were sometimes fakes, and they criticized the shows for not making more of an effort to check people's stories.

Generally, however, talk shows are more authentic than most media forms, because only portions such as the opening and cut-away statements are scripted on most shows in the genre. Individuals represented on the news and documentaries, forms considered highly authentic, clearly have self-presentational strategies operating as well. Studio audiences at talk shows often attempt to rattle the guests, to shake the frame, so that authenticity is better revealed. This may explain why these shows are so appealing to audiences; they seem real in a world in which the news as well as other media products increasingly rely on simulations and prepackaged elements.

Presentational strategies were at the forefront of participants' concerns, but the disclosures were still revealing and risky. Clearly, strategic planning as to what to suppress occurs in more routine settings as well, in which self-disclosure is also useful as a currency in maintaining and initiating relationships.[31] There are differences, then, as well as similarities between the use of disclosure in the mediated forum of the talk show and in interpersonal settings. In either case, disclosure can productively be used to tell one's own story in an act of self-construction that can be highly influential in shaping others' impressions.

David Shaffer, J. Smith, and Michele Tomarelli found that a key construct in social psychology—self-monitoring—impacted disclosure levels.[32] Mark Snyder defined the concept as follows:

> High self-monitors usually use their harvest of information [garnered from their ability to size up situations and other individuals] to tailor their public images to fit their social circumstances by using techniques of impression management—words and deeds chosen not so much for what they say about private attitudes and feelings, but rather for their tactical value in setting up appearances.[33]

The prevalence and breadth of the reported strategies suggest a tendency in this group toward a proficiency at self-monitoring. Snyder's characterization of high self-monitors seems to fit this group well: "They monitor or control the images of self they project in social interactions to a great extent."[34] Members of stigmatized groups may have more refined self-monitoring abilities because they so often face what Fred Davis called "strained interactions" with "normals." Patrick said, "Growing up gay, you know, dealing with your parents, answering all those questions . . . if you can handle them in a justifiable manner, then the public kind of falls into line." This lifetime of confronting questions about the stigmatizing features of one's life, in addition to the preplanning strategies employed, partly explains why talk show panelists often appear very much at ease in front of a national audience.

Furthermore, participants may have developed impression management skills in earlier attempts at "passing" as a "normal."[35] Lorretta said, "But I'm finding for myself and some other survivors of incest, we've had to survive over the years, so that's one of our—the things we can do, is to stay real poised, and particularly myself." Participants situated on the furthest margins of society were more accustomed to and more adept with the contested space. In other words, they were better contestants; they played the game well. They had a lifetime of practice behind them. During television appearances, this mastery of impression management techniques was no longer used to pass, which is a strategy of invisibility. Instead, the skills were utilized during a ritual of heightened visibility, television disclosure, in an effort at normalization geared toward a reinterpretation of the stigma.

The orchestrated nature of a talk show appearance points to an emphasis on descriptive rather than expressive disclosure. In fact, Dan Coates and Tina Winston found that high self-monitors received less therapeutic value during distress disclosures because of their focus on pleasing others and acting appropriately. The affective component is what James Pennebaker identified as crucial for precipitating a cathartic benefit. However, as mentioned earlier, the talk show participants I talked to were beyond a stage in which they were seeking a catharsis. For most, the aim was evangelical rather than therapy-based.

NOTES

1. In this chapter, I touch on the highlights of the extensive literature on self-disclosure, most of which has been generated by
   scholars in the fields of social and clinical psychology. Only
   one study of talk shows (Haag's 1993 work) specifically draws
   from this enormous body of literature, although many mention
   such relevant concepts as honesty or confession. For a compre-
   hensive review of the self-disclosure literature, see Derlega and
   Berg, 1987; Derlega et al., 1993; and Tardy, 1985.
   The usual pattern for studying self-disclosure is to manipulate
   the disclosure levels of confederates in experimental settings
   and then measure one or more of the various dimensions of
   the subjects' responses. Earlier studies used questionnaires in
   an effort to identify personality variables that correlated significantly with self-disclosure levels. However, these measures were largely abandoned after they were found to lack
   predictive validity (Cozby, 1973), and contextual factors were
   determined to play a critical role.
2. An early criticism by Archer, 1979, remains largely true
   today: "The weakest point in the basic superstructure of self-
   disclosure is the concept of disclosure itself" (p. 57). Worthy
   et al., 1969, provide one of the most commonly used definitions: "that which occurs when A knowingly communicates to
   B information about A which is not generally known and is
   not otherwise available to B" (p. 59).
3. Fisher, 1984, p. 278.

4. For reviews, see Archer, 1979; Cozby, 1973; and Gilbert, 1976.

5. Oprah Winfrey, for example, read many pages from her diary in a program in late 1993 that focused on her struggles with her weight. The episode included unflattering videotaped footage of the early stages of her dieting efforts. I believe her willingness to reciprocate disclosure plays a key role in her enormous popularity.

6. It is interesting to note that participants are called "guests," yet there are very firm expectations for what job they will do for the host. When I related the incident from *The Oprah Winfrey Show* that first prompted my interest in this study to informants, they often sharply criticized the woman for breaking an unspoken pact to give over the details.

7. See also Berscheid, 1985.

8. Lowery, 1991, p. 1D.

9. "Everybody's Talking!" 1992, p. 37.

10. Archer and Earle, 1983.

11. Bochner, 1984.

12. For reviews, see Archer, 1979; Cunningham, 1981; and Hill and Stull, 1987. Indeed, women seem to appear more often on talk shows; it may be that men more frequently refuse to be on the program, or they may be asked less often. I think that *Donahue* probably has a more even balance of men and women on the program, perhaps because of the mix of topics.

13. See Archer, 1979.

14. Hill and Stull, 1987.

15. Rubin and Shenker, 1978.

16. Slobin, Miller, and Porter, 1968.

17. Miller, Berg, and Archer, 1983.

18. Hendrick, 1987.

19. Shaffer and Ogden, 1986.

20. Donahue's receptivity is notable. He assumes a humanist posture, encouraging both disclosure and a tolerance for diversity. His accepting attitude toward what others might call deviancy is clearly exhibited in this passage from an episode on "sexual minorities" of August 15, 1991: "These live, irreplaceable sons and daughter of God, human beings all, want you to

know, among other things, that that's exactly what they are, human beings, and there [is] an awful lot of nervousness attending to their particular personal situations which provoke a lot of prejudice. The whole point of—the whole fuel of prejudice is ignorance today."

21. Stiles also argues that heightened states of private self-consciousness, an inner clamoring for attention to one's own feelings and thoughts, often prompts this feverish state.

22. Jourard, 1964, p. 24.

23. The outpouring of support from similarly marginalized others sometimes contains an element of reciprocated disclosure after the airing, however. Wendy, for example, talked about how often people would quietly reveal to her that they were also rape survivors.

24. Working definitions of self-disclosure in the fields of counseling and social psychology are not rigorously defined to exclude strategic but truthful revelations. There is not yet a consensus about the boundaries of the self-disclosure construct.

25. Kenneth Gergen's (1991) erudite book, *The Saturated Self,* traces this shift, as does Michael Wood and Louis Zurcher's (1988) text, *The Postmodern Self.* Lyotard, 1984, and Baudrillard, 1987, are key postmodern writers who write of individuals as relationally situated.

26. Davis and Sloan's (1974) rating guidelines are frequently used to judge levels of these components.

27. Sandi was miffed that a staff member at *Sally Jessy Raphael* anxiously inquired in preliminary interviews about whether Heather would break down in tears while telling her story. Sandi felt the producer was angling for just that dramatic effect. They were not invited as panelists, perhaps because Sandi's answer was "no" or because they had recently appeared on *Donahue.*

28. Dyer, 1991, pp. 138-139.

29. "Untrue Confessions of a Devious Duo," *Newsweek,* 1988, p. 80.

30. Ollove and Zurawik, 1994, 1A.

31. Derlega et al., 1993, described various studies in which self-

disclosure is used strategically to indicate the desired status of a relationship with another person.

32. Shaffer et al., 1982, found that high self-monitors patterned their disclosures more closely to the level of intimacy and emotional tenor of the disclosures of the person they were paired with in experiments than did low self-monitors. In addition, people who have high levels of private self-consciousness (see Davis & Franzoi, 1987), the tendency to be in tune with one's feelings, are likely to disclose more. The public component of self-consciousness is of particular interest here, because studies have shown that the presence of a camera in experiments increases the awareness of one's public self. When disclosure is expected in such situations, it is often characterized by the use of impression management techniques because of the saliency of an audience (see Scheier & Carver, 1981). Respondents realized that they served as representatives of stigmatized groups and were therefore acutely aware of themselves as social objects who would be studied by the audience. It is not surprising, then, that television disclosure in front of an audience of millions would be shaped by impression management techniques. However, as reported earlier, the studio cameras and monitors apparently did not serve as an environmental press on self-disclosure during the event, probably because of the already high level of self-monitoring tendencies in this group. None of the informants said that they had revealed more than they intended. Instead, most came away feeling that they had not been able to say everything they wanted to get across because of the time constraints.

33. Snyder, 1987, pp. 35-36.

34. Snyder, 1987, p. 5.

35. The fact that impression management occurs as a strategy of resistance is important to note. Erving Goffman, and symbolic interactionists in general, seem to downplay the limitations placed on the individual by the system, concentrating instead on each individual's role in the performance. The concept of impression management needs to be expanded to include larger issues of power differentials in society.

CHAPTER TEN

TRUTH AND CONSEQUENCES

Despite differences in primary motivations for television disclosure and in degree of affinity for the medium, the outcomes were roughly the same for each group. Somewhat surprisingly, the consequences of this rather risky behavior were almost universally positive in terms of increased self-esteem, in responses from the mainstream, and from people for whom the topics resonated.

REACTIONS FROM FELLOW OUTGROUP MEMBERS

An appearance on a daytime television talk show generated an outpouring of support from similarly marginalized others via calls and letters, what both Michael and Kate called "fan mail." These responses were almost entirely favorable; people contacted participants to provide encouragement, send donations, or seek help. Lorretta, for example, received about 40 calls and letters, and the clinic where she had been counseled was deluged with hundreds of calls. Craig and Patrick garnered thousands of dollars in donations for their legal battle from their various talk show appearances.[1]

Connections were established with others confronting similar problems or those open to unusual lifestyles. Will, who received calls from around the country, said men phoned to ask, "Is there a priestess I can go to bed with here in my area?" Jenny, who works at an organization that plans events for swingers, said, "You wouldn't believe the phone calls that come into this office. Every time we go on a program,

135

the phone rings for days—and sometimes months." Jim Cobb, a member of a ministry that helps gays convert to a heterosexual lifestyle, described the responses:

> Everyone who wrote was a Christian . . . there was no negative . . . and was either struggling with it now, or had, or one woman didn't struggle with it at all but was just very impressed that we gave the testimony and—and just wanted to write to encourage us about doing it. . . . And the—the couple of them we're still corresponding back and forth or on the phone, one of the guys is from Georgia who'd just attempted suicide, so you know, we've had some relationships with these people now that the show's over.

Responses often pertained to the powerful influence the episode had had on individuals grappling with similar lifestyles or problems. Joy, a gay parent, said:

> The people who took the time to search me out were universally positive, either you know, "Gee, after we watched the show together my daughter turned to me . . . and said, 'Mom, I have something to tell you,' and thank you for opening my eyes so I could hear her say that." I've had lots of grandparents. Or "You gave me the courage to own up to . . . myself."

Charlotte found it gratifying that one woman had used a tape of her *Donahue* appearance to come out to her husband as a lesbian.

In a few cases, informants reported that they had received marriage proposals and other propositions from strangers scattered around the country. Donna, who had appeared with her husband to discuss their sometimes clashing levels of sexual desire, said:

> Max and Della [Their therapists who appeared on the show with them] informed us uh during the following week of the show that people called them from all over the United States to uh, find locally where they could seek help, so the responses did get to some people and then in the course of the conversation, people said, "That couple that was on with you, they were knockouts, and you know, either one of them want to have a little roll in the sack with me or something, we'd be glad to do it." So we got a lot of propositions.

136

Everyone seemed slightly flattered but also somewhat unnerved by these infatuated responses. Kate said, "That someone could write me a love letter from South Carolina, saying that I'm so attractive, that she would really like to blah, blah, blah, and I go, 'You don't even know me.' . . . I want to laugh about it." Ross found that he was sometimes uncomfortable with the level of "adulation" he received from males who had applied his seduction techniques after they saw him on various shows and bought his book. He said, "When they get in the messiah level stuff, I start going, 'Whoa!'"

Participants were fairly confident that members of their marginalized group would react favorably to their evangelical disclosure, but they seemed surprised by the level of support. Formerly invisible group members revealed themselves to them and commended them warmly. The television disclosure was often a type of "coming out." Pete and Charlotte, for example, highly respected in their church and neighborhood, essentially discredited themselves with the mainstream by appearing but gained a newfound sense of fellowship within the gay community. Pete said, "It was a total turnaround to where people that were friends were gonna wind up foes, and people that were foes—."

After connections were established with members of one's group, talk show participants often quickly came to be seen as leaders within that social circle. For example, Craig and Patrick were asked to be grand marshals in the gay pride parade in Atlanta. Joy said, "It has, within my own [lesbian] community, given me somewhat, again, of that celebrity status." This was due in large measure to the activism that originally generated the publicity, but the leadership process was accelerated when participants stepped forward to speak on television about issues confronting the stigmatized group.

Many who wrote were thrilled that their out-groups had been portrayed so positively. Dolores commented: "I started getting letters and phone calls from people all over the country who said they were glad I had been on. . . . A lot of women who had been to college said they were glad I had broken the stereotype of what a prostitute is."[2]

Bud's response from leaders of the pro-marijuana movement was one exception to the outpouring of support. Bud, whose shtick includes lighting up a joint on stage and using the Bible to promote the decriminalization of drugs, said of the complaints from NORML and other groups who seem moderate by comparison:

They don't want me getting out there putting my opinions on. I said right to a guy, I said, "Look, I'm not just a pro-marijuana advocate, I'm a revolutionary," and unfortunately, the pro-marijuana movement is very conservative. And that's exactly the crux of the matter. They're trying to call me a self-promoter. I don't promote myself. I promote revolution. I don't make a dime off this.

Several in Bud's movement seek to promote a more moderate image of those who smoke marijuana; others complain that he should substitute more positive phrases such as "teaching plants" for his use of the term "drugs."[3] Bud said, however, that he had received letters from people in prison and from many others who wrote to tell him they appreciate his efforts to legalize marijuana. He discounts the criticism from leaders of other organizations as jealousy.

Most outgroup members expressed gratitude merely to see the topic addressed on television. Jenny, a swinger, excitedly described the following incident:

Within . . . a month after we were on, must have been *Donahue*, there was a woman . . . and her partner. . . . They had seen us on television, and the fact that they saw us on television allowed them to go out and "Oh! People do this! Oh! Neat! I'd like—we'd like to try that!" And so they went out; it gave them the opportunity to go out and explore something they may have thought was secret and bad about themselves. And for me, that's what this is all about.

The perception of legitimation conferred from television's treatment of a topic was affirming to members of the television audience who engaged in similar behaviors or held parallel interests or points of view.[4] As I discuss in greater detail later, media appearances often spark this validating effect. Paul Lazarsfeld and Robert Merton contend:

The mass media bestow prestige and enhance the authority of individuals and groups by legitimizing their status. Recognition by the press on radio or magazines or newsreels testifies that one has arrived, that one is important enough to have been singled out from the large anonymous masses, that one's behavior and opinions are significant enough to require public notice.[5]

138

Marginalized viewers apparently believed that television exposure grant-ed a measure of legitimacy to the issues and lifestyles discussed as well as to the speakers.

The gratifying identification of others out there who share an interest in a rarely mentioned or taboo behavior was discussed on a *Montel Williams* episode concerning infantilism.[6] Two of the panelists had previously been guests on *Donahue*. One man described the "40 or 50" letters he had received after his *Donahue* appearance from others who also engaged in the practice of dressing as babies. He said, "They thought they were the only one—[and] realized they're not crazy, haven't gone berserk in some way."

Addressing a topic on television seems to put the issue on the cognitive map of American consciousness. With visibility, various lifestyles emerge from out of bounds and come within the realm of possi-bility and normalcy. Gerre Goodman, George Lakey, Judy Lashof, and Erika Thorne explain their view:

> Homosexuality is rarely an option that is presented to us. Thus, it is a major struggle to define, let alone feel comfortable with, an identi-ty and way of life which should naturally give us joy. The lack of recognition by our culture is one of the reasons why we need to keep on publicly affirming our existence.[7]

Stewart Hoover identified a similar desire for visibility in a study of contributors to *The 700 Club*, a Christian television program once hosted by Jim Bakker. Hoover found that their financial support of the program stemmed from their belief in the importance of a national forum for their fundamentalist Christian views. He wrote:

> They said until recently, most people thought of them as being rep-resentative of rural, backwater, "fringe," sectors of American soci-ety. . . . [They were enthusiastic about] introducing their worldview into the public stage where it can receive the respect and the hearing that it deserves. The program enhances the credibility of their beliefs and affirmations, which were previously marginal in American social and intellectual life.[8]

Hoover discovered that, as with television disclosers, contributors were not frequent viewers of the program. They simply wanted to help finance the evangelical message each one fervently believed needed to be represented on the national medium of television.

In summary, marginalized group members responded with an outpouring of support. Connections were made with others interested in nontraditional lifestyles, religions, or causes. The attention often earned participants increased status in their marginalized communities. Fellow outgroup members were grateful that the discloser had stepped up to broach the subject on television in an act they believed brought greater legitimacy to stigmatized lifestyles.

RESPONSES FROM THE GENERAL PUBLIC

Many informants expected a negative backlash from the public at large, but they strongly believed in the importance of their efforts to strip their lifestyle of its deviant connotations and to tell their side of their stories. Although they steeled themselves for harsh repercussions, they were very pleasantly surprised by highly favorable public responses when they returned to their communities. Charlotte, whose newly discovered lesbian identity had strained her marriage, said:

> And our life has been—different. Different. Then they re-aired it in August and people are still recognizing us. "Hey, great." Thumbs up all around. Yeah. They went, thumbs up, "Hey, I remember you two. Great show, fantastic. You two looked good," you know, positive feelings, from the gay community and the non-gay community, too.

Jenny and Jim, the swingers, gleefully related a story about some people in a truck who recognized them after their appearance on *Sally Jessy Raphael* and asked, "Can we get out and shake your hand?"

Inmates at Leanne's prison responded with cheers and refrains of "Go, girl, go!" as they watched the show in crowded TV rooms in jail units. Then, during a moment in which Leanne confronted her chief accuser about the money the woman had made from selling the story, the crowd sat stunned. She said: "There was drop dead silence, and everybody looked at me, especially the girls that just really do know me, and they're like, 'Leanne, I just did not know you had it in you.' They were like, 'We are so proud of you,' 'cause I stood up for myself."

Carol, who modeled the results of her various plastic surgeries on *Donahue*, *The Oprah Winfrey Show*, and in *People* magazine, described how people cheered enthusiastically when she went to the grocery store soon after her appearance on *Donahue*. Wendy, a survivor of acquaintance rape, said people were very supportive when they recognized her: "They were all very nice, the times it happened. It's happened in shopping malls; it's happened in all sorts of places."

Dennis and Raymonda, who appeared on a show celebrating exceptional husbands, described the reactions of neighbors who told them, "We really appreciate what you did for our town . . . because you mentioned Perry [their small home town in Georgia]." Sandi and Heather, however, whose story partly indicts their Iowa community for its lax response to sexual harassment claims, found that people of their city were somewhat threatened by the negative coverage and therefore less friendly toward them. Yet, when Heather ventured out into neighboring towns, teens excitedly recognized her from a news story on Whittle's *Channel One* and from other appearances.

An electrified response was quite common. "Sam" spoke of the small town atmosphere in her community: "There's not a whole lot that goes on, so when this happened, it just sort of shot us to celebrity status." She noted that the delighted recognition of "I saw you on *Sally Jessy!*" was still happening a couple of years after their appearance. She added, "It was like rooting for a football team, the same kind of enthusiasm." Carl, whose fiancée is 40 years his junior, said, "We get a lot of compliments. From both shows. Lots of compliments. . . . 'You did fine on there, Carl; we were proud of ya.'"

Sherrol's straight-talking and humorous manner made her very popular with talk show audiences, who often waited around to get a chance to talk to her after the show:

> Sometimes, I'll be up there two or three hours. It's just phenomenal. People just line up—They line up just like they're getting tickets to go see Clint Black or Garth Brooks or something. . . . And they want my autograph, and I tell 'em, I say, "Honey, my hand to God, I'm telling you, I am nobody special. You know, I empty bed pans and give pain shots for a living. I'm nobody"—and they go, "You're going to be famous someday; we just know it. We want your autograph." And they won't shut up, so I just say, "well," scratch "Sherrol Simpson Miller." Oh, they just kiss me and hug me and carry on. I'm thinking, "What would it be like to be a real celebrity?"

Sherrol is an interesting case because of her extreme popularity with viewers. She has received thousands of letters and has answered every one. The *Donahue* staff has told her that they have received more mail directed to her than for any other panelist. Oddly, she has also received two dozen plane tickets from viewers around the country who have invited her to visit their towns.

People who recognized television disclosers away from the studio were enthusiastic and encouraging regardless of the topic. Bert, part of a gay parenting trio, commented that people said things like, "Good for you!" and "You were great!" Craig, championing the legal right for gay marriage, said, "When we go out, people always talk to us. And, you know, 'I support what you're doing,' want to shake our hands, 'I believe what you guys do.'" Charlotte, who had appeared on *Donahue* twice to discuss her struggle to reconcile her new lesbian identity with her long-standing marriage to Pete, said:

> We were getting positive feedback from the community—positive feedback in where we were living; so it didn't get that, I mean, "You guys gotta be kidding." You didn't—what you saw on the show today [a negative response from the studio audience], that's an exception to the rule in our case.

Indeed, members of the studio audience often had been rough on panelists, condemning their lifestyles, and participants often came away thinking that the show had been disastrous. The positive regard seemed to be triggered largely by the broadcast nature of the event. Michael, for example, had been extremely worried about a *Donahue* episode on which he had been labeled a prostitute, with Donahue intimating he might have put 100 or so people at risk for AIDS. Members of the studio audience were sharply critical, but, after the show aired, he was extolled by people he met.

Michael felt very uncomfortable, however, believing that people were saying unkind things behind his back. Although the responses had virtually been wholly positive, he still seemed to be struggling with making sense both of that brief period in his life and with the resulting depiction on *Donahue*. Nevertheless, he said he would appear again, because of the high-profile status he has achieved among AIDS activists and in the larger community. Michael said, "I don't want to use the word celebrity, but, in the eyes of people who know you, you are a celebrity.

Because you've done something that they can't do, and that you have put yourself before the public."

Some participants speculated that people responded to them favorably because viewers considered them courageous. Carol, whose on-screen photos of her plastic surgery were very revealing, said: "I think they admire me because they know, number one that I put myself in some positions that I don't look good and that I did it anyway. . . . I think people think I'm brave. Because it's scary." Catherine said, "And I think other people have said, 'Wow. That took a lot of courage and guts to do that.' And with that audience and all. So I think I—you know, people respect me more for that." Rocki said, "People think it's a lot more than it really is." Kate mused about the reactions of strangers, which she described as "100 percent friendly": "I like to think it was because I was honest and people kind of like that. That's what I like to think." Sherrol said of people's enthusiastic response to her feisty demeanor: "I think a lot of people kind of live through some of these talk show personalities, and they say, 'Boy,' you know, 'I wish I could be like her; I wish I could kick some ass.'"

Informants described disapproving public reactions when prompted but stressed that these negative incidents were rare. In fact, however, several experienced drastic consequences.[9] Pete felt he had been blacklisted, because offers for speaking engagements on Christian broadcasts as a speaker and performer came abruptly to a halt. Jenny believed she lost her job as a result of coming out on television as a swinger. Patrick, too, lost his job at a major department store after his appearances. Sabrina and Will suffered a string of dire effects from discussing their unconventional religious beliefs on *Sally Jessy Raphael*, their first mainstream talk show appearance. The ensuing police surveillance caused a sharp decline in their church membership. They later served jail terms for prostitution and pandering, were ex-communicated from the Mormon church, and received death threats.

Despite these negative outcomes, Sabrina and Will seemed very positive about their various appearances, even returning to *Sally Jessy Raphael* after their release from prison. Will said, "Ninety-nine percent of the people are really very friendly. We'll be driving down the street, and some Mexican kids the other day honk and say, 'Hey, that's Sabrina! That's Sabrina!'"

A handful of painful incidents involving the general public

occurred that colored the experience for several respondents. Cutting remarks were made to Donna and Dale, the couple with disparate sexual desires. They were badly hurt by the sexually suggestive comments of co-workers that Donna described as "the hardest, hardest part we had to come back to." Ross has been attacked by a woman in a bar. Ross, however, is someone who does a lot of posturing on talk shows, slinging insults and affecting mannerisms more common to pro-wrestling matches.

Patrick described a frightening incident on the metro that occurred after he appeared on *The Oprah Winfrey Show*:

> A group of youths, black youths, were looking at me. . . . They went, "That fag on *Oprah*!" or something like that and they all ran over to the door of the train and they tried to reach in the train, but the doors shut on them, and then the others were banging on the windows and glass and no one else on the train understood why, but I was certain that that was why. But that was—that was really the only threatening—physically threatening thing.

On the other hand, however, Patrick's partner Craig felt that the media exposure often protected them. Craig, who repeatedly stressed the importance of using the forum to humanize the image of gays and lesbians, said:

> We've been treated worse as anonymous gay people. . . . People see Craig, us, as a gay couple, they don't know who we are on the streets, you know, we receive abuse, you know, harassment, they'll yell, "Faggot!" at us. One time someone tried to shoot us as we were leaving the club. Uh, if—when people know us as Craig and Patrick, if they're anti-gay, they aren't anti-Craig and Patrick. You know, we don't receive the—the same anti-gay violence.

Similarly, Norma Jean asserts that her notoriety garnered from her many talk show appearances saved her life. She believes her high-profile position kept the Los Angeles police, whom she says were furious at her for the tell-all book she was writing about the department, from quietly getting rid of her.

Most outcomes were less dramatic, certainly, than those described by Norma Jean. Participants reported that the overwhelming majority of the feedback was limited to brief, friendly exchanges. Significantly, responses were often merely the simple but excited recognition, "I saw you on TV!" Kate, a transsexual lesbian, said:

> When people come up and say those kinds of things like, "Oh, I saw
> you on *Donahue*." But then they don't go and try to engage in con-
> versation, like, you know, "What you said about this, I would really
> like to talk." There's nothing to do with that. [Instead,] with "You,
> it's you!"

Ken, married to his ex-wife's sister, said, "A lot of people talk to you that
didn't really talk to you before: 'Hey, I saw you on TV.'" His wife,
Susen, added, "Yeah, total strangers come up and say, 'You're the one on
TV!'" Michael described the reaction of a friend he had known in high
school who ran into him at a store:

> He almost was more impressed with the getting on *Donahue* than
> saying, "I'm sorry you are HIV positive." I think because it's some-
> thing that most people can't even believe that—I guess average
> America doesn't think they could ever get on a talk show, because it
> seems like celeb—what's that word?—celebridom?

Terry Prone, a British author, also has noted the limited nature of
the public response to speakers who have appeared on television. She
points out that there is often no comment on the content of the remarks
made during an interview. Instead, people simply say, "I saw you on television."[10] In the present study, this brief and congenial recognition is particularly remarkable, because revelations of discrediting stigmas are generally the focus of the appearances. Importantly, as I discuss at greater
length later, it seems that the special status conferred by appearing is
almost entirely independent of the topics discussed.

Stuart Ewen writes of the media's power to bestow significance to
individuals: "In their ability to magnify, and to create near universal recognition, the mass media are able to invest the everyday lives of formerly
everyday people with a magical sense of value, a secularized imprint of the
sacred."[11] This newly minted value accorded to those who have appeared
on television may explain the outpouring of friendly responses.

Alternately, the expressions of support by strangers may simply
mirror findings in the self-disclosure literature of increased liking for disclosers who discuss intimate topics. There is no conclusive evidence as to
whether the underlying trigger for these positive responses is the status
conferred by television or more routine patterns of liking for disclosers. In
addition, liking and understanding may have resulted from the extended

opportunity afforded the discloser to disavow stigma.[12] Although the particular mechanism for the perceived attitude shift is yet to be identified, the reported responses of friendly recognition are a consistent finding.

Respondents also found that they were more popular with friends and associates after their appearance. Carol said, "And it really does make you a big deal with your friends. . . . It's very interesting how some people really really really think that's a big deal; I mean, like it influences their being with you, which blows my mind." Joy commented, "There are some people, yeah, like casual friends, I guess, um, that did treat me kind of different. They'd somehow act like my opinion is more valuable than it used to be." Donna said her boss watched the show three times and told her he had a newfound respect for her.

Participants on *Donahue* whose social standing situated them furthest from the center of society expressed the strongest feelings of validation from the experience. These outgroup members had, in many cases, already been discredited and so had the most ground to gain. Respondents characterized as moths, plaintiffs, and marketers, who tended to be less ostracized generally by society, reported a little less satisfaction with their experiences on talk shows. This can be traced in part to the discrediting information they brought to light or exaggerated, which caused them to fall away from the center slightly and lose ground.

An appearance on the show seems to function somewhat differently for marginalized group members and other participants, as if fun house mirrors were reflecting the images of each in distinct ways. Members of outgroups stepped up, small and sometimes reviled, and were made to appear life-like, normalized, for the first time. Marketers, moths, and plaintiffs, on the other hand, often presented themselves feeling "normal" and came away feeling fractured and slightly discredited due to the nature of the forum.

Donna and Dale, for example, expected some degree of sensationalism but felt that, after they had had a chance to talk on *Donahue,* they would be seen as very healthy for discussing and seeking help for their bouts of sexual incompatibility. They cited statistics provided on the show that 61 percent of couples suffer from some degree of sexual dysfunction as part of their rationale for feeling that their problem was not freakish or rare. Dale, whose label read "Treated for sexual desire problem," felt a better label would have read simply, "Just a couple." They felt they came across as more impaired than was really the case, partly because they were teamed on the show with a married woman who had not had sex in a year and a half.

Similarly, a studio audience member said to *Donahue* during Susen and Ken's show taping, "I don't think you'd be doing a show about it if there wasn't a problem here. I mean, there's obviously something wrong." The "freak" nature of the show may be most harmful, then, for those are already "inside" but whose appearances on the show to talk about a feature of their lives marks them as outside the bounds of normalcy. Furthermore, the less marginalized participants, who had less experience with stigma management, also were unaccustomed to feelings of negativity expressed by the studio audience. Harsh comments seemed to sting the moths and plaintiffs, whereas this type of reaction hardly fazed the more evangelical disclosers or the marketers. Everyone reported favorable reactions from the public after the broadcast, but those with membership in the most stigmatized groups were almost ecstatic about a new level of acceptance, whereas several moths and plaintiffs were discomfited by a measure of criticism brought on by their disclosures.

CHANGES IN SELF-ESTEEM

Many felt that weathering the experience was a thrilling accomplishment. Michael said, "And I think in essence for me, that's kind of a neat feeling, because it's kind of—sometimes, I'll just be riding along in the car, and I'll be like, 'Wow! I did that!' You know, it's kind of like a rush." Participants were buoyed by newfound feelings of self-worth and self-efficacy. Wendy, who had spoken about acquaintance rape on *Donahue*, said, "It made me feel good about myself; it really did. I was really proud." Heather said, "It made me a lot more stronger than I was, that I was able to stand up for myself. I had more self-confidence—by doing this." Lorretta, an incest survivor, said:

> Uh, I like myself, and I think that may even have intensified it, that uh, I really know that I'm okay. After that show, people came up and were putting their arms around me and just very—guys too, very nurturing, very caring . . . and so I just really felt like what I had done was really okay. I felt like I had contributed something, uh, to society.

Leanne said, "It's gave me—I realized that I didn't just have low self-esteem, I had no self-esteem. And now I've managed to get it up to low self-esteem."

Debra Bailey, a counselor for troubled teens in Miami's project areas, said that the two teens who appeared with her on *Donahue* began to show signs of improved self-esteem before they even arrived on the set. She said of the young women, who, at Donahue's urging, detailed a litany of crimes during the show's taping: "They began to feel very important, like they were actually going to do something to help people."

Importantly, participants received feedback that let them know the evangelical message they were trying to get across was being heard. Lorretta, for example, described an incident after her appearance on the *Good Day* show in Boston, in which two women approached her to ask about incest. She said, "I was glad. It told me that what I had set out to do is starting to work. Even if it only reaches 1 in 100,000 right now, that's 1 in 100,000 that wasn't hearing it before."

Feelings of self-worth were enhanced because informants felt they had made an important contribution to society. Bert said:

> But, um, in my down times, and when I think I'm useless or something like that, I think, "But, wait, I have touched these people." You know, I have said, "not only through acting, but just being able for that one hour, I was able to touch a bunch of people and move them in some way." And uh, it makes me feel good about myself.

Informants felt brave for taking up the banner for their group and serving in the vanguard. Michael said, "I accomplished something that most people are afraid of."

Patrick, who appeared on the show as an advocate for gay marriage rights, said, "My belief, how confident I was on those shows and how positive they came across. . . . Seeing their faces turn around confirms to me that what I'm doing is, it's right, and it's progressive, but it's a civil right." Catherine, Kate's lesbian partner, said: "Another thing I guess I feel good about is that—I will stand by my convictions. I will take a stand for something that I believe in and be out there with it and [for] that I think I feel really good about myself."

Respondents felt special for having been chosen to appear. This, too, often bolstered their self-esteem.[13] Dale remarked, "We got this like awesome compliment that for some reason we're like you know, invited in to appear." Jim Cobb felt that God had chosen them to be on *Donahue*. He said: "We felt special in our relationship to God, because both my wife and I have in those—some areas of low self-esteem because we weren't valued, you know, a lot by our parents and uh, it feels special in God's eyes—that was very encouraging." Each was aware that there were others who were similarly situated (for example, other transsexual lesbians or other prostitutes—other "others"), and they were pleased that they had essentially won the casting call to represent their groups.

Sometimes the heightened self-esteem was linked to feelings of mastery. Many mentioned their delight in watching the program and seeing how composed they appeared or how well they were able to stand up to the negative members of the crowd. Joy said, "Watching them [the media appearances] and seeing that I was able to handle it was very good for my self-esteem." Catherine said: "It gave me a lot of confidence that I didn't know before that I could be articulate. . . . I could actually acknowledge that about myself and [say], 'Oh. I sound intelligent, or I actually have something to say that—' and, you know, 'I can look good on camera.'" Jim Cobb commented: "My wife was very uh, I think it really helped her self-esteem a lot . . . seeing herself on the show and her composure and her answering the questions and everything, she was really—and the way people treated us afterwards, it was really, it was nice."

Significantly, informants often referenced their screen image as the trigger of these feelings of self-worth. Jim Cobb said:

> Having been on the show and then watching ourselves on the show—I mean it's not often that you get to watch yourself on TV and how you really come across to people. And I really liked myself. I mean, it was like, it really improved my self-image. By seeing myself on TV, both my wife and I. Uh, 'cause I mean, you talk to people and you have a perception of yourself while you're doing it . . . and you really don't know exactly . . . but I really liked myself, my tone of voice. I mean, you don't even know how your voice sounds to a degree, but to hear yourself, and see yourself in action, uh, it's like, I liked myself.

Bert said, "I was happy with how I looked because I thought I was horrible, you know, and I thought, 'No, you're not bad at all,' you know, 'You look all right.' And the makeup helps too." Kate explained how she felt when she glimpsed herself in the monitor: "That was really nice, it was so nice, because I felt, fine, OK, I don't look like, you know, a complete jerk. I don't look like a travesty, and I'm okay." This verification of being "okay" and "not bad" appears to be particularly important for those who have played out stigmatized lives.

Television seemed to serve as the quintessential looking-glass self for those who appeared on the medium. Charles Horton Cooley wrote, "The thing that moves us to pride or shame is not the mere mechanical reflection of ourselves, but an imputed sentiment, the imagined effect of this reflection upon another's mind."[14] The "imputed sentiment" of the televised reflection may be one of specialness, being chosen and certified worthy of joining the ranks of those whose images have been broadcast on television. Carol, whose body and face had been reshaped by thousands of dollars of plastic surgery, said of her appearance on *Donahue*: "So it's given me permission, it's almost like it's given me permission that I'm really okay."

Interestingly, because many utilized impression management techniques, the reflected image was sometimes skewed. Joy, who had downplayed some of the wilder parts of her personality in order to foster positive views of gay parenting, said, "I found myself . . . being only one side of myself in a real public way and playing down the other side and was starting to fall into it. And I got some stress-related illnesses from all of that." Later, she commented, "So I lost track internally of my own self-image."[15]

More generally, however, the reflected view of a larger-than-life status was extremely gratifying. Carl said that it felt wonderful to see himself on the monitor: "Here I am, a little boy from a little town in Pennsylvania, on TV!" Carol, too, marveled at how far she had come, saying: "You're meeting a star, you know—he's famous. You know, I mean, I'm from, you know, originally, Norton, Mass. You know, I'm a little kid from a small town, And I'm thinking, Does he really know who he has here?" Pete and Charlotte also stressed their humble beginnings, saying, "Now you understand, Pat? We are nobodies, come from nowhere." Pete reminded me that they returned to "no man's land," a city housing project in Sacramento, after the show taping.

Rocki was pleased to be singled out for recognition by being asked to appear:

I went to a rural school, you know, graduated in a class of 70 kids, and went through the routine that most everybody did around here, and it's, I just never really expected to be on any kind of a television show—far from being anything like any kind of an actress—and I never considered it being anything like that, but I just never expected to even be called to do anything like that. I didn't expect anything in my life to happen that was important enough for anybody to want to hear about.

The transition from "nobodies, come from nowhere" to someone whose story is worth hearing happened in a catapulting leap when producers tapped outsiders to come in.

"Sam" expressed a feeling of disbelief at seeing herself framed on television:

You see yourself and it's just like—you know, I really can't believe that that's me. You know, here we are—you know, you know—we're in New York City, we're on *The Sally Jessy Raphael* show? You know, of all things, you know, she's just so world-known, and so famous, and, you know, here we are, nobodies, and we're on this show, and it's just hard to believe, really hard to believe. I mean, we watch all these stars and, you know, all these famous people, and suddenly there *you* are? You know— most assuredly not a star! It's like, "Gosh!"

Respondents often conveyed their excitement about the red carpet treatment they received as guests of a talk show. Dale, who discussed his sex life on the show, was most enthusiastic:

It's very cool like you know, they send the limo and you ride over in a limo and pull up to the 30 Rock, and you walk beneath the canvas . . . like in the old days, you know. . . . Then they ah make mention to the guard and these people are waiting in line to be audience participants, the lengthy lines, and somebody comes out of the elevator and greets you . . . and you're just really glad that you got this really fancy Swiss hotel and we go back and jump on the bed, yell out the window.

The limited potential for access to television means that participants join an elite community of those who have appeared on screen. The exclusive nature made the experience all the more valuable to Bert, who said:

Before the *Donahue* show, uh, I was unemployed, looking for work, and after I was on that, and realized that me, Bert Lacquement, was on this and these people that I was interviewing on had never reached that fame and it was sort of like a status, in like the world: this is my perception of it, that I could indeed do anything and have anything I wanted. And uh, so just that self-worth of knowing that I had been on TV. You know, in front of millions. And ah, I carried it off, didn't make a complete idiot of myself, that um, I could find something other than a minimum wage job. And I did.

Many expressed generalized feelings of empowerment. Carol, who had had multiple cosmetic surgeries, said of her appearances on *Donahue* and *The Oprah Winfrey Show*:

So, I'm learning to speak up . . . the couple of things it's done for me, I'm more conscious of my time . . . because I know that I can do these things . . . like I feel real pressed about the animal work—I want to do more. . . . I think being on the show and realizing that I can make even more of a difference, that it's possible, I used to think, "well, there's the famous people, and then there's us," but I realized it doesn't take that much to get to be known . . . and I went, "I'm like an ordinary person, and if I can get this much publicity without trying," and I'm talking about without trying. Imagine what you could do if you really—I noticed I did a thing the other day—I wrote to the head of animal control. . . . She's invited me, I'm going to this Doris Day Committee in Washington. I just realized that it probably doesn't take that much to be known. 'Cause so many people are in apathy; they think you can't do anything anyway, so they don't.

Susen commented:

Well, I think it's a kick, cause if you can go on national television, and sit in front of those people, what can't you do? I mean, it's like college, I keep thinking I'm never going to make it. . . . But if I've been on television, and I've got this far in my life, why can't I finish that?

Wendy said, "I think it was probably a major stepping stone in giving me a boost of confidence to go out there and do public speaking seriously." Carol, who began to take a more active role in animal rights causes, said, "I don't want to make a difference anymore, I mean, I want to make a *huge* difference. . . . It has empowered me . . . that people really want to listen to me, like I'm interesting, My God!"

152

Several believed that being singled out by *Donahue* and his staff was an achievement of the highest order. Carol said, "If you're on the *Donahue* show, you've made it. There's nothing else other than maybe we could be invited to President Bush's for dinner." Bert said passionately, "And that show [Donahue] was sort of like, I want to say a second honeymoon, but that's not quite it. It was like a toast from a country that we were doing okay, that's how I felt . . . being asked on to do it and also to get the feedback that we got from that show." Later, Bert added, "It was nice to be able to ah, be presented by him or something."

In her book, *Mediaspeak*, Donna Cross discusses celebrity appearances on gossip-oriented talk shows: "Today, of course, an appearance on a television talk show is the ultimate certification of 'making it' in America . . . simply to gain recognition, to prove, merely by showing up, that they are 'somebody.'"[16] Talk show participants do not need to display any particular talent or speak as experts on anything other than their own lives, but they do need to trade their privacy to get over the wall and onto center stage.

Joshua Meyrowitz contends that narrow parameters of information shared across groups in the era prior to television "distinguished insiders from outsiders."[17] Shifts in social distinction that result from a TV appearance benefit the marginalized participants, who become "insiders" alongside celebrities and politicians, other groups allowed access to this hallowed place. Participants' membership shifts from the outcast status to celebrity, from margin to center, outside in.

Part of the certification effect stems from the national reach of the program. Several stressed the word when discussing their appearances. Carl, for example, said that his former wife had always held him back from the fame he felt was his due as a dancer. He said of his young fiancée, "I give Michelle a lot of credit. For going on television. *National* television." Many people amended their comments about television in this way. Marty extended the geographic coverage of the show further still. She said, "Is it a big deal? Yeah, cause it's national. *International!*" Susen's comment was similar: "It aired all over the world, you know."

The attention, then, was particularly affirming for those like Sherrol, who had been told she would never amount to anything. The stream of attention directed at her came rather abruptly after a difficult childhood and a humiliating divorce from the conman who bilked her. She said: "It's a broad step. I feel like God gave me a little breather, you know, God said, you know, 'You had a miserable childhood,' and, you know, 'you had a miserable life 'til you were 37,' and all the sudden, 'Time for you to have some sunshine, kid.'" Sherrol and others seemed to struggle slightly to make sense of the outpouring of affection and support. She said of the fan-like behavior people exhibit toward her: "Oh, it's just phenomenal. . . . And I tell 'em up front, I say, 'Look, I'm nobody special. I'm just some everyday nurse that married a homosexual and got on television.'" And yet, repeatedly, she is thanked by many who say she saved them from getting involved with con artists and is warmly greeted by people—including patients groggy from surgery.

Negative consequences did occur but were downplayed in their accounts, apparently because the balance was one of affirming support. The overriding sentiment expressed was that the "greater good," as Sabrina termed her crusade, was served despite these negative consequences, and that "greater good" was repeatedly confirmed by the responses of the public.

OTHER OUTCOMES

Only occasionally did participants report that the experience had therapeutic advantages. "Sam," for example, said that she and her daughter had learned a few things about their relationship from the expert, a therapist, who appeared on the show. Kate noted a therapeutic release: "It's a relief, it's like, um, well, there's a few less secrets I have in my life." Sherrol said:

> It is pretty therapeutic. You know, it gives you time—it gives you time to kind of step by step tell what happened, because people will say to you, "Okay, when did you first find out about your husband, what started cracking your story?" And you kinda start putting a to b and b to c, and you just, you know, gradually kinda recall what happened to you, and it seems like it kinda smoothes down a lot of the pain. And it really does.

I asked Sandi how she felt about Donahue's prompting Heather to detail the hateful phrases that had been scrawled on school walls by schoolmates who repeatedly harassed her. She said:

154

As ironic as it sounds, it's when she finally started publicly saying what people were saying about her is when she started to heal. And that sounds . . . like maybe it's revictimizing her, and to an extent it is, but—those are the things that she's been called everyday of her life, and it took her a long time to understand that it's not her fault.

Oprah Winfrey, too, believes her show can have therapeutic outcomes. She said of her disclosure on her program about childhood sexual assault, "It helped me release some of personal shame about sexual abuse."[18]

Perhaps because participants were sometimes talking about family secrets, responses from family members were often the source of the harshest feedback. For example, Sabrina's parents had virtually disowned her after she appeared on a variety of talk shows to describe the sexual rituals she practiced as part of her religious beliefs. Carl and Michelle's families were very upset and made repeated calls to urge them to cease their appearances. His children felt that he had embarrassed the family; one son suggested he see a psychiatrist. Charlotte sadly described her family's reaction:

I had trouble because my sisters called me, my mother called me, my father-in-law talked to me since that show. My father's very macho, extremely sensitive. He could not have a lesbian child. My sister could not deal with having a child [sic] who was going to hell . . . how could we possibly bring that on the family? . . . I didn't want to bring it all up again. I just hang; there's phone calls back at the house waiting for me that I don't want to get.

Sherrol's family has largely shunned her for bringing a "black spot on the family" by appearing. She said, however, "I did help people, and consequently I found out that these strangers nationwide and worldwide have turned out to be more precious to me than my entire family I've known for 44 years, so go figure." There were exceptions to this trend of familial dismay, but many informants reported that their parents, especially, were humiliated by their adult child's revelations on television. Processes that foster liking or status conferral may not work as effectively with others who know the discloser more intimately and whose reputations are also perceived to be at stake in the television arena.

The exceptions may have to do with the relatively mainstream character of some of the revelations. Craig, for example, described how his mother received extensions of the positive feedback he and Patrick had encountered: "She become a little minor celebrity in her mah-jongg club. She got lots of support. People say, 'My son's gay, my brother, etc.'" Many of the respondents, however, had gingerly avoided discussing their talk show appearances with their parents.

Ralph's relationship with his daughter began to be strained over time. He said, "It's caused a lot of problems for my family." For example, he described how teachers at his daughter's school callously mentioned in class that they had seen her father on *Donahue*.[19] Although he has always received her permission before his participation on any show, he acknowledged that conflict looms, because his daughter has asked him to turn down future opportunities. She wants to begin to put the terror-filled event behind her, yet Ralph feels compelled to carry on his crusade as his only way to counteract feelings of helplessness. Family members do not always share the evangelical zeal to carry on the quest at all costs, and, certainly, the costs to privacy and the suffering that stems from opening up old wounds are different for Ralph and his daughter. Family members, then, hold disparate views about talk shows as a valued forum worth the price of renewed pain and loss of privacy.

Despite the negative fall-out that some experienced, all but Michael and Dale were extremely upbeat about their appearances. Most felt they accomplished what they had set out to do. The difference in outcomes is one of degree, with the evangelicals attaining a level of acceptance that they had never received before, and the others garnering more of a mixed response, but one they still interpreted as affirming.

Several later capitalized on their appearances as a sort of calling card. Michael discussed how he was on a friendly basis with the actor Dack Rambo:

> But without the *Donahue* show, I don't think he would have given me the time of day. And um, I have met a lot of neat people, and people do—I think when you go on a talk show, it's your automatic in. You can call up anywhere and "blah blah blah, I was on the *Donahue* show," and all the sudden, people want to talk to you.

Rocki said that strip club owners used her talk show credits as "an extra draw" when she made special appearances at their clubs. Ross said his opening paragraph in direct mail appeals for the catalog he markets often contains a reminder that his name was recognizable from his many talk show appearances. He said, "I use it as a legitimizer." He went on to describe how the process of certification could be abused:

> If you get a mailing from, you know, John Doe, who says, "I can teach you how to seduce a woman in seven minutes," you know, yeah, right. But if you've seen him on TV—. TV—this is the frightening thing, TV gives you an enormous credibility that's totally undeserved. I mean, it's deserved in my case.

The status accorded those who had appeared on television occasionally worked to the disclosers' disadvantage, however. For example, Jim Lightner, the swinger, when asked whether his appearance had attracted sexual partners, replied:

> Actually, in some ways, I think it's had some of the opposite effect. In some ways, I think, with a few people that we've ended up encountering in the past months, it's been a bit of an intimidating effect on them because we're quote too well known. . . . Well, some of the people we know that we meet haven't been involved in this for quite some time, so, I guess, they may end up thinking we're a little more hardcore about this than they are . . . and they may think that we're just a little too fast for them, if you want to use that term—which isn't the case, but I think the aspect of being on television magnifies that a bit.

Similarly, Dolores found that her high-profile status as "America's most notorious prostitute" (a moniker accorded her by the *Atlanta Journal*) often adversely affected her business. Although some "clients" found her fame a bewitching attraction, others were uneasy about being seen in public with her.

A related drawback was that some participants felt they had to match the image they were representing. Craig said, "People see us as an ideal couple, and that's the hardest thing to live up to." Bert and Joy related how they found it very stressful to play the perfect family on TV talk shows and return home to bicker about the stresses of working out their complex parenting arrangement. Michael said he felt very much on display as a well-known symbol of AIDS activism because of his two *Donahue* appearances, and he was therefore especially careful to limit his alcohol intake and to behave in an exemplary manner while at gay clubs.

"It really forced me to watch my actions," he said. "You are always watching yourself differently now." Participants seemed to feel they would be held to a higher standard or accountability. Generally, however, disclosers found this newfound status useful as well as affirming.

Norma Jean, who had just moved to a new part of Los Angeles, said she was throwing an open house, during which she planned to show her new neighbors the segment of *60 Minutes* that featured her. She explained, "I want to get it out in the open, so it's not a rumor." She added, laughing: "I'll say, 'This is who I am, by the way.'" She also shows the *60 Minutes* tape each time she lectures at colleges. Many others noted that they used segments from their various appearances as opening gambits when they spoke publicly.

As predicted by Paul Lazarsfeld and Robert Merton, media attention snowballed in a spiraling fashion, such that an appearance on *Donahue* led to other offers for many respondents. Catherine, who was later interviewed for a feature story in a lesbian magazine and asked to appear on a local talk show, said, "I'm sort of looked at differently in that, 'Oh, I guess she has something to say.'" Sabrina, head priestess in the controversial Church of the Most High Goddess, said:

> I'm very thrilled, and I would even like to be more well known because of the good you can do. The—the more people that know about you, the more will listen to what you have to say. And that's great. So I've, I have enjoyed being like at that rally against police brutality and having a—one of the channel people come up an say, "Oh, hi, Sabrina; I recognize you. What do you think of this?" And say, "Hey, someone wants to listen to me." I can say something and the people out there watching TV will take my opinion and maybe think about things.

Several reported they frequently were contacted during sweeps periods by various shows and asked to recommend people as guests. Joy said, "Not just gay people, but other odd folks." She continued: "I'll periodically get a letter, 'I've left so-and-so, and I'm now with *Joan Rivers*,' for example, um, 'If you have any ideas for me, send them in.' Once you've done it, the circuit, you actually have input into the process." Dolores calls herself a talk show "pimp" because she often serves as a paid liaison between the shows and potential guests, many of whom she knows as colleagues in the sex industry.

In summary, participants reported that being chosen to present one's life story on the show was very gratifying. The aggregate impact of affirmation from the public, expressions of gratitude from people who share a stigmatizing feature, being treated like a celebrity the day of the taping, and private feelings of mastery and specialness resulted in a surge in self-esteem for most informants. Many felt empowered by the experience and channeled their newly expanded sense of self-worth into projects important to them. After seeing themselves on television, many felt that they were "okay," or, in Kate's case, not a "travesty." The cultural underpinnings of the certification of value and normalcy that television imparts are addressed in the next chapter.

NOTES

1. Ralph also received donations, but I am unsure as to whether contributors were struggling with their own rape-related issues or not. He donated these funds to the local rape crisis center and other charities.
2. French and Lee, 1988, pp. 178-179.
3. I talked to one man in the studio audience of *The Jerry Springer Show* who had written a letter to the show to complain about Bud's earlier appearance and had been asked by the staff to rebut Bud's views during a segment of the program.
4. This notion of legitimation had played a part in Charlotte's rationale for appearing on the show to discuss her efforts to come to terms with her lesbian identity in the context of her marriage to Pete. She said, "So I knew again, there's that old— Is this gonna . . . help somebody? Yes, I did step out . . . they did, I did, I'm normal. I validate them. Come on out. Let's deal with it." Later she added, "I got a chance to validate people. I got a chance to validate the gay and lesbian community."
5. Lazarsfeld and Merton, 1948, p. 101.
6. *Montel Williams*, February 13, 1992.
7. Goodman et al., 1983, p. 21.
8. Hoover, 1990, p. 240.

9. Negative repercussions are occasionally reported in the press. I have heard rumors, for example, that a man killed himself after being portrayed on one program as a "bad influence." Ben Stocking, 1994, reported a separate case in which a high school teacher was suspended after appearing on *The Montel Williams Show* to discuss the pain his affairs had caused his family. Calls came into the principal's office minutes after the show began, although the man, his wife, and daughter all wore disguises. The man's supporters said the matter was private and should not jeopardize his job. The lawyer representing the school district asserted: "When you go public with it, it's no longer a private issue" (pp. 1A, 10A).

10. Prone, 1984, p. 72.

11. Ewen, 1988, p. 93.

12. An anonymous reviewer noted that the genre may be an example of one in Frye's (1957) typology in which the audience is set up to feel superior to featured performers. The reviewer then remarked that panelists have an hour to work the crowd using persuasive techniques to convince the public of their status as equals.

13. This theme is occasionally voiced on talk show special episodes in which stories of popular panelists are updated. In 1990, for example, on the January 2nd episode of *The Oprah Winfrey Show*, a letter was read from a rape survivor who had appeared on the show during the previous year. She wrote, "I feel that because you felt my story was worth telling and I was articulate enough to tell it, I now have some self-worth and am of value. You've given me much more self-confidence."

14. Cooley, 1902, p. 152.

15. Arkin, 1986, noted that the roles adopted for self-presentation by an individual are often internalized and become a part of one's self-concept.

16. Cross, 1983, p. 148.

17. Meyrowitz, 1985, p. 131. Meyrowitz's compelling argument about television's part in the blurring of social distinctions concerns the fact that audiences can glimpse the inner workings of a wide array of situations formerly roped off from scrutiny. Hence, in his view, there is less of a schism between

what insiders and outsiders know. I am taking his terms *insiders* and *outsiders* to underline my idea that stepping inside television reality provides a new social distinction for participants. His ideas about blurring apply in the sense that access enables marginalized group members to garner a measure of acclaim granted previously to a much narrower group.

18. Oprah mentioned this on *Good Morning, America* on September 8, 1986.
19. The show aired in New York City on Veteran's Day, when many people were home because of the holiday.

CHAPTER ELEVEN

"GILT BY ASSOCIATION":[1] EXAMINING TELEVISION'S POWERS OF CERTIFICATION

Participants were only vaguely aware of the potential to earn a larger-than-life status. Many often aspired merely to be deemed acceptable, with their ideas espoused as worthy of consideration. Avidly seeking visibility in what Joel Carpenter calls the "show windows of modern publicity" is motivated by marginalized individuals' thirst for certification of legitimacy.[2]

As noted in earlier chapters, most participants explicitly stated this desire as part of their rationale, explaining that they were actively trying to disavow the stigmatized connotations others apply to their lifestyles or life predicaments. Jenny said, "Basically, the whole idea is that there are other ways to live one's life that are just as acceptable, and the people in them are just as good quote unquote people as everybody else." Many hoped their television appearances would signal that their lifestyles or beliefs were viable alternatives to the status quo.

Closely related were longings frequently expressed for one's life story to be validated as important and certified as true. A thirst for validation was seldom voiced concretely but was an elusive theme that surfaced repeatedly. Lorretta, an incest survivor, clearly stated her desire for validation, but others did not. She said, "It goes back to being validated. Uh, and people knowing that—I hadn't made this up all these years." Later, she continued: "It's a relief. 'Cause I know that there's people over the years that I worked with who thought I was a little odd. . . . [They] can sit there now and go, 'Well, I'll be. There was a reason.' And then they can sit there and see how far I've come." Michael said of his former partner, who had deceived him and others about his HIV status:

People were disbelieving in my story, because he had convinced them, because he looked so healthy . . . [that I was] just making this whole thing up. . . . I think my going on the show was my way of proving some credibility to my story. Because I thought if—if a talk show is willing to talk about it, then they must be willing to—or at least there's some credibility there.

The longing for television's stamp of certification often hovered at the subconscious level and seemed to take many forms. Informants implied that the various claims they were advancing, in effect, would simply be proven true if seen or told on television. Carl mentioned briefly on *Donahue* that Michelle's former boyfriend had abused her. I asked Michelle if she minded that he brought that up during the taping. She replied that the negative portrayal was important to "show that he really did that and he hopefully at this day is sorry that I left." Carl told me: "I want all his friends to know what kind of man he was, how he treated this girl. . . . I wanted them to know how I cared for this girl. . . . I said she was like a ragamuffin when she came to me—Now she's out there, dressed like fit to kill."

Raymonda expressed a related desire to use her *Donahue* appearance as a testimony to the strength of her relationship with Dennis. She said, "My mother's always kind of thought I was kind of a gypsy . . . but I wanted her to know that, 'Look, mom, I've really settled . . . finally at last,' and that I am happy." Similarly, Dennis sought a sort of ratification by being presented as a finalist in the show's best husband contest. He admitted that he had avidly hoped to win, but the yearning for validation seemed deeper than being honored with a first-place finish. He said, "We've got acquaintances, ex's or whatever, that we would like to prove a point to, that I ain't as bad as you thought, and maybe you did lose an opportunity."

A prize was not necessary for the experience on *Donahue* to feel validating to participants, especially those in society whose relationships are generally considered illegitimate and abnormal. Kate said of her appearance on the show with her lesbian partner:

I don't know if it's the same, but maybe it fulfilled the same function as . . . witnessing love, I mean to have one's love witnessed. That's—that's really good. . . . I've always been able to walk down the street and hold hands with my lover when I was a boy. It's a little different now. And in San Francisco, I can do it, but not many other places. But to do it on national television, that's—that's—that's a big joy. That's a big, big joy. That approached holiness.

Catherine's remarks in a separate interview echoed this sentiment: "It was liberating. It was really nice to just be out there to affirm, and affirm that [her relationship with Kate]."

Indeed, the conventions of the genre are that both members of a couple appear together on the show and that several "exhibits," essentially, of the outgroup are on display. Such pairings work in the outgroup's favor and are particularly important when gay topics are broached, because researchers such as Alfred Kielwasser and Michelle Wolf have stressed the general pattern of solo gay depictions in most media forms. Each coupling, then, speaks volumes to viewers at home grappling with feelings that they will always be alone because of a marginalizing feature.

Although many were hoping their visibility would precipitate a simple normalizing effect, gains exceeded expectations, as participants were enveloped in a mantle of distinction. Certification involves the newfound celebrity status triggered by having appeared on television. Paul Lazarsfeld and Robert Merton refer to this process as status conferral: "The audiences of mass media apparently subscribe to this circular belief: 'If you really matter, you will be at the focus of mass attention and if you are at the focus of attention, then you surely must matter.'"[3] This theme was later addressed by Daniel Boorstin, who defined 20th century fame in this oft-quoted line: "The celebrity is a person who is well-known for his well-knownness".[4]

The process of status conferral seems to spin into effect in a rather content neutral way, transferred regardless of the topics brought forward. James Monaco calls the perception of worthiness which emanates from a television appearance "gilt by association."[5] Cecelia Tichi traces this cognitive shift to the prominence of advertising in society:

> From the earliest days of network commercial broadcasting, television has been a showcase for commodities whose salient selling point was their onscreen simulation. "As seen on TV" has been a mark and stamp from the early 1950s. . . . Over time, the very phrase has become a media seal of approval.[6]

Tichi provides fascinating examples of early advertisements for television sets that imply that real life pales in comparison with televisual reality.

The author Walker Percy is often mentioned in discussions of certification because of a character's musings in *The Moviegoer* about locales being made "real" when captured on film. Robert Snow compares television's power of certification to that of dictionaries, in that people believe a word is not legitimate if it does not appear in this sanctioned source.[7]

Participants wanted viewers to know that nontraditional lifestyles existed, could work, and were legitimate. Their talk show appearances signaled new or more expanded and nuanced listings in television's dictionary of represented images. Bert, who was primarily seeking his "15 minutes of fame," was also earnest about the message he hoped to convey: "that it is possible to be a loving family, be homosexual or lesbian, be a single parent, you know, whatever that may be, it doesn't have to be, you know, 2.4 children or whatever that statistic is." Susen, married to her sister's ex-husband, said, "We just wanted to go on and tell people that we get along really good. . . . We just wanted to show 'em that kids can be raised normal, with two different sets of parents."

Many felt that a degree of normalization had successfully taken place as a result of their television appearances. Patrick, a gay male, said:

> I carry myself in a more confident manner now. Um, there's no one who I feel like I have to hide who I am from. And, uh, it's as if there wasn't this thing that's different about me, different than normal society, that I'm homosexual, um, to me, it's not. I mean, if someone wants to know, I'll tell them. I don't hide it anymore.

Both Susen and Patrick seem to use the word *normal* to refer to an ideal. Similarly, Jim Lightner, a swinger, said:

> One of the things Jenny's mentioned, about the fact that we can end up showing people that we're quote normal people . . . is that we actually hear that from a lot of people in the audience during commercial breaks. They might come up and say, "But you look so normal."

Dale's comments about normalcy were somewhat quixotic. He said of his decision to appear on the show to discuss his sex life: "Maybe I was just trying to legitimatize my own life. . . . Nothing's really normal about like what it is we've ever done, so that pretty much kind of fits. . . . So like I said, maybe I was trying to do something normal for a change."

166

Participation in the freak show, quite paradoxically, offered a certification of normalcy. Pete, who appeared with his wife to talk about her newfound lesbian identity, said, "Because again, you want to make some sort of contacts and know that you're just not uh, freak of nature." Bert, a gay parent, said, "I think the agenda was, if I had any agenda, was that uh I'm just as normal as anybody else." This finding of a quest for validation among many of the respondents is perplexing when one considers the sensational nature of the genre. Importantly, participants did not expect the wildly positive responses they received, but they sensed the normalization that mass media can bestow.

Significantly, these glimpses of a pattern of normalcy seeking may provide evidence of the ontological change concerning televisual reality that Cecelia Tichi argues has occurred. Pointing to advertisers' use for more than 40 years of the phrase "As seen on TV" to certify a product's value, Tichi contends:

> The slogan points further, toward the cultural change wrought by television in the introduction of a new set of cognitive and perceptual categories in which what is real or unreal is superseded by what is televised and what is not. . . . To be transposed onto television is to be elevated out of the banal realm of the off-screen and repositioned in the privileged on-screen world.[8]

In their sometimes plaintive cry for inclusion as "normals," respondents expressed their perceptions that the hyperreality of the television landscape is the valued reality to aspire to. Richard Schickel writes of television: "What matters is that if we do not somehow insert ourselves into this reality, we run the danger of being, in our own eyes, unpersons."[9] The corollary to the status conferral function in which individuals are singled out as worthy of attention, then, concerns the impact of omissions. If the topic is not broached, it is considered out of bounds.

Individuals may feel similarly unworthy if never allowed to represent themselves.[10] Daniel Schorr argues that television is the "arbiter of identity:"

> "I think, therefore I am," Descartes had said. "I am seen, therefore I am" was the new version. Television had created a new class distinction of the Visible and the Invisible, and the most extreme are ready to muscle their way into visibility.[11]

It is the ability to represent oneself that seems most powerful.[12] Leanne's story, for example, had been told in a variety of news and tabloid stories in which her edited comments had been pieced together in representations she decried as inaccurate. Although she had received 100 supportive pieces of mail from her *Donahue* exposure, she described the outcomes after the other shows this way: "Nothing good happened, but people turning their heads from me when I'd go into a store, a lot of whispers, got evicted from a house I was living in, two days after the show aired, a lot of people that—I mean, I was labeled really bad." Only on *Donahue*, where she was able to assume more control over her representation, did the certification effect kick in.

The handful of respondents classified in Chapter 4 as moths—those whose primary rationale for appearing was a quest for 15 minutes of fame—clearly articulated a desire to be seen on TV. When Carl, an avid viewer of television talk shows, was asked what he thought of the genre, he replied, "I thought, 'My God. I ought to be on there. I'd love to be on there. I gotta have a reason.' Well, my reason is perfect. I have a woman 40 years younger than me." Donna let her husband make the decision about whether to appear on the show because the topic of his comparatively diminished sex drive was particularly sensitive for him. However, she said:

> Not to say that I didn't want to go, I mean, [she turned to her husband] like you said, you know, who gets the opportunity to be in front of national television? What's your comment about what Andy Warhol says, "Everybody gets to be a star 15 minutes of their life"?

After the show aired, she jokingly asked her daughters if her agent had called. Recounting this, she added, "You know, well, a dream."

Sometimes these moth-like tendencies were an outgrowth of fantasy, and several used that very word. Bert said:

> I used to fantasize when I was 12 or 13 watching *Donahue* how I would love to be on that show and be such an individual that people would, you know, clamor, you know, hang on my every word. . . . It was in those dreams of being a movie star. You know, and then my life progressed, then I wasn't that movie star, but was just ultimately myself. And people were interested in me.

Lorretta, evangelical in her intentions to awaken the public to the critical need for changes in legislation pertaining to incest, said: "My fantasies were to go on *The Oprah Winfrey Show* and expose my father, and it ended up being done for a healthier reason. In the beginning it was anger. . . . In the end, it was because I had gotten well and could help others."[13]

Joy said of her various appearances in the media, "It fulfills, in some ways, a fantasy. I used to listen to the late night radio talk shows and imagine what I would say." When asked to elaborate, Joy replied:

> You know, kids have fantasies. I know more people who have fantasies [about] being on the Johnny Carson show. . . . Whether it's playing the spoons or, you know, bringing their 18-foot python or something on. We grew up with it, it's part of our American culture, um, and I think everybody who dreams of being famous . . . [thinks], "I'll be so famous, Johnny Carson will invite me on his show."

Craig and Patrick watched an episode of *Oprah* some time ago that featured two gay bodybuilders who were "out" about their relationship. Patrick recalled that day:

> In fact, I even kidded to Craig at one point while we were watching the show. We couldn't believe what we were seeing, first of all. . . . Then the conversation went to . . . wouldn't that be interesting if we actually went this far and pursued for the marriage to be legal—[in unison with Craig] and got on *Oprah*!

Viewers who later saw participants responded effusively, joining in the celebration of fantasy fulfillment. An appearance on television provided much more than a certification that a participant is legitimate, "normal," and no longer a nonperson. Joy discussed the responses her daughter had received: "It actually worked to her advantage. Kids—she's still at that age—where, 'Oh, wow, you're cool, you've been on TV' that they didn't really notice the subject matter all that much." Surprisingly, it was not just children who often did not weigh the content of the message heavily in their appraisals of the television discloser. "As seen on TV" enveloped those who appeared on television with a newfound aura of celebrity.

This engulfment suggests that "As seen on TV" constitutes a new and powerful "master status determining trait." Howard Becker described the term:

> Some statuses, in our society as in others, override all other statuses and have a certain priority. Race is one of these. Membership in the Negro race, as socially defined, will override most other status considerations in most other situations; the fact that one is a physician or middle class or female will not protect one from being treated as a Negro first and one of these other things second.[14]

Garnering an appearance on television—for whatever reason—similarly subsumes other attributes of the individual. The important role television plays in modern life and the exclusivity of the experience have fueled this creation of a relatively new master status trait. This phenomenon of status conferred regardless of actual accomplishment seems to be evidence of Marshall McLuhan's claim that "the medium is the message."[15]

The content of the disclosures on talk shows was often overridden by image. Charlotte and Pete said the public had responded with the comment, "You two looked good." If family members were not estranged after the appearance, their response generally involved compliments about the way panelists looked on television. Donna said:

> There has not been one member of our family who will discuss it with us. And I'm a little bit miffed with that because I'm very close to my family, and I don't mind sharing with them the fact that you know, I have done this or that and I'm proud of it. And yet, they almost do not want to discuss it or mention it because that's—it's like something to be ashamed of. My sister . . . said, "You looked fabulous on TV.' That's . . . my sister's only—[I'm] very close to my sisters; that was her only comment. . . . My sister's husband, his only comment was I showed too much leg. I said, "What a bizarre comment."

Catherine said: "My dad thought I looked good. . . . It was very interesting what he said [about her transsexual partner], 'She has a nice, she has a nice face.'" Michelle reported that her mother, who had not wanted her to appear on the show, said, "They were giving you all those nice clothes shots. You really looked good on there."

The continuing trend of image transcending content has troubled critics monitoring political campaigns and governance. Jerry Mander said of Nixon's presidential campaign in 1972, "Even though many people understood that his change was only cosmetic, he won. This confirmed for me the idea that something in the nature of television imagery allows form to supersede content."[16]

Image is not based solely on appearance on television. Also necessary is an element of mastery of the situation. However, if both appearance and manner, to use Erving Goffman's terms, are carried off relatively well, strangers and acquaintances accord a new status to those who have successfully negotiated the gauntlet of attack from the studio audience.[17] Goffman also notes the range of props that individuals use to telescope status. Apparently, appearing framed in a 19-inch television set is a prop that prompts extravagant, unstudied respect from others. Dale pointed this out. He said of the "big deal" acquaintances made of his appearance: "It's the context. People get to see you framed at that 21-inch electronic—."

Informants characterized as moths seemed to be oriented in their impression management toward their appearance rather than larger concerns of issue presentation. Bert said: "I never really had an agenda. I didn't. Keep my hair, you know, look good." Interestingly, the presence of the cameras, when they were noted, seemed to make one's appearance more salient than self-disclosure levels or expectancies. Moth-like participants were most likely to notice the cameras. Susen said, "It was the cameras. . . . You keep thinking in the back of your mind, you think, 'Gosh, I'm going to be on national television. I wonder if my eyebrows—.' My shirt kept coming unbuttoned right here, and I didn't dare move."

The lack of preparation for concerns beyond appearance seemed partly responsible for the differential outcomes for the evangelicals and the other groups. Those characterized as moths, particularly, were usually not advocacy-oriented and had little of the life-long practice of stigma management that the more marginalized respondents had mastered. As a result, the moths did little planning and were less focused during the taping. Members of the studio audience seemed to attack more assertively because of the hedging done by these moth-like disclosers who tended to be less prepared for the onslaught of questions. Those in the moth category were not as polished in a venue in which image is paramount. However, as described previously, the accord heaped on participants was still profuse despite these minor differentiations in outcomes.

GETTING IN: THE MAGIC OF STEPPING
INTO TELEVISUAL REALITY

Kate was cognizant of television's magical ability to grant celebrity status:

> This is going to be real—I haven't got this one all together, but, you know, we—it's all very interesting, the Joseph Campbell books that talk about, "Oh, those people with their myths." But we have our myths. And I think our myths, or gods and goddesses or demons or demi-gods and goddesses are our celebrities. The myths are their stories, and—and in a way, I think that by appearing on there—that kind of elevates you into this kind of like, hierarchy of a myth maker, and it does.

A young man who appeared on a *Donahue* show that highlighted past guests described the response from the public after the earlier broadcast:

> It was great. It was right after we did the show. I felt like Bo Jackson. It's like, "I know you!" It felt good because I guess you find out where people really are, like how many people are actually involved in interracial relationships. . . . We were walking around the Village about a week after the show. It was a couple from Philly. They stopped like they seen God.[18]

Marty said acquaintances often exclaimed, "You've met him!" when they learned she had been on *Donahue*. A common question asked of participants after their experience was "What's Donahue like?" Talk show panelists had gained access to an inner sanctum populated largely by deities viewers know intimately but are separated from by the glass wall of the set.

The actual experience of the show taping was described as somewhat unimpressive. Participants were treated well and appreciated the first-class accommodations, but they seemed to find the event itself rather lackluster. Dale compared the sensation to the slight letdown he experienced when he lost his virginity. Their impressions reversed, however, when they began to receive the positive responses from strangers who had seen them on television and when they saw themselves situated within the set. Only then did they seem to be aware of the impact of the medium and did the cycle of positive effects begin.

Participants were puncturing the glass veneer and stepping in to what seemed like a seamless entity. Richard Schickel suggests that the suprareality situated on screen holds mythic characteristics because of changes in society:

> This [television] reality is so attractive because many of the conventional realities have either diminished in their power to sustain and nurture us psychologically, or are in a state of transition. . . . The celebrity community, which has about it—as small-town life once did—aspects of the extended family, offers a kind of compensation. . . . In the dimmest motel room in the farthest reaches of the nation, we can always find that community.[19]

Stuart Ewen argues that the yearning for inclusion in the televisual realm is largely due to feelings of anomie that characterize modern life:

> In a society where conditions of anonymity fertilize the desire to "become somebody," the *dream of identity*, the *dream of wholeness*, is intimately woven together with the desire to be known; to be visible; to be documented, for all to see . . . when "being no one" is the norm. . . . Becoming "someone" is a gift bestowed upon people by the image machine.[20]

The value placed on "As seen on TV" can be traced to the exclusivity of the medium, the sense of stepping from the anonymous outskirts of banal reality to join a favored community of elites and the long-term use of the slogan by advertisers to connote a stamp of certification. The result is a wash of respectability for those who appear, and this seems to occur even when participants provide discrediting information during their brief sojourn to this esteemed and seldom-visited place of television land.

Television disclosers can indeed capitalize on this content-blind certification process. Donal Carbaugh, in his analysis of the *Donahue* show, expressed concern about the potential for certification regardless of what is discussed on the program:

> As a valued form of speech in which the saying of improper things is acceptable, being honest can be easily abused if uncritically used to legitimate the illegitimate actor. . . . Further, the marginal person's face can be enhanced, if ever so directly and slightly, by exploiting the freedom to speak, and making valued information public in a proper honest way.[21]

173

Daniel Boorstin commented about the celebrity as hero: "His relation to morality . . . is highly ambiguous."[22]

Talk shows are occasionally taped from prisons around the country, from which rapists, serial killers, and other criminals have spoken to plead their cases directly to the public. Donahue has been criticized by family members of victims for providing air time to heinous criminals who often defend their actions and appear without apology.[23]

Many organizations who fight bigotry feel the forum grants the Klan and other dangerous groups too much legitimacy. Rona Feder describes how anti-Klan groups often turn down opportunities to appear on talk shows to refute white supremacists' world view because, as the Simon Wiesenthal Center's Mark Weitzman told her, "We refuse to give them intellectual legitimacy."[24]

On a *Nightline* discussion, attorney Alan Dershowitz said:

> Television legitimates in a way that's very different from the way, for example, just the speaker on a soapbox legitimates. Because we've had a long history of only having mainstream items on TV—of having censorship, as it were, of having the FCC decide what does and doesn't go on—to now put the Klan on TV, it has a legitimizing effect.[25]

The resulting potential for normalization is indeed troubling, given the range of subjects discussed, but democratic ideals played out in other forums also can be worrisome, when racists and other extremists exercise their rights of free speech.

DEVIANCY DISMANTLING

Although participants were primarily seeking to delabel or divest themselves of their deviant status, the ramifications of a television talk show appearance are better characterized as a *re*labeling. The stigma that once engulfed many of the participants is expunged and replaced with a new master trait: "As seen on TV." This relabeling theory I am advancing here relies solely on informant reports of responses received from neighbors, family members, and strangers and therefore is not a firsthand assessment of the attitudes held by those parties. Participant reports are valuable, however, because they provide insights into aspects of the

media's influence that have been difficult to capture in more conventional and straightforward ways. Furthermore, participants' perceptions are
important because the "imputed sentiment" that Charles Horton Cooley
described is a crucial component of self-concept formation.

Respondents may indeed be correct that audience members now
see them as certified, but there are many possible artifacts. Informants
might selectively remember or report only the positive feedback.
Members of the public may keep negative comments to themselves or
might not know what else to say in what they may perceive as an awkward situation. It is possible, too, that respondents could feel certified
such that they then interpret public responses favorably. Carl, for example, said, "We feel like celebrities. We know people are staring at us, and
we know what they're saying." In fact, the observers could be whisper-
ing any number of things, but Carl viewed this attention positively, perhaps influenced by televisually enhanced levels of self-esteem.

Future studies need to directly assess the attitudes held by viewers who later interact with talk show panelists. It is important to know
whether the positive response from the mainstream is merely another
example of what Fred Davis identified as "fictional acceptance" in relationships between stigmatized individuals and "normals" or is an indication of true approbation.

In a related vein, it is unclear whether other members of the stigmatized group receive a measure of the benefits of the normalization
process that appears to result from television disclosure. The increased
acceptance may be directed only to the individuals from the stigmatized
group who appeared on television and who received the opportunity for
more lengthy deviance disavowal than is normally afforded to marginalized individuals. Joan Emerson details the possible conclusions drawn by
"normals" toward members of groups considered deviant. She suggests
that they may decide that (a) the member is, as previously surmised,
deviant; (b) their beliefs about the group are incorrect; (c) the individual
group member is not a "monster," as formerly believed; or (d) the shorthand rule that deviants are "monsters" is not tenable.[26]

Anecdotal evidence suggests that increased understanding and
acceptance does extend to people who are similarly situated. A colleague
of mine married to a man 10 years her junior remarked that his sisters
accepted her more readily after seeing an episode of *Donahue* that profiled the happy marriages of couples with varying differences in age. She

said, "They were excited about it. They were smiling, eager to tell me all about it. Maybe it was a relief for them."

It is paradoxical, still, that the general public seems to scoff at the freak show nature of the forum yet then lavishes participants, when seen in person, with newfound respect. These findings suggest that age-old mechanisms for defining the boundary lines of normalcy that work by trotting deviants out for ridicule may work differently in the age of television. Kai Erikson wrote:

> In our past, both the trial and punishment of deviant offenders took place in the public market and gave the crowd a chance to partici-pate in a direct, active way. Today we no longer parade deviants in the town square or expose them to the carnival atmosphere of Tyburn, but it is interesting to note that the "reform" which brought about this change in penal policy coincided almost precisely with the development of newspapers as media of public information.[27]

Erikson argues that press coverage of transgressions replaces the pillory to mark out the boundaries of deviancy in similar ways. However, television's preeminence in society appears to have altered these cen-turies-old processes of delineating deviancy; the expected reinforcement of the boundaries of normalcy buckles because of the medium's power to confer status to those who are seen there. Members on the periphery of society seem to grasp this potential of the medium better than those inside the margins and are capitalizing on it when the opportunity arises.

The powerful, still-rather-exclusive television medium invests disclosers with a certification that they were worthy for having been cho-sen to participate as a contestant and for successfully braving the onslaught of questioning. Viewers do not closely examine how partici-pants gained access, just as the public does not look very carefully at how power brokers and millionaires have earned their way to the top. What matters is getting there.

Even children seem to glimpse this idea of a televisual reality that is difficult to access yet "real." A colleague told me about his son, who asked to be able to participate on a children's show. He assured the child that he would arrange a visit and later found his son behind the TV set, tinkering, inquiring, "But how do you get in?" Morning news anchor Paula Zahn described her child's comment about her work: "[My moth-er] lives in a box."[28]

Joshua Meyrowitz has discussed "the unique power of television to break down distinctions between here and there, live and recorded, and personal and public."[29] Self-disclosure on television is a clear example of boundary permeability; the membrane formerly separating private and public becomes more porous by the day. Shifting concepts of "here and there" that Meyrowitz points to are just as revolutionary, however, because the transformation is causing abrupt changes in how Americans assign value to individuals.

Although Meyrowitz contends that the resulting effect of television technology and conventions is a feeling of "no sense of place,"[30] I believe the effect is of an ever-increasing certainty that television has created a *new* sense of place. Wayne Munson also uses the phrase "a new sense of place."[31] His meaning is similar, too, in that he sees talk shows as a new place where community can be forged through discussion. My use indicates the wider sense of place that television inhabits in our cultural consciousness as a hyperreality of utmost import in shaping identity and cultural consciousness. Talk show guests jump rather spontaneously at the chance to enter, to move from outside in, while viewers then marvel at participants' success at reaching the mystical ground-zero of television transmission.

NOTES

1. This phrase was taken from James Monaco, 1978, p. 6.
2. My use of the terms *legitimacy* and *validation* are sometimes used interchangeably to emphasize the perceptions held by many that the treatment of a topic on the preeminent medium of television confers a public sanction of the behavior as within the boundaries of discussion. At other points in my argument, I use both *validation* and *certification* to indicate participants' yearnings to be declared the one who is telling the truth. My use of these words throughout this chapter is sometimes muddled, I believe, due to the perplexing paradox of television's simultaneous ability to both certify as simply legitimate and to certify as demi-celebrity.
3. Lazarsfeld and Merton, 1948, p. 102. Italics in the original.
4. Boorstin, 1982, p. 243.

5. Monaco, 1978, p. 6.
6. Tichi, 1991, pp. 131, 133.
7. Altheide and Snow, 1979, argue that the "legitimizing function of media is the essence of media influence" (p. 237).
8. Tichi, 1991, pp. 138, 140.
9. Schickel, 1985, p. 263.
10. Didion, 1992, described a press conference in which a 10-year-old girl who brought charges of sexual assault against the "Spur Posse" mentioned her frustration that her mother had appeared on *Donahue*, but she herself had not. The child said, "I have been upset because I wanted to be on TV. To show how I feel. I wanted to say it for myself" (p. 65).
11. Schorr, 1977, p. 164. Cross, 1983, argues that the "validating eye of the television camera" is so enticing that people who cannot achieve fame through talent "will offer to reveal intimate and embarrassing secrets about their personal lives to gain entree" (p. 154). She mentions the number of individuals who wrote to *Real People* volunteering to carry out dangerous stunts as evidence that people are willing to take great risks in order to be on television.
12. It is interesting to note the number of celebrities who are well known for doing little more than being themselves on TV. People such as Vanna White, Ed McMahon, and the hosts of the various talk shows do not play a range of roles and are revered despite a lack of manifest talent.
13. Lorretta's rationale for appearing includes this strain of fantasy fulfillment, to step forward as a plaintiff on *The Oprah Winfrey Show*. It is interesting to note that Oprah's newly redesigned stage vaguely resembles a courtroom, and I would classify a hefty proportion of her guests as plaintiffs.
14. Becker, 1963, p. 33.
15. McLuhan, 1964, p. 7. While this is a simplistic shorthand for McLuhan's complex body of work, I am using this well-known phrase to summarize his theory that characteristics of the television medium, and not programming content, are paramount.
16. Mander, 1978, p. 34.
17. Goffman, 1959.

18. April 29, 1991 episode of *Donahue*.
19. Schickel, 1985, pp. 264-265.
20. Italics in the original. Ewen, 1988, pp. 94-95.
21. Carbaugh, 1989, pp. 138-139.
22. Boorstin, 1982, p. 243.
23. A member of Donahue's staff admitted in an article called "Everybody's Talking!" in the magazine *For Women First* that the show regretted airing a 1985 episode that profiled a murderer. The victim's wife had written to complain about the hour-long showcase the unrepentant killer had received.
24. Feder, 1993, p. 31.
25. *Nightline*, June 3, 1988. (As quoted in Feder, 1993, p. 32.)
26. It would be interesting to know more about frequent viewers of the genre. It is possible that they develop a world view consistent with the "mean world syndrome" (Gerbner et al., 1978) from their repeated exposures to an array of social problems discussed on the shows. What Munson calls the evershifting, ever noisy "constellation of voices" on daytime talk shows may prompt mainstream viewers to retrench toward conservatism, feeling the "center cannot hold" due to the straining of the boundaries when group after group asks to be let in. On the other hand, because members of diverse groups are given the opportunity to proclaim their similarities with the mainstream, heavy viewers may develop an increased understanding of and tolerance for diversity. This does not necessarily mean that viewers would lose their capacity to differentiate between right and wrong, as many critics of talk shows fear. The genre may provide lessons in the value of multiculturalism, an ethic important for peaceful coexistence in modern society, and in democratic ideals of free speech.
27. Erikson, 1981, p. 27.
28. Zahn described this incident on the December 14, 1993 episode of *Donahue*.
29. Meyrowitz, 1985, p. 18.
30. In fact, this is the title of his book.
31. Munson, 1993, uses the phrase for the title for his epilogue.

CHAPTER TWELVE

MARGIN TO CENTER, OUTSIDE IN

The afterglow of participation may not be long-lasting. Daniel Boorstin wrote of the fleeting nature of fame:

> The white glare of publicity, which first gave him [the celebrity] his specious brilliance, soon melts him away. . . . Now when it is possible, by bringing their voices and images daily into our living rooms, to make celebrities more quickly than ever before, they die more quickly than ever.[1]

The public response toward talk show guests will probably wane, because participants will be recognized less frequently as time passes. However, the positive effect on self-concept may be more permanent. Everyone owned videotaped copies of their appearances and had other souvenirs of the experience as well. Several brought out photographs of themselves with various hosts of the talk shows. Dennis and Raymonda showed me press clippings from the local newspaper pertaining to their appearances and even took my picture to add to their *Donahue* collection. Susen started a scrapbook of the press response to her TV appearance.[2]

Raymonda was surprised that there were no formal tokens of appreciation for participation on the show: "That's what cracked us up, you don't get any money. Gee, I thought we'd get something, you know, a 50 cent piece, something with Donahue's face on it or something, nothing."[3] As the attention from the public ebbs, informants can pour over the collected keepsakes to recapture feelings of specialness and mastery. The relative permanence of the experience in this crystallized state highlights its distinctiveness. Friends or acquaintances who missed the event often asked to see the tape, and several participants admitted that they had watched the episode repeatedly.

A guest's comment on an April 5, 1990 episode of *Sally Jessy Raphael* indicates that declining levels of public affirmation may be quite difficult for some participants. The panelist was an advocate for the mentally ill who was on a day pass from a psychiatric institution to discuss the fall-out that occurred after his appearance on *The Oprah Winfrey Show*. He described the red carpet treatment he had received from Winfrey's staff and said, "You really think you've arrived. You go back to the dirty dishes. . . . You feel like a star—people ask for your autograph. When it dies down, you want that feeling back. It's like a drug." Although many of the people I interviewed had been called back to participate on *Donahue* or had appeared on other shows, most disclosers on talk shows do not have the broadcast longevity of experts repeatedly called on over a period of years on programs such as *Nightline* or the news.[4]

Time Warner executive Jim Paratore commented in *The Wall Street Journal* that topics that suddenly become the rage and fuel a feeding frenzy by talk show staffs have a "half-life of a week to two weeks."[5] The commodification of otherness entails a built-in process of discarding the topic after it serves its purpose; however, because of ongoing pressures to find topics that are titillating, guests who are willing to talk about sensitive subjects are, in fact, sometimes marketable over an extended period.[6]

Furthermore, participants have succeeded in "stepping in" to a valued place, and, rather like the limited number of men and women who have orbited the earth, one only has to get there once to have that lasting credit. As long as access to television remains limited, then, the specialness of participation is likely to last.

APPROPRIATENESS

The impetus behind this examination of self-disclosure concerned the public nature of a behavior normally conducted in private settings. This context makes television disclosure seem out of place, but questions of disclosure propriety can now be examined more closely in light of the findings. Sidney Jourard argues that appropriateness of disclosure is determined by the mental health gains involved. In the present study, informants reported higher levels of self-esteem, so the mental health benefits seem clear for this group of participants, although the duration of effects is uncertain.

Valerian Derlega and Janusz Grzelak suggest different criteria. The authors argue that appropriateness is best evaluated in a functional framework with a focus on the perceptions of the discloser as to whether goals have been attained and on prevailing norms for the appropriateness of self-disclosure.

The evangelical rationale for participation in the television talk show forum expressed by the informants indicates that their goals usually were not geared toward expressive or self-clarification functions. Participants seeking fulfillment of these needs might be sorely disappointed, considering the disjointed and superficial nature of the discussions on the programs. Instead, informants reported they were striving to influence others' impressions so that acceptance and inclusion could result, goals that appear to fit the function referred to by Derlega and Grzelak as social control.[7] The public affirmation directed toward participants indicates that respondents were successful, at least to some extent, in these ventures. In fact, the positive nature of the response from both the mainstream and fellow outgroup members greatly surpassed their expectations.

Derlega and Grzelak stress that goal attainment must be balanced by the cost to relationships. As described earlier, many family members of the disclosers were deeply upset by the revelations on television of what was often discrediting information. In most cases, however, disclosers whose families had severed ties had already developed new primary groups that supplanted the loss of family support. Furthermore, participants felt the negative response from family members was outweighed by the potential to increase public understanding.

The operational norms, Delega and Grzelak's second factor, are detailed in Donal Carbaugh's work.[8] He describes the expectations on *Donahue* for honesty, which is rewarded with polite listening by the studio audience because of society's need for information. More generally, too, society places a value on truth telling, as evidenced by the rising tide of celebrity confessions endlessly recited in the media.

Joshua Meyrowitz traces the late 20th century's blurring of lines of propriety to television, arguing that the medium's boundary-breaking characteristics allow topics formerly not discussed in front of certain groups to become transparent to all. Robert Kubey's critique of Meyrowitz's seminal work points to additional social forces that explain historical trends Meyrowitz attributes to television. Kubey's list includes Freud's impact (and its reverberations of expressing and being yourself) and—even—the rise of method acting. Cultural drifts that include coming out proclamations by gays, feminist activism espousing the "personal is political," and 12-step programs advocating declarations of addiction also work to create a climate in which self-disclosure is encouraged and sanctioned. The cultural climate, then, for public self-appraisal makes television disclosure more acceptable than it might appear at first glance. These norms are not universal, however, as is evident in Donal Carbaugh's recent study that found that Russian youths were loathe to discuss sexuality to the degree that Donahue demanded in a special program broadcast from the former Soviet Union.[9]

In the United States, given the varied criteria of mental health gains, goal attainment, and social expectations, television disclosure seems appropriate as a strategy. Participants on *Donahue* successfully utilized self-disclosure as a rhetorical tactic to educate others in a venue in which such declarations are sanctioned. Informants also experienced an unexpected bonus: a boost in self-esteem.

The tactic seems especially risky, however, when used by disclosers not yet firmly beyond a period of period of raw vulnerability and self-examination. Psychologist Herbert Freudenberger suggests that "it can kick off stuff and there's no one there to clean it up."[10] This sort of feverish disclosure was rare in this group, but the genre seems to be moving more toward this type of participant as the competition for ratings and guests grows ever fiercer. Choosing unbalanced disclosers may make for gripping television, but it can be dangerous. One man who had discussed his incestuous relationship with his daughter called the *Geraldo* staff when he returned home to say he was considering killing her.[11] Staff members at various shows claim that they try to procure professional help when guests seem at risk after participation, as did *Geraldo*'s staff in this case.

Dr. Peg Ziegler, a rape crisis counselor who accompanied Wendy on *Donahue*, was annoyed that the staff whisked them offstage when the show wrapped and provided no place for the panelists to gather afterwards to take stock of the emotional toll of talking about rape. She said, "These women had bared their souls. The show could have at least let them bond."

Although Dr. Ziegler came away miffed with the show for this reason, she noted the powerful boost to Wendy's confidence and recovery.[12]

Although strong contestants may suffer the slings and arrows of the taping well and emerge feeling victorious, relationships can be terribly—and perhaps irrevocably—strained when public revelations include intimate details about others.[13] A striking example was a case before the Texas Supreme Court in 1994 that centered on *Donahue* panelist Miriam Booher's disclosure that her husband had impregnated her daughter years earlier.[14] After the show aired, the daughter—and her son, now a teenager—sued Booher, Donahue, and one of his former producers for emotional distress and loss of privacy. The court upheld Booher's free speech rights; the family remains torn asunder. The teen has since switched schools because the teasing became intolerable after his paternity was revealed. Clearly, the risks can be heavily borne by significant others when family skeletons coming tumbling out of closets.

Recent trends toward the use of props and recreations on daytime television talk shows make the genre riskier still. For example, a shocking *Donahue* episode about infantilism opened with the adult male panelists dressed as infants and shown sitting in a crib, high chair, and playpen. A *Sally Jessy Raphael* episode about men whose wives were angry that their husbands routinely described their sex lives to their best friends situated the man, his wife, and friend on large beds on stage. A *Donahue* episode concerning male rape featured a reenactment by the teenaged victim of the gang rape situation. This sort of highlighted sensationalism would appear to make it all the more difficult to resist stigmatizing processes. Legitimacy may be especially difficult to procure under these negative trappings despite careful attempts at impression management.[15]

Although television disclosure seems generally appropriate by the standards put forth by Derlega and Grzelak, questions of co-optation remain. Although the absorption and undermining of groups resistant to dominant norms is a characteristic and frequently noted feature of hegemony, the difficult issue of gains made by individuals at the forefront of the group being coopted is not often addressed. Participants believed they had been successful and felt empowered and special as a result of the experience, although they themselves recognized the freak show nature of the proceedings. Steadfastly insisting they had not been used, they argued that they had strategically taken advantage of the show as an avenue to further their goals.

Ralph, who doggedly spoke about his daughter's rape on show after show in an effort to apprehend the rapists, said: "Whatever I could do to try and fight I used. I used the media and they used me." Marty talked about the number of times she and Brett had related the painful story of his coming out during show and tell as the child with AIDS at school. "But," she said firmly, "if it changes an attitude, or opens somebody's eyes about it, then, you know, why not?" Carl, who was very proud of his relationship with Michelle, 40 years his junior, said:

> My son, my brother-in-law, they said the same thing: "He used you."
> "Yeah," I says, "Dave, I let him use me." I says, "That's fine. Let him use me. He's making a fool out of himself. I'm the good person. . . . I have nothing to hide. I am not ashamed of anything I say or do."

Michael said, "No matter what the end results are, of how they use you, if you really think you have a good cause, there's something—then you become driven to do it." Respondents expressed an eagerness to appear again if the chance arose.

Talk show panelists, who are relatively powerless players on television's hegemonic turf, made the best of an uneven playing field through active preparation. Importantly, participants had no other court in which to plead their case. Talk shows are a type of "freak" people's court; otherwise, they are never given a hearing. Television disclosers are capitalizing on producers', and, by extension, the audience's thirst for intimate details while they carry out their goals to evangelize, sell products, garner attention for themselves, and tell their sides of a story.

bell hooks declares the need for "coming to voice, articulating and redefining reality"[16] without suggesting practical forums in which resistance can currently be voiced. Television talk shows, imperfect as they are, are seen by some marginalized group members as viable vehicles to serve just such a purpose. The value of the opportunity for those languishing on society's periphery to speak for themselves via the central medium of modern culture cannot be overestimated. Therefore, whereas gains in acceptance might be fleeting or illusory and the end result be cooptation, informants were not embittered but delighted by the opportunity and the positive responses garnered. Rather curiously, whereas commodification is of great concern to critical scholars, participants and viewers alike reveled in each participant's new status as commodity. In this era of image, commodification is highly valued when the stamp of "As seen on TV" is affixed.

A nagging concern persists in my mind, partly because this work paints almost without qualification a rosy picture of the disclosure experience as reported by informants. I have also talked to women who have been featured in *Playboy* magazine who are similarly upbeat, feeling special for having been chosen and feeling empowered by positive responses from the public. It appears that those with the least power in society who are seldom singled out for representation find attention from the media the most affirming. Perhaps this is the Hawthorne effect of media attention, an improvement in morale prompted by the slight notice paid yet disconnected from the actual specifics of the experience.

As Akiba Cohen, Hanna Adoni, and Charles Bantz point out, the privilege of appearing on television, especially on the news, is generally denied to those not already established in positions of power.[17] This practice further entrenches present hierarchies in society because of the status conferral processes that unfold. Talk show participants seem to grasp intuitively the idea that social norms are negotiated and partly played out on television. Furthermore, they sense that bargaining chips are doled out in large measure according to one's access to television visibility.

John Fiske and John Hartley cast the yearning for validation discussed in the last chapter in terms of power rather than perceptions of the risk of being a nonperson if television credentials are lacking. They wrote of the "desire to be on television, and thus to be an active cultural agent at the transmitting rather than the receiving sector of the communication circle."[18] An appearance on a talk show is not an unfettered opportunity to control the transmitting end because of the variety of constraints determined by broadcast standards, the genre, and the host, but it is a moment or two to speak—live (or live-to-tape)—to a potential audience of millions.[19] Only Sabrina, who hosts a cable access program, can to a large degree control the representation of herself that is sent out over the airwaves, but the size and variety of her audience is severely limited in a narrowcast venue.

As pointed out by Joshua Meyrowitz, the resulting blurring of private and public boundaries provides more extensive information about the "other" to viewers,[20] but the freak show nature of the forum would seem to severely limit more substantial gains. The extent of the progress toward understanding when talk shows are utilized strategically is unclear. Although outgroup members were gamely participating because of the potential to change consciousness and force visibility, they were sometimes disappointed by how little progress was made, how little advancement was gained in the dialogue about the topic.

Dale, whose show topic centered on married couples' differing levels of sexual desire, said, "On the range of a to z, we never got to b with the issue." Kate felt she was rarely able to get beyond viewers' basic questions about her new anatomical features and believed that many interesting questions about gender were never broached because of the elementary level of discussion on talk shows. Sandi brainstormed, searching for other forums on which to discuss related and less sensational aspects of sexual harassment such as the enduring effects and a more detailed treatment of what parents can do. Gains in knowledge seemed agonizingly slow and appeared to inevitably plateau at an elementary level, no matter how many shows each person appeared on or whether producers put a different spin on the topic. Yet, participants believed that both humanization and public awareness were critical, and perhaps neverending, first steps.

Less prejudicial arenas are needed in which members of marginalized groups—indeed, ordinary citizens of all stripes—could plead their cases. In 1980, a UNESCO commission decried the vertical, one-way nature of communication flow radiating downward to inactive recipients of broadcast messages. The committee called for a more dynamic, participatory system:

> Democratization can be defined as the process whereby: a) the individual becomes an active partner and not a mere object of communication; b) the variety of messages exchanged increases; and c) the extent and quality of social representation or participation in communication are augmented.[21]

The talk show forum affords active participation and a diversity of voices, as espoused by the UNESCO Commission. However, their last point—the quality of representation—is limited by the sensational nature of the forum. The spectrum of debate on more legitimate programs needs to be widened so that access is not limited to established power brokers of society, what Marc Cooper and Lawrence Soley call the "Golden Rolodex" of experts regularly called to speak on public issues. Herbert

Gans recommends the inclusion of individuals on the news who represent diverse backgrounds and points of view in order to provide "multiperspectival coverage." Instead, marginalized groups are herded into the freak show ghettos of daytime television and seldom allowed access to the nightly news or such shows as *Nightline*, on which the gains might be even greater.[22]

In fact, however, because of the generalizing character of the certification process, the ghetto nature of the forum may not really matter. What matters is access. Participants' reports of the certification processes set in motion even when discrediting information is revealed on air provides evidence to support Cecelia Tichi's claims:

> If the on-screen world is the place to be, then, inevitably, a complex of human concerns—identity, experience, locale, action—these, too, must migrate to the TV screen. Inevitably, the status of these human phenomena will rest on their being "seen on TV."[23]

Most of us, however, have very limited access to this influential medium in which concerns could be validated and brought to light.[24]

Ralph's plaintive refrain when talking about the number of people who get away with heinous crimes, was "This just is not acceptable." Participants were clamoring for the public's attention for issues they believed were urgent yet neglected by the media. Most had turned away from television as they struggled with harsh realities in their lives that the medium ignored or treated frivolously. Each refused to passively let others set the public agenda.

Sally Steenland calls the genre's showcasing of noncelebrities an "ultimate democracy":

> People who are heavy, plain-looking, without a persona—who act like themselves in front of the camera—have their day on "Oprah" and the rest. Such ordinary citizens—not celebrities, not especially articulate or outstanding men and women—are invisible in nearly every other inch of the landscape.[25]

Denise Kervin points out differential patterns of representation on the news that include inequities in who addresses the camera, who is allowed to speak for longer durations, and who is seated during interviews.[26]

189

Although talk shows seem a lowly and freakish forum, in fact, certain features are far less constricting than those in more "legitimate" forums.

However, participants have to be willing to pay the price to enter these valued sites by trading personal disclosures in a set-up that is hardly democratic.[27] Self-disclosure is a form of a poll tax far less regularly required of experts or politicians in order to gain access to the very airwaves owned by the public. Participants trade their privacy for the chance to place their items on the agenda. Importantly, too, not everyone willing to self-disclose is allowed access; the topic must be deemed one that will pull viewers while not offending advertisers or affiliate stations.

THE PUBLIC SPHERE

Self-disclosure serves as a powerful currency when it is used to enter the fray, where a rhetorical struggle can then begin. The risks, however, as Anita Hill and others have found, are great. As Nancy Fraser points out, parties in public disputes are not always accorded equal levels of consideration when sensitive areas of inquiry are rooted up. Generally, more leeway and greater opportunities for self-definition are given to privileged members of society. A leveling of the terrain is underway, however, as both private and public persons are being asked to come clean with personal details.

Traditional patterns of privatization favor certain power imbalances. In her analysis of Anita Hill's public disclosures of sexual harassment, Nancy Fraser argues that hush-hush attitudes toward topics such as incest, sexual harassment, spousal abuse, and other "private" issues have worked to favor those who commit crimes and then hide behind the taboos for speaking that silence victims. The actress Roseanne, an incest survivor, said, "This is a disease that can only thrive in silence. I have a social and moral obligation to speak out."[28]

Public disclosures are often dismissed as vindictive and self-serving. For example, the woman who claimed that William Kennedy Smith raped her has been criticized for continuing to speak out about her allegations beyond the point at which the jury found him not guilty. Media forums increasingly serve as useful extralegal venues when individuals feel the system of justice has failed them.[29] No wonder, then, that long lines of people are waiting their turn at the court of public opinion to argue their cases for themselves and/or for their groups.

Politicians utilize the power of strategic self-disclosure, too, in impression management. Charles Krauthammer describes the spiraling increase in the use of what he calls the "pornography of self-revelation" in politics. He calls the Democrat's high levels of self-disclosure at the 1992 convention the "Oprahtization of politics." The crucial difference, however, is that the public has virtually no other options for getting its messages out.

There is power, then, in disclosure, particularly when it is carefully employed. However, Susan Bordo contends that "creative interpretation" of issues is not enough, that there must be "ongoing political struggle."[30] As Christina Reynolds has pointed out, the talk itself is not the point; social action must be. Michael Chatman, an activist for teens at risk in inner cities, told me that he was chagrined at the unfolding dialogue on a *Donahue* episode he appeared on in 1993. Donahue prompted the teens to recount a long list of misdeeds in elaborate detail; there was no time for the many solutions Chatman came prepared to discuss. A former gang member himself, he expected to have to give over the goods about his checkered past. He said: "I don't mind the risks of doing that, only if in fact, like the girls expected, it was going to help someone. But not in the situation whereby I just tell the story and it's a meaty sensational story with no solutions attached to it."

The genre's almost exclusive focus on the sensational aspects of issues is where the public is terribly underserved. Episodes generally end after a too-large group of panelists has doled out the tantalizing details, with no time left for some of the pesky particulars that might address pending legislation, for example.[31] The public is partly to blame for this, of course. If viewers turn to competing fare the moment the titillation ends, then little wonder producers hustle to keep the plates spinning, faster and faster. A related problem occurs when topics are turned down because producers feel the story lacks certain saleable elements that will grab and keep viewers.[32] The resulting gate-keeping severely restricts the range of topics to which Americans are exposed; unfortunately, these trends are evident across the spectrum of the broadcast medium and are not limited to talk shows.

Members of the public chosen by producers to enter the ring felt empowered, and some utilized newfound feelings of potency toward social activism. Others, however, seemed to languish at this stage, riding the carousel of talk show appearances as a vehicle to get their word out. Few seemed to apply energy toward more conventional methods for affecting political change. Bud, for example, who repeatedly insisted that he is a radical, bemoaned the time-consuming nature of trying to drum up talk show appearances. He routinely called producers, angling for more publicity for his cause. This, then, may be how potential gains made on the program are neutralized; participants get caught up in the attention and cease their efforts on other fronts.

bell hooks cautions that speaking of one's experience "is only part of the of the process of politicization, one which must be linked to education for critical consciousness that teaches about structures of domination and how they function."[33] In a similar vein, Linda Alcoff and Laura Gray express concern that media coverage of rape and incest survivors often focuses on the woman's emotional state: "The discussion of the survivor's 'inner' self and feelings replaces rather than leads to a discussion of links to the 'exterior' and ways to transform it."[34] Televised self-disclosures seem particularly useful as a starting point, both as a call for solidarity and for providing information to the mainstream about social problems that warrant attention.

Upon cursory examination, television disclosure seems inappropriate, rather vain, and potentially dysfunctional for participants. The rationale offered by participants forces a different orientation toward this genre of television programming and perhaps television in general. Talk show forums can now be seen as opportunities for deviance disavowal and agenda setting. I view the phenomenon of television disclosure as a plaintive cry for inclusion in society via a medium that blithely ignores topics participants feel must be addressed and excludes marginalized groups except for rare treatments in which they are stereotyped or vilified.

Indeed, many may cringe at the kinds of groups who are receiving a measure of legitimacy in this forum. Nonetheless, individuals working for social change can learn from these tactics. Noted advertising creator Tony Schwartz argues: "It is more important to learn how to use the power of media than it is to attempt to curtail that power, to use media not to achieve trivial ends but in the cause of those social and political struggles that involve ordinary people."[35] Certification processes are set in motion largely because of the relative exclusivity of the medium. The nondiscerning status conferral that occurs can best be counteracted by opening up access to national forums that allow members of the public greater participation in voicing their concerns.

Currently, public dialogue on television occurs either between elites on news and information programs or on talk shows, where invited guests must have salacious items to trade. These high brow and low brow offerings provide narrow windows of opportunity for most members of the audiences to be anything other than mere spectators. Guy Debord argues that those in power want citizens' desires for change to be both anesthetized and diverted by the constant parade of spectacle. Interestingly, Daniel Dayan and Elihu Katz contrast the spectacle, which sharply limits the range of responses from the audience, with festivals, which they describe in the following paragraph:

> No simple picture or pageant is imposed monopolistically on participants. The occasion offers many different foci and much room for ad hoc activity. . . . Interaction is obviously called for, since the roles of performers and spectators are neither fixed or irreversible.[36]

I say until we develop widely democratic forms of television, burst in on the spectacle if you can. This is the sobering reality: It is here, at this carnivalesque and often ridiculed site, that citizens have the greatest prospect of speaking about their concerns on the powerful medium of television. So, step right up, folks. Talk shows can be bustling festivals of competing rhetorics, but members of the public must learn both to muscle their way in and to protect themselves from corrupting influences while at the carnival.[37]

CONCLUSION

This text, which was initially conceptualized simply as a study of self-disclosure in an unusually public context, developed into a broadly interdisciplinary work that draws from the deviancy labeling literature, readings on social activism, and new ideas from the field of mass communication about television's powers of certification. This work provides a link between these diverse fields and offers new insights into marginalized groups' use of television and of private disclosures to resist deviant labels.

Significantly, an unusual number of informants were virtually nonviewers of television. As members of marginalized groups, they reported that they rarely watch television because they believe the medium neglects and stereotypes them. They are, however, aware of its importance and are therefore willing to step forward to attempt to counteract its negative influence through self- and group representation that is carefully managed to put the best possible image forward. It is interesting that they are aware of the need to use advertising-based ideals of packaging predominant on television despite their low reliance on the medium.

This proactive response to the media is a new type of activity level seldom noted in the range of involvement described in theories of audience response.[38] This work turns the tables on the conventional emphasis on audiences in mass communication studies. Here, the investigation of media effects is extended to those impacted by the medium yet independent to some degree of viewing habits.

Participants are off the map of conventional models of mass communication processes in this way. For example, Melvin DeFleur and Sandra Ball-Rokeach's broad theory of media dependency and effects identifies three types of dependency relations for individuals that include understanding, orientation, and play. Omitted are conceptions of self-determination or "talking back." The existence of these active nonaudience members who are not identified in mass communications models reveals a hegemonic blindspot of many researchers. Conventional media practices that virtually deny participation except in limited freak show forums are not generally questioned. As a result, the possibility for participation does not even show up on models in the field.

In the critical literature, in which issues of power imbalances are foregrounded, the emphasis on creating meaning is generally situated in the reading of the text. This study presents a unique example of resistance based at the encoding level. Rather strikingly, much of the current writing about audience members' engagement in texts is even more pertinent to talk shows because of viewers' ability—when chosen by producers—to literally play themselves within the scene. Eric Michaels wrote, "In postmodernist space, the activity of the audience is self-inscription. One is invited to create meaning in the text by writing oneself there. . . . Within the text, we displace the star."[39] I believe this rare opportunity for actual displacement is a key factor in the certification processes that occur.

These programs provide a text rich with unusually diverse meanings. Although all media texts are considered by cultural theorists to contain a variety of potential readings,[40] talk shows are laden with particularly diverse meanings because they are multiauthored. The mainstream public generally seems to regard daytime talk shows as frivolous and often inane. Members of marginalized groups, however, appear to take the genre more seriously, attending more closely to the dialogue rather than the circus-like elements.[41]

Talk show guests willingly stepped forward to discuss taboo subjects to expand society's boundaries pertaining to normalcy and to neutralize the negative cast of common stereotypes. Craig continued, "If you're humanized, people will have a harder time hating you. It's, uh, I think if we each reach the process of humanizing the concept of gay, of all gays and lesbians, that there will be a lot less hatred." Self-disclosure serves as a strategy for those otherwise relatively powerless to affect social change. Unexpectedly, an appearance on the national medium of television, whatever the role played, conferred status and fulfilled a normalizing function that afforded a patina even to those previously tarnished by deviancy labels.

The proactive stance exhibited by participants is a type of agenda setting by crusaders who want to change society, and the same strategies can be effective for a variety of causes. The gains to society can be great, from increased public awareness of health issues such as the risks of penile implants to more information about outgroups. Importantly, the dialogue about these topics is spoken by the people whose quality of life is at stake.

NOTES

1. Boorstin, 1982, p. 247.
2. Part of the spiraling attention Susen received occurred after I had given her name, with her permission, to reporters writing magazine articles about talk shows.
3. Therese, who appeared on *The Oprah Winfrey Show* in 1994, told me that each participant was given a mug with Winfrey's name on it as they were "shuffled out" of the studio. She also noted that panelists were not given an opportunity to have

their pictures taken with Oprah, nor did they even receive a handshake on that particular day.

4. See Cooper and Soley, 1990; Hoynes and Croteau, 1989.

5. Jensen, 1993, p. A6.

6. Jensen, 1993, talks about the talk show circuit, which Sherrol most notably has successfully ridden for an extended period. However, Sandi noted that staff members at two shows had recently talked to her about Heather but then declined to offer her a spot on the panel when they found she had already appeared on several shows. Producers did not seem to find repeated appearances a problem in other cases, but this may be a fairly new response to a sense that the public is increasingly weary of seeing—as Norma Jean had been described—"the same deviant" on show after show. Sandi also noted that many others were also willing to step forward to talk about sexual harassment, and she was often asked to suggest names of those ready to go public.

7. Participants' behavior seems rather similar to the authors' concept of social validation, but Derlega and Grzelak use the term to refer to self-validating attempts. As discussed earlier, outcomes did entail an increase in self-esteem, and participants often described feeling validated, but the overall goals were directed toward stigma management. There is a pejorative sense, certainly, about the authors' phrase—social control. Talk show guests generally are not trying to "control" or convert others, but are instead seeking to represent their own realities. Stewart et al.'s (1989) work on social movements notes that "persuasion and coercion are often inseparable" (p. 15).

8. Carbaugh, 1989.

9. Carbaugh, 1993.

10. Kolbert, 1993, p. 2E.

11. Kolbert, 1993, p. 2E.

12. It seems that participants most familiar with standards for therapeutic exchanges were most critical of the talk show format. This was the case for Dr. Ziegler as well as Dale, who seemed to expect that the show would handle the topic sensitively, with time to reel out a delicate issue, as did his therapy sessions.

13. One of the women I spoke to who had appeared on *Ricki Lake* said she was very concerned about how the show would affect her strained but cordial relationship with her ex-boyfriend: "Because they try to get you to say things you would never, ever say."

14. Gordon, 1994, relates this court case in an article in *The Washington Post.*

15. One strategy is to act very much like the celebrities who generally inhabit television land, so that certification processes are most likely to spin into motion. Glamour, too, despite its sometimes campy dimensions, seemed to work effectively for several participants. I saw this tactic work when I appeared on *The Jerry Springer Show* with an odd bunch of participants who had been guests on countless programs. Several were dressed extravagantly, and people in the studio audience during the taping and afterward complimented the participants effusively about their exaggerated outfits and makeup.

16. Galtung and Ruge, 1973, wrote, "In our elite-centered news communication system ordinary people are not even given the chance of representing themselves" (p. 66).

17. Fiske and Hartley, 1978, p. 148.

18. The programs are generally either shot live (as in *Donahue's* case) or live-to-tape; the latter is a production pattern that allows greater leeway for tardy guests and for editing a variety of mishaps. Editing out portions is rather rare except when certain profanities are used or when information such as a private phone number is inadvertently provided. Comments made during the live-to-tape shows are occasionally shaved for time, but extra editing adds to the expense.

    Creative topic selection on *The Oprah Winfrey Show*, especially, is shifting generic conventions of the talk show form best characterized by its static place—the studio—and by its freeform discussion. Increasingly, shows are folding in edited pieces culled, for example, from several hours of tape shot by a production team at someone's home or at Oprah's office. These trends leave less time for participants who hope to play a large role in structuring the debate.

19. hooks, 1989, p. 16.

20. Meyrowitz, 1985.
21. UNESCO International Commission for the Study of Communication Problems, 1980, p. 166.
22. Hoynes and Croteau, 1989, also argue that mainstream news and public affairs programming should extend their guest lists. The focus of their research concerns the highly regarded program, *Nightline:*

> The program should regularly and systematically include representatives of citizen organizations, especially organizations which represent groups different from the white, male, power establishment. Peace and public interest groups, unions, women's groups, church-based organizations, minority and civil rights groups, and other social movement organizations, to name a few, should be granted regular access to the arena of debate now so closely guarded by "Nightline" (p. 32).

23. Italics in the original. Tichi, 1991, p. 136.
24. This certification process is unlikely to be in effect in countries where a staple of the TV diet is inexpensive game shows in which many citizens compete for minor prizes, because the sense of exclusiveness and glamour is lacking.
25. Steenland, 1990, p. 12.
26. Kervin, 1985. Cohen et al., 1990, provide a model of levels of representation on the news. A mere description of the position held by a group or person is indicative of the lowest level. Increasing representation is shown when the reporter (a) quotes the speaker, (b) shows the party speaking on screen, (c) interviews the person on air, or (d) advocates the position held by the individual of group.
27. Levin (1987) touts the democratic potential of talk radio. He wrote: "Working men and women may be emboldened to participate by the absence of video, which relieves them of the shame that bourgeois society imposes on the unfashionable and less well-educated . . . and it is the only medium not dominated by established figures, romance, cops and robbers, or celebrities" (p. 16). Levin admits that the radio host can interrupt, deride, screen, bait, and dominate callers, but he believes

the genre provides a necessary outlet for expression for disenfranchised citizens.

28. Roseanne was quoted in an October 7, 1991 *Newsweek* article
written by Darnton et al., p. 71.

29. An interesting exchange on *Donahue* on March 5, 1991 highlights the talk show as a forum especially useful for those who
feel the standard judicial process works against them. The
topic that day was a sting operation that targeted gay sex in a
remote section of a public park in a midwestern town. A fundamentalist Christian minister on the panel defensively
responded to Donahue's complaint that none of the city offi-
cials consented to appear. He replied, "They regard you as a
very skilled ring master; frankly they're not interested in being
in this circus." One of the gay men who had been arrested then
countered, "The only difference . . . is our ringmaster is in the
courtroom." Leanne, too, spoke of the relatively free flow of
conversation on talk shows as more equitable than her trial:
"It's as fair as fair can be. You get to say what you couldn't
say in court, what they wouldn't allow."

30. Bordo, 1993, p. 280.

31. Therese called the number of guests which overflowed the
stage the day she appeared on *The Oprah Winfrey Show* a
"cast of thousands."

32. Heather told me that one of the tabloid shows dropped the idea
of doing a story about her when they learned that she had chosen to attend an alternative school. They were very disappointed and told her mother that they felt this decision was cowardly. Heather's life choices, shaped largely by social forces outside her control, did not make for a good story in their view.

33. hooks, 1989, p. 108.

34. Alcoff and Gray, 1993, p. 280. Furthermore, they caution that
the incitement to speak should not be exclusively championed,
because the emotional toll and the ramifications of public disclosures can be brutal.

35. Schwartz, 1981, p. 29. Feder's (1993) work also mentioned
Schwartz.

36. Dayan and Katz (1992), p. 93. The authors use MacAloon's
(1984) work entitled *Rite, Festival, Spectacle, Game* to dis-

cuss the different ways media cover public events.

37. The postmodern age is largely characterized by its coopted and chaotic flood of representations. Gergen, 1991, writing about the postmodern age, also uses images of the carnival to describe participation in social life: "Life itself may become a form of play, in which one transforms ventures into adventures, purpose into performance, and desire into drama. Culture seems a carnival with a never-ending array of sideshows" (p. 193).

38. See, for example, Levy and Windahl, 1984.

39. Michaels, 1987, p. 91.

40. See Fiske and Hartley, 1978; Parkin, 1972.

41. Elucidating different readings would be valuable, as these may be important factors determining participation when the opportunity to appear arises and would impact attitude changes that may result from viewing. The elements of the program that foster this polysemic quality would also be interesting to examine, as would the range of rhetorical devices utilized.

METHODOLOGICAL NOTES

The methodology for this work is an odd mixture of invention (the use of a toll-free number[1] and the investigative tracking of informants) and tried and true methods (for example, standard focused interview techniques). The end result was a rich data pool of well over 1,000 typed pages.

Respondents include: two female prostitutes, two gay parents, a rape survivor, a woman who had had 10 plastic surgeries, a lesbian transsexual and her partner, a gay couple waging a legal battle for marriage rights, two swingers, an incest survivor, a married couple with different levels of sexual desire, a former homosexual, an intergenerational couple, a couple who head a church that espouses sexual intercourse with the priestess as the route to salvation, and a couple who appeared on a show entitled "sisters who swap husbands." Other informants include a woman briefly married to a gay con man bigamist; a man labeled on the show as a "former male prostitute"; a woman and her son, who has AIDS; a married couple grappling with the recent discovery that the wife is a lesbian; a man labeled as having had 100 affairs; a sperm donor; a vigilante dad ready to avenge his daughter's rape; a "speed seducer"; a woman in prison for adoption fraud; a mother and her daughter, who has been sexually harassed at school; and a happily married couple who appeared on a *Donahue* episode profiling superb husbands.

Three additional informants had not appeared on *Donahue*—yet—but had been guests on a variety of other shows. These were a man seeking to legalize drugs as a way to foster revolution, a woman with large breasts, and a mother who appeared on two talk shows about "sexy moms and jealous daughters."

Disclosers who were patently crusading for a cause were usually not pursued. For example, a woman who discussed the debilitating depression and physical ailments she suffered after her hysterectomy was excluded because she was the president of an organization called Hysterectomy Educational Research Services. However, when another informant in the same city had been located, efforts were made to maximize time and minimize expense by lining up interviews with others as well, even though their formalized links with an organization might be apparent. In addition to making the trips more cost effective, this strategy increased the range and number of informants, providing a spectrum of discloser types.

INTERVIEWS

The initial contact usually occurred in a phone call to respondents' homes. In these cases, after introducing myself, I asked if they were willing to be interviewed about their talk show experience(s). All but 1 person who could be reached by phone agreed to participate, and 7 of 12 who received letters of intent accepted as well, although 1 man, the "heavy drinker," later slipped out of the sample when he moved without leaving a forwarding address before he could be interviewed. An advocate for survivors of spousal abuse, a former battered wife, was reached at the shelter where she worked. She seemed somewhat hesitant and wary, and I did not press her to participate.

The heterogeneity of the participants was bolstered by limiting the selection to two people per panel.[2] The programs are usually designed to showcase two or three disclosers and their significant others. This coupling might be with a spouse, relative, or gay partner. Whenever possible, both members of the pair were interviewed.

Informants were allowed to decide whether they wished to be interviewed together or apart. Most chose the former. These were challenging encounters, because an effort was made to record both members' responses to each query. These dual interviews were richly fertile and dynamic.

Interviews lasted roughly two hours. All were audiotaped. The interviewing style was patterned on suggestions from two sources. Michael Patton's many practical recommendations for interviewing proved helpful. Robert Merton, Marjorie Fiske, and Patricia Kendall's focused method of in-depth interviewing was useful because of its emphasis on an open-ended examination of the informant's definition and description of a situation.

Merton and his co-authors advise a thorough preliminary investigation of the situation to be discussed so that a portion of the interviewing can be targeted to specifics. This was accomplished through a careful review of the videotapes of the program episodes in which the television disclosure had occurred. In this way, elements of the show that the informant chose to discuss could be delved into further, but particular incidents that had transpired on the show could also be investigated. Merton et al.'s suggestions for using verbal cues that emphasize the past tense were especially important, because in much of the questioning, respondents were asked to describe views they had held prior to the very dramatic experience of being on the program.

A flexible, open-ended questionnaire was used as a rough guide for conversations with informants (see Appendix B). Initial sensitizing concepts gleaned from the literature included parasocial interaction, social support networks, public self-consciousness, and affinity for the television medium. Questions roughly adapted from a dependency scale developed by Sandra Ball-Rokeach, Milton Rokeach, and Joel Grube explored this latter concept, as did information about general television viewing levels and attitudes toward daytime talk shows. Lines of inquiry were developed based on Alan Rubin, Elizabeth Perse, and Robert Powell's parasocial interaction scale and on Mary Procidano and Kenneth Heller's scale for perceived social support. Allan Fenigstein, Michael Scheier, and Arnold Buss's scale pertaining to public dimensions of self-consciousness was also adapted by asking questions about the saliency of the cameras and monitors as well as the studio and television audience.

Informants were asked to reconstruct their initial decision to disclose on television, with particular attention paid to the goals each person sought to fulfill by accepting the invitation. The degree to which respondents expected to and were willing to disclose were important areas of inquiry. Informants provided their views on the other daytime talk shows and were asked to describe their experiences on other programs on which they had appeared. To procure a better understanding of the consequences of being on the show, each person was questioned about both positive and negative repercussions. Information about outcomes was easy to obtain, because informants peppered the conversation with concrete examples of what had transpired since the show taping and airing; the challenge was in redirecting their thoughts to their prior views of the situation for other elements of the inquiry. The content of the interview guide continued to evolve as new concepts surfaced during sessions with respondents.

Interviews began with brief pleasantries exchanged, after which the purpose of the research was explained and the consent form reviewed. Informants were told how they came to be selected and were assured of confidentiality. Interestingly, all but three declined this offer and asked to have their names used.

After the various areas of the interview guide were covered, additional queries were generally asked of informants about elements of the show that seemed notable, such as a particularly hostile audience member or a remark Donahue had made. At the close of the discussion, respondents were asked if there was anything that they wanted to add and were encouraged to call the toll-free number provided if they later wished to make further comments or relate a new incident that had occurred as a result of their appearances.

A thank you note was mailed to informants after each interview. Approximately six months later, respondents who were participants in the dissertation phase of this work were sent a summary of the study results and were encouraged to respond if they had comments or questions. A self-addressed, stamped envelope was included in the mailing, as was information about the researcher's toll-free number for those who wished to call. Five informants responded after this mailing to comment or to update the information held about them.

DATA ANALYSIS

The analysis unspooled in several overlapping phases. The process began early; I kept a diary of analytic memos as I encountered my informants and studied diverse areas of literature. This type of journal keeping is geared toward recording insights generated through readings, conversations, and semi-structured interviews. As suggested by Anselm Strauss, both methodological and theoretical issues were addressed in the more than 200 pages of notes that resulted. These memos were highly speculative in the beginning but became increasingly specific as time progressed.

Barney Glaser and Anselm Strauss's analytic technique of constant comparison proved useful in several stages of the analysis. The method serves as a powerful aid in developing insights into theory, as speculative hunches are systematically compared in diverse circumstances. For this reason, constant comparison played an especially important role in phase one, the selection of informants. The authors' emphasis on extremes prompted me to increase the heterogeneity of the selected sample so that evolving theories could be tested across disparate situations.

Phase two involved the construction of data templates, a design that involved fitting the results of each wide-ranging interview session into clusters of information so that informants' responses to particular topics could be compared. The template covered such areas as concerns about appearing, previous levels of disclosure, prior attitudes toward Donahue and the show, conceptions of the audience, genre viewing levels, outcomes, and many other topics. The template evolved to encompass additional categories that became salient over time. These included stipulated restrictions on appearance, preparation tactics, assessment of one's performance, and prior television and radio incidents reported as significant by informants.

In phase three, the body of data within template items was assessed across informants to determine patterns in critical areas of inquiry that included respondents' rationale, television affinity, conceptions about the genre, and outcomes. A particular emphasis was placed on working from in vivo codes, as suggested by Anselm Strauss. These are respondent descriptions that have imagery and analytic potential. Informant Pete Lumpkins's use of the term *evangelism* and Kate Bornstein's reference to Erving Goffman's work on stigma management are examples of two in vivo codes that proved valuable. In a similar vein, Judith Preissle Goetz and Margaret LeCompte suggest working with metaphors as a method for organizing the analysis. Informants supplied the rich metaphors of a public soap box and freak show. Glaser and Strauss's constant comparison tactics were used in this phase to develop emerging concepts. This method advocates ceaseless efforts at fitting data into evolving categorizations that are strengthened or discarded as the analysis proceeds.

Phase four entailed a close analysis of discrepant cases so that developing theories about television disclosure could be delimited and necessary conditions identified. Categories of moths, plaintiffs, and marketers surfaced over a period of time as new informants were added who extended the typology. Patterns of differential outcomes for each group became clearer under close scrutiny of these discrepant cases.

It is important to note the spiraling nature of the analysis stages. For example, as the core concept of evangelistic disclosure began to build in importance, additional informants were chosen in order to inspect this concept more thoroughly. In effect, this meant cycling back to phase one of the analysis. Respondents who were clearly evangelical as well as others who did not appear to be were included to examine budding theories.

After the interviewing was completed, the templates were scanned to look for verification or refutation of trends. As the core categories became firmer, the fifth phase began. This was the writing stage, and analysis continued as weaknesses and gaps were found in the fabric of the grounded theory and repaired with additional information gleaned from the data.

In summary, five stages of analysis were conducted. These included (a) a preliminary, open period in which informants were selected to begin to test emerging ideas about the findings; (b) the construction of templates; (c) a period of constant comparison that sought patterns, which often surfaced in in vivo codes, across parallel sections of informants' templates; (d) the examination of discrepant cases; and (e) the writing. Analysis continuously cycled back to previous stages and overlapped considerably but gradually moved toward greater specification of concepts and theories.

The present study bears interesting methodological implications, particularly due to the straightforward reporting of the respondents' identities. Informants, as a result, have distinct voices rather than anonymous ones folded into the mix of research findings. This infuses the data with a robust vigor; however, it presents unique problems as to exactly how much of their testimonies should be revealed in the reported findings. Generally, this was not a problem, because the informants had already appeared on national television to intimately discuss their lifestyles or situations. However, some revealed additional information in the interviews that had not been discussed on the show. Lorretta, for example, specifically gave me permission to discuss her sexual preference, and the disclosure is significant because it is evidence of impression management concerns. Nevertheless, I thought long and hard about revealing this fact. Social scientists rather routinely avoid these dilemmas—and the often unknown risks—by assuring confidentiality. Participants' voices are muted, however, using conventional methods.

Another methodological point that needs addressing concerns the difficulties encountered in tracking down informants. Areas of research in mass communication and other fields are frequently limited by pragmatic considerations of how to gain access to key players. Indeed, difficulties in locating respondents made this project much more time-consuming and expensive. Furthermore, access to the inner sanctum of production houses is extremely difficult to procure. Scholars must continue to clamor for access beyond the blackout curtains private companies and other organizations use to shield their activities from public scrutiny.

VALIDITY CONSIDERATIONS

This section addresses the trustworthiness of the present study, primarily relying on criteria advanced by Robert Merton et al. and Yvonna Lincoln and Evon Guba. Efforts made to safeguard the credibility of the findings are also described. Merton et al. stipulate four criteria to evaluate the success of a focused interview. These include the specificity, range, depth, and personal context of the responses.

Specificity was a strength of this study for a variety of reasons. During the interview sessions, informants often recounted specific incidents that occurred during the show taping or after their return to their communities. The researcher's close examination of the episode(s) the informant had participated in as well as long-term viewing of the *Donahue* show and others in the genre allowed discussion in minute detail. For example, some respondents mentioned episodes in which they felt the panelists had been glaringly unsuccessful in their attempts to communicate, or they commented on particularly objectionable episodes. Furthermore, specificity of description was repeatedly stressed because informants were so heterogenous that the researcher was continually oriented to diverse world views that were important to capture in order to understand the unique disclosure situation faced by each.

The range of replies to queries was evidenced by a number of unexpected responses. Unanticipated information included the low television affinity levels and informants' responses about yearning to be seen as normal through their participation in the show. The depth of the inquiry was indicated by the strong affective component often expressed in poignant testimonials about past discrimination and earlier feelings of self-loathing. These accounts of painful incidents also bolstered the personal context component.

Lincoln and Guba place primary emphasis on assuring the credibility, or truth value, of a qualitative work. Two safeguards that enhance credibility are (a) the use of adequacy checks by informants of the final or evolving interpretations, and (b) systematic and wide-ranging data collection and analysis. The insider checks were carried out in the present study when letters summarizing the working findings were sent to each informant while the study was still in process to provide them with a chance to question or comment about the results. Lincoln and Guba stress the importance of member checks as "the most crucial technique for establishing credibility."[3]

The emphasis on systematic methods was accomplished primarily through the diary keeping mentioned earlier. The methodological and theoretical notes written almost daily fostered orderly and regular assessment of biases, negative cases, and neglected or underdeveloped areas. The use of a journal also enhances what Lincoln and Guba call *confirmability*, their term roughly equivalent to objectivity. The notes provide a record of attempts made to remain neutral and pursue negative cases.

Lincoln and Guba warn of the potential to overidentify with informants' perspectives and thus weaken study credibility. Increasingly, I found as I thought through issues in the diary that I held a fairly positive view of my informants, considering them brave and well-meaning. I speculated that it was possible, as with other viewers, to fall prey to according informants respect simply as a response to the status conferral processes operating due to their television appearances.

I confronted this issue by asking my transcriptionist for her views about my subjects, because she, too, had come to know them through careful attention to the tapes. She had not, however, seen them on television. The woman, a 61-year-old administrative secretary, said her views had changed about such subjects as homosexuality and transsexualism. When asked about Craig and Patrick, gay men battling for marriage rights, she replied, "That's another one I didn't expect to like. . . . I see it in a totally different light. . . . It's terrible to admit, but I felt a little repelled, but [now] I see what they feel—It's an education."

Lincoln and Guba also stress the use of triangulation of data points. Access constraints limited data gathering to some degree, but televised episodes provided an important additional data source. Although the archived copies of six months of *Donahue* episodes did not constitute a formal part of this study, they did provide useful validity checks. For example, consistency of informant rationale could be examined in cases in which the respondent had previously addressed a similar question on the show—or on others in the genre.

Lincoln and Guba's equivalent conceptualization of generalizability, transferability, clearly exists to a large degree for this group of informants, who generally would appear on any show which came their way. The typology of disclosure categories also seems transferable. During long-term viewing of the diverse array of talk shows that now spans the broadcast day, I repeatedly saw plaintiffs, evangelicals, moths, and marketers surface, their faces and stories floating through the gestalt of images that make up daytime television.

LIMITATIONS

A potential deficiency is that a goal-based model of self-disclosure may not cover the full range of self-disclosure behaviors and has the potential to be unnecessarily limiting. Expressive aspects of self-disclosure are not addressed well in a goal-based model, perhaps because these needs for expression or catharsis are not readily verbalized or conceived as goals by informants. However, the instrumental use of the medium exhibited by the informants appeared to be intensely goal-oriented, and therefore the goal-based model seemed fruitful to explicate the television disclosure phenomenon. Although Lynn Miller and Stephen Read's model was known to the researcher before the design was implemented, it resurfaced as an analytic tool when the evangelical intent of the respondents became clear.

An unavoidable artifact in this study was that the selection of informants comprised those who could be tracked down. The results were probably skewed toward evangelical disclosure, because advocates of social causes want viewers to be able to reach them. However, those in the group who were most difficult to locate were generally similar in evangelical intent.

The two-hour interview sessions limited the amount of data that could be fully developed. When procuring consent, I was hesitant to ask informants for a longer time commitment, because their cooperation was key to the research. The study was perhaps too broadly defined, given those time constraints, but there was so much about the phenomenon that had not yet been examined, so many puzzle pieces yet to be fitted.

Another potential pitfall concerns the high self-monitoring tendencies of the respondents. Their well-honed skills of impression management make them particularly capable of crafting and executing a socially acceptable rationale for their television disclosures. However, their evangelical fervor held throughout each interview, from heartfelt testimonies about feeling like "freaks" to their expectations that the studio audience would reflect the same disgust and hostility many informants had faced throughout their lives.

Another possible artifact is that the staff of the various shows winnows the potential guests. This may be why other disclosure processes such as those described by William Stiles's fever model are not operating here. The patterns pointed out in the present study may not be applicable for those who do not get a chance to appear but petition shows for the opportunity.

In hindsight, there were two deficiencies that, if addressed earlier, might have strengthened this study. The first concerns the finding of low levels of television viewing on the part of the disclosers. The focus of inquiry during the interview stopped at current viewing habits, which, at the time, seemed sufficient. A closer examination of the role of television during childhood and adolescence might have teased out a better understanding of the yearnings for certification. The childhood fantasies fortuitously described by several informants provided an important clue to the validation seeking that was not otherwise clearly articulated by respondents.

The second weakness is related to this need for a deeper understanding of the somewhat elusive concept of validation. Only after repeated readings of the transcripts did the notion of normalcy become salient, and I wish I had followed up with questions when that term was mentioned. Although I could have called later to probe, I felt that questions after the fact about issues held at a rather tentative level of consciousness would have been jarring and ineffective.

The strength of this study, however, is in the grounded nature of the theory. Barney Glaser and Anselm Strauss summarize the benefits of emergent designs: "In short, our focus on the emergence of categories solves the problems of fit, relevance, forcing and richness."[4] The interpretation presented here with rich complexity intact works to explicate the meanings inherent in the social act of television disclosure embedded in the strains of the diverse voices of the informants.

NOTES

1. For a discussion about the advantages and disadvantages of using toll-free numbers in qualitative research, see Priest, 1993.
2. Mike Elmeer and the Lykins are a slight exception to this. Mike appeared with the Lykins on a broadly defined show about AIDS. Later, both Mike and the Lykins appeared again on separate *Donahue* episodes.
3. Lincoln and Guba, 1985, p. 314.
4. Glaser and Strauss, 1967, p. 37.

APPENDIX B

INTERVIEW GUIDE

[Reconstructing the decision experience:]
How did it come about that you were on *Donahue* [or other shows]?

What incentives—if any—were given by the show's staff?
What line of reasoning was given to convince you to participate?

As you tried to decide, what did you see as the pros and cons? [Any others?]
Was it difficult to make up your mind?
What were some concerns?

Did you have second thoughts after you agreed to participate? [If yes:]
What were they?
Did you ever think seriously about backing out? [Why?]

Were there people who tried to influence you to be on the show—or who tried to convince you not to participate? [Who were they?/Why?]

What were your expectations about what being on the show would be like?

When you thought of the audience who would see you, who did you picture?
Were there certain people you felt uneasy about, knowing they might see the show? [Why?/Who were they?]

213

Had you disclosed this information in other places/shows? [Where?]
How was your life going at the time you were asked to be on the show?

[Demographic information:]
Age, education level, occupation, marital status.
What role has religion played in your life?

[Television viewing habits:]
How does television fit into your life?
Are there programs you try to watch regularly? [What are they?]
Are there shows you clear time for, that you really settle in to view?
Do you have a general pattern of viewing during prime time?
How about daytime viewing?
How would you feel if your television was taken from you for a month?

[Television talk show viewing:]
What were your feelings about *Donahue* before you appeared on the program?
Do you watch other daytime talk shows? Are you a fan? Do the shows seem different from one another? [In what ways?]
Would you be willing to participate in these other shows if asked? [Why?/ Why not?]
Has being on the show changed your viewing habits of daytime talk shows?

[Prior opinion of the host:]
Think back to your feelings about *Donahue* [or other hosts whose shows they had appeared on] before you were on the show. Would you consider yourself a fan?
What were your feelings, before going on, about their abilities as hosts? Their sincerity? Their therapeutic expertise?

Radio listening? Any talk/advice shows?

[Relationship information:]
Are there other people you can talk to about this issue?
Can you describe the level of emotional support you received from people before you discussed this topic on the show?

Let's briefly talk about the relationships you have with people like your spouse/partner, family, friends, and co-workers. How would you characterize these relationships?

[Counseling background:]
Have you ever talked to a counselor or therapist about the same thing you discussed on the show?

[Describing the experience:]
Was there much contact with the producer before arriving for the taping?
Could you describe the day of the show taping?
What was it like being in the studio?
What kind of briefing were you given?
What effect did the presence of the studio audience have?
What was it like to see yourself in the monitor?
What effect did the camera have?
Did you say more than you expected to say? Did you feel you were able to get your point across? Was it difficult to hold yourself together?
You don't have to tell me what they were, but were there things you decided to hold back?
Were there times you felt like crying but you felt it would not be appropriate?

How would you evaluate *Donahue* as a host?
How would you evaluate the staff?
Do you feel you were treated fairly? Taken advantage of?

[Describing outcomes:]
Did you watch the show when it aired?
What was it like to see yourself?
Who was with you when you watched the show?
Did you contact anyone and suggest that they watch the show? [Why?]

Did you tape the show?
What feelings do you have when you watch the program?

What has happened as a result of being on the show? Any life changes? Any new insights?

Have people treated you differently? [In what ways?]
How have people close to you responded? Have there been changes in your relationships with your family or partner/spouse?
How do you feel about your life now?

[Overall evaluation of the experience:]
So how would you summarize the advantages and disadvantages? [Probe may be necessary if only one part of the question is described.]
Would you recommend this experience to others if they had the opportunity to appear on the show to discuss a sensitive topic? [Why?/Why not?]
What would you do differently if you had it to do over again?
Would you appear for other topics? [What topics come to mind?]
Are there topics you would not go on to discuss? [What topics?]

Is there anything else you would like to mention about your experience?

Alcoff, L., & Gray, L. (1993). Survivor discourse: Transgression or recuperation? *Signs, 18*(2), 260-290.

Altheide, D.L., & Snow, R.P. (1979). *Media logic* (Vol. 89, Sage Library of Social Science Research). Beverly Hills, CA: Sage Publications.

Althusser, L. (1971). *Lenin and philosophy and other essays*. London: New Left Books.

Altman, I., & Taylor, D.A. (1973). *Social penetration: The development of interpersonal relationships*. New York: Holt, Rinehart & Winston.

Archer, R.L. (1979). Role of personality and the social situation. In G. J. Chelune (Ed.), *Self-disclosure: Origins, patterns, and implications of openness in interpersonal relationships* (pp. 28-58). San Francisco: Jossey-Bass.

Archer, R.L., & Earle, W.B. (1983). The interpersonal orientations of disclosure. In P. B. Paulus (Ed.), *Basic group processes* (pp. 289-314). New York: Springer-Verlag.

Arkin, R.M. (1986). Self-presentation strategies and sequelae. In S.L. Zen (Ed.), *Self representation: The second attribution-personality theory conference, California School of Professional Psychology* (pp. 6-25). New York: Springer-Verlag.

Ball-Rokeach, S.J., Rokeach, M., & Grube, J.W. (1984). *The great American values test*. New York: The Free Press.

Banks, J. (1990). Listening to Dr. Ruth: The new sexual primer. In G. Gumpert & S.L. Fish (Eds.), *Talking to strangers: Mediated therapeutic communication* (pp. 73-86). Norwood, NJ: Ablex.

Bass, T.A. (1972). *Sojourner Truth: A rhetoric of reform*. Unpublished master's thesis, University of Georgia, Athens.

Baudrillard, J. (1987). *The ecstacy of communication*. New York: Autonomedia.

REFERENCES

Becker, H. S. (1963). *Outsiders.* New York: MacMillan.

Becker, H.S. (1986). *Writing for social scientists.* Chicago: The University of Chicago Press.

Berg, J.H., & Archer, R.L. (1982). Response to self-disclosure and interaction goals. *Journal of Experimental Social Psychology, 18*, 501-512.

Berscheid, E. (1985). Interpersonal attraction. In G. Lindzey & E. Aronson (Eds.), *Handbook of social psychology* (3rd ed., Vol. 2, pp. 413-84). New York: Random House.

Bochner, A.P. (1984). The functions of human communication in interpersonal bonding. In C.C. Arnold & J.W. Bowers (Eds.), *Handbook of rhetorical and communication theory* (pp. 544-621). Boston: Allyn and Bacon.

Boorstin, D.J. (1982). From hero to celebrity: The human pseudo-event. In G. Gumpert & R. Cathcart (Eds.), *Inter/Media: Interpersonal communication in a media world* (2nd ed., pp. 242-249). New York: Oxford University Press.

Bordo, S. (1993). "Material Girl": The effacements of postmodern culture. In C. Schwichtenberg (Ed.), *The Madonna connection: Representational politics, subcultural identities, and cultural theory* (pp. 265-290). Boulder, CO: Westview.

Brooks, T., & Marsh, E. (1979). *The complete directory of prime time network TV shows.* New York: Ballantine Books.

Brown, L. (1977). *The New York Times encyclopedia of television.* New York: New York Times Books.

Carbaugh, D. (1989). *Talking American: Cultural discourses on DONAHUE.* Norwood, NJ: Ablex.

Carbaugh, D. (1993). "Soul" and "self": Soviet and American cultures in conversation. *Quarterly Journal of Speech, 79*, 182-200.

Carey, J.W. (1989). *Communication as culture: Essays on media and society.* Boston: Unwin Hyman.

Carpenter, J. (1985, April). *Tuning in the gospel: Fundamentalist radio broadcasting and the revival of mass evangelism, 1930-1945.* Paper delivered to the Mid-American Studies Association, University of Illinois at Urbana.

Carpignano, P., Andersen, R., Aronowitz, S., & DiFazio, W. (1990). Chatter in the age of electronic reproduction: Talk television and the 'public mind.' *Social Text, 9*, 33-55.

Carter, B. (1992, February 22). One offended viewer tries to hit "Donahue" in wallet. *The New York Times*, pp. C1, C6.

Carter, B. (1992, June 22). Talk is cheap, but profitable, on TV. *The New York Times*, pp. D1, D8.

Coates, D., & Winston, T. (1987). The dilemma of distress disclosure. In V.J. Derlega & J.H. Berg (Eds.), *Self-disclosure: Theory, research, and therapy* (pp. 229-256). New York: Plenum Press.

Cohen, A.A., Adoni, H., & Bantz, C.R. (1990). *Social conflict and television news*. Newbury Park, CA: Sage.

Cohen, S., & Young, J. (1973). Effects and consequences. In S. Cohen & J. Young (Eds.), *The manufacture of news* (pp. 337-349). Beverly Hills, CA: Sage.

Conrad, P. (1982). *Television: The medium and its manners*. Boston: Routledge and Kegan Paul.

Cooley, C.H. (1902). *Human nature and the social order*. New York: Charles Scribner's Sons.

Cooper, M., & Soley, L.C. (1990, February/March). All the right sources. *Mother Jones*, pp. 20-27, 45-48.

Cozby, P.C. (1973). Self-disclosure: A literature review. *Psychological Bulletin, 79*, 73-91.

Cross, D.W. (1983). *Mediaspeak: How television makes up your mind*. New York: Coward-McCann.

Crow, B.K. (1986). Conversational pragmatics in television talk: The discourse of "Good Sex." *Media, Culture and Society, 8*, 457-484.

Cunningham, A. (1993, September). Sex in high school. *Glamour*, pp. 252-255, 318-322.

Cunningham, J.A. (1981). Effects of intimacy and sex-role congruency of self-disclosure (Doctoral dissertation, University of Utah, 1981). *Dissertation Abstracts International, 42*(8-B), 2597.

Darnton, N., Springen, K., Wright, L., & Keene-Osborn, S. (1991, October 7). The pain of the last taboo. *Newsweek*, pp. 70-72.

Davis, F. (1979). Deviance disavowal: Management of strained interaction by the visibly handicapped. In V.L. Swigert & R.A. Farrell (Eds.), *The substance of social deviance* (pp. 153-161). Sherman Oaks, CA: Alfred Publishing.

Davis, M.H., & Franzoi, S.L. (1987). Private self-consciousness and self-disclosure. In V.J. Derlega & J.H. Berg (Eds.), *Self-disclosure: Theory, research, and therapy* (pp. 59-79). New York: Plenum Press.

Davis, M.H., & Sloan, M. (1974). The basis of interviewee matching of interviewer self-disclosure. *British Journal of Social and Clinical Psychology, 13*, 359-367.

Dayan, D., & Katz, E. (1992). *Media events: The live broadcasting of history.* Cambridge, MA: Harvard University Press.

Debord, G. (1990). *Comments on the society of the spectacle* (M. Imrie, Trans.). London: Verso.

DeFleur, M.L., & Ball-Rokeach, S.J. (1982). *Theories of mass communication* (5th ed.). New York: Longman.

Denzin, N. (1991). *Images of postmodern society.* London: Sage.

Derlega, V.J., & Berg, J.H. (Eds.). (1987). *Self-disclosure: Theory, research, and therapy.* New York: Plenum Press.

Derlega, V.J., & Grzelak, J. (1979). Appropriateness of self-disclosure. In B.J. Chelune (Ed.), *Self-disclosure: Origins, patterns and implications of openness in interpersonal relationships* (pp. 151-176). San Francisco: Jossey-Bass.

Derlega, V.J., Metts, S., Petronio, S., & Margulis, S.T. (1993). *Self-disclosure.* Newbury Park, CA: Sage.

Didion, J. (1992, July 26). Trouble in Lakewood. *The New Yorker*, pp. 46-50, 60, 62-65.

Donahue, P., & Co. (1979). *Donahue: My own story.* New York: Fawcett Crest.

Dyer, R. (1991). *A Star is Born* and the construction of authenticity. In C. Gledhill (Ed.), *Stardom: Industry of desire* (pp. 132-140). New York: Routledge.

Emerson, J.P. (1973). Nothing unusual is happening. In T. Shibutani (Ed.), *Human nature and collective behavior* (pp. 93-207). New Brunswick, NJ: Transaction Books.

Erikson, H. (1989). *Syndicated television: The first 40 years, 1947-1987.* Jefferson, NC: McFarland and Co.

Erikson, K. (1962). Notes on the sociology of deviance. *Social Problems, 9*, 307-314.

Erikson, K. (1981). Notes on the sociology of deviance. In E. Rubington & M.S. Weinberg (Eds.), *Deviance: The interactionist perspective* (4th ed., pp. 25-28). New York: MacMillan.

Everybody's talking! (1992, November 30). *For Women First*, pp. 31-37.

Ewen, S. (1988). *All consuming images: The politics of style in contemporary culture.* New York: Basic Books.

Farrell, R.A., & Morrione, T.J. (1979). Social interaction and stereotypic responses to homosexuals. In V.L. Swigert & R.A. Farrell (Eds.), *The substance of social deviance* (pp. 122-139). Sherman Oaks, CA: Alfred Publishing.

Feder, R. (1993). *A qualitative study of white supremacists on daytime television talk shows: Is it hate TV?* Unpublished master's thesis, Boston University, Boston, MA.

Fenigstein, A., Scheier, M.F., & Buss, A.H. (1975). Public and private self-consciousness: Assessment and theory. *Journal of Clinical and Consulting Psychology, 43,* 522-527.

Ferguson, R. (1990). Introduction: Invisible center. In R. Ferguson, M. Gever, T.T. Minh-ha, & C. West (Eds.), *Out there: Marginalization and contemporary cultures* (pp. 9-14). New York: The New Museum of Contemporary Art.

Fisher, D.V. (1984). A conceptual analysis of self-disclosure. *Journal for the Theory of Social Behaviour, 14*(3), 277-296.

Fiske, J. (1987). *Television culture.* London: Routledge.

Fiske, J., & Hartley, J. (1978). *Reading television.* London: Routledge.

Foucault, M. (1978). *The history of sexuality* (Vol. 1: An Introduction). (R. Hurley, Trans.). New York: Pantheon.

Fraser, N. (1992). Sex, lies, and the public sphere: Some reflections on the confirmation of Clarence Thomas. *Critical Inquiry, 18,* 595-612.

French, D., & Lee, L. (1988). *Working: My life as a prostitute.* New York: E. P. Dutton.

Frye, N. (1957). *Anatomy of criticism.* Princeton, NJ: Princeton University Press.

Galtung, J., & Ruge, M. (1973). Structuring and shaping news. In S. Cohen & J. Young (Eds.), *The manufacture of news* (pp. 62-72). Beverly Hills, CA: Sage.

Gamson, W.A., & Modigliani, A. (1989). Media discourse and public opinion on nuclear power. *American Journal of Sociology, 95,* 1-38.

Gans, H.J. (1979). *Deciding what's news: A study of CBS Evening News, NBC Nightly News, Newsweek and Time.* New York: Pantheon.

Garfinkel, H. (1967). *Studies in ethnomethodology.* Englewood Cliffs, NJ: Prentice-Hall.

Geertz, C. (1973). *The interpretation of cultures.* New York: Basic.

Gerbner, G., Gross, L., Jackson-Beeck, M., Jeffries-Fox, S., & Signorelli, N. (1978). Cultural indicators: Violence profile No. 9. *Journal of Communication, 28*(3), 176-207.

Gergen, K.J. (1991). *The saturated self: Dilemmas of identity in contemporary life.* New York: Basic.

Gilbert, S.J. (1976). Empirical and theoretical extensions of self-disclosure. In G.R. Miller (Ed.), *Explorations in interpersonal communication* (pp. 197-216). Beverly Hills, CA: Sage.

Gitlin, T. (1987). Television's screens: Hegemony in transition. In D. Lazere (Ed.), *American media and mass culture: Left perspectives* (pp. 240-265). Berkeley: University of California Press.

Givens, R. (1989, July 17). Talking people into talking. *Newsweek,* pp. 44-45.

Glaser, B.G., & Strauss, A.L. (1967). *The discovery of grounded theory: Strategies for qualitative research.* New York: Aldine de Gruyter.

Goetz, J.P., & LeCompte, M.D. (1984). *Ethnography and qualitative design in educational research.* San Diego, CA: Academic Press.

Goffman, E. (1959). *The presentation of self in everyday life.* Garden City, NJ: Doubleday Anchor Books.

Goffman, E. (1963). *Stigma, notes on the management of a spoiled identity.* Englewood Cliffs, NJ: Prentice-Hall.

Goodman, G., Lakey, G., Lashof, J., & Thorne, E. (1983). *No turning back: Lesbian and gay liberation for the 80s.* Philadelphia: New Society Publishers.

Gordon, M. (1994, May 22). Incest on TV: Whose life is it anyway? *The Washington Post,* p. G4.

Gramsci, A. (1971). *Selections from the prison notebooks.* London: Lawrence and Wishart.

Griffin, C.W., Wirth, M.J., & Wirth, A.G. (1986). *Beyond acceptance.* Englewood Cliffs, NJ: Prentice-Hall.

Gross, L. (1991). The contested closet: The ethics and politics of outing. *Critical Studies in Mass Communication, 8*(3), 352-388.

Gusfield, J.R. (1986). *Symbolic crusade: Status politics and the American Temperance Movement* (2nd ed.). Urbana, IL: University of Illinois Press.

Haag, L.L. (1993). Oprah Winfrey: The construction of intimacy in the talk show setting. *Journal of Popular Culture, 26,* 115-121.

Habermas, J. (1989). *The structural transformation of the public sphere:*

An inquiry into a category of bourgeois society. Chicago, IL: University of Chicago Press.

Hall, S. (1981). A world at one with itself. In S. Cohen & J. Young (Eds.), *The manufacture of news: Social problems, deviance, and the mass media* (pp. 147-156). London: Constable.

Hendrick, S. (1987). Counseling and self-disclosure. In V.J. Derlega & J.H. Berg (Eds.), *Self-disclosure: Theory, research, and therapy* (pp. 303-327). New York: Plenum Press.

Herman, E.S., & Chomsky, N. (1988). *Manufacturing consent: The political economy of the mass media.* New York: Pantheon Books.

Hill, C.T., & Stull, D.E. (1987). Gender and self-disclosure: Strategies for exploring the issues. In V.J. Derlega & J.H. Berg (Eds.), *Self-disclosure: Theory, research, and therapy* (pp. 81-100). New York: Plenum Press.

Hilton, J., & Knoblauch, M. (1980). *On television! A survival guide for media interviews.* New York: Amacon.

Hofacker, K.H. (1979). *An analysis of the "Donahue" show from 1967-1978.* Unpublished doctoral dissertation, University of Michigan, Ann Arbor.

hooks, B. (1989). *Talking back.* Boston, MA: South End Press.

hooks, B. (1990). Marginality as site of resistance. In R. Ferguson, M. Gever, T.T. Minh-ha, & C. West (Eds.), *Out there: Marginalization and contemporary cultures* (pp. 341-343). New York: The New Museum of Contemporary Art.

Hoover, S.M. (1990). The meaning of religious television: The "700 Club" in the lives of viewers. In Q.J. Schultze (Ed.), *American evangelicals and the mass media* (pp. 231-249). Grand Rapids, MI: Academic Books.

Horton, D., & Wohl, R.R. (1956). Mass communication and parasocial interaction: Observations on intimacy at a distance. *Psychiatry: Journal for the Study of Interpersonal Processes, 19,* 215-229.

Hoynes, W., & Croteau, D. (1989, February). *Are you on the "Nightline" guest list? An analysis of 40 months of "Nightline" programming.* Available from Fairness & Accuracy in Reporting, 130 W. 25 St., New York, NY 10001.

Hughes, E.C. (1945). Dilemmas and contradictions of status. *American Journal of Sociology, L,* 353-359.

Hunter, J.D. (1983). *American evangelicalism.* New Brunswick, NJ:

Rutgers University Press.

International Commission for the Study of Communication Problems. (1980). *Many voices, one world.* Paris: United Nations Educational, Scientific, and Cultural Organization (UNESCO).

Jensen, E. (1993, May 25). Tales are oft told as TV talk shows fill up air time. *The Wall Street Journal*, pp. 1, 6.

Jones, E., Farina, A., Hastorf, A., Markus, H., Miller, D., & Scott, R. (1984). *Social stigma.* New York: W. H. Freeman.

Jourard, S. M. (1964). *The transparent self.* New York: D. Van Nostrand.

Katz, E., Blumler, J.G., & Gurevitch, M. (1974). Utilization of mass communication by the individual. In J.G. Blumler & E. Katz (Eds.), *The uses of mass communications: Current perspectives on gratification research* (pp. 19-32). Beverly Hills, CA: Sage.

Kervin, D. (1985). Reality according to television news: Pictures from El Salvador. *Wide Angle, 7*, 61-71.

Kettering Foundation & The Harwood Group. (1991). *Citizens and politics: A view from main street.* Available from the Charles Kettering Foundation, 200 Commons Rd., Dayton, OH, 45459.

Kielwasser, A.P., & Wolf, M.A. (1992.) Mainstream television, adolescent homosexuality, and significant silence. *Critical Studies in Mass Communication, 9*, 350-373.

Knapp, L. (1988). Oprah Winfrey presents: The lesbian as spectacle. *Feminisms, 2*(2), 4-7.

Kneale, D. (1988, May 18). Titillating channels. *The Wall Street Journal*, pp. 1, 25.

Kolbert, E. (1993, July 18). When baring all to 4 million viewers doesn't help. *The New York Times*, pp. 2E.

Krauthammer, C. (1992, August 10). The pornography of self-revelation. *Time*, p. 72.

Kubey, R. (1992). A critique of "No Sense of Place" and the homogenization theory of Joshua Meyrowitz. *Communication Theory, 12*(3), 259-271.

Kuehn, L.L. (1976). The only game in town: Subcultural development among game show contestants. *Pacific Sociological Review, 19*(3), 385-400.

Laskas, J.M. (1991, November). What's happened to Phil Donahue? *Redbook*, pp. 44, 46, 48-50.

Lazarsfeld, P.F., & Merton, R. (1948). Mass communication, popular taste and organized social action. In L. Bryson (Ed.), *The communication of ideas* (pp. 95-118). New York: Harper.

Levin, M.B. (1987). *Talk radio and the American dream.* Lexington, MA: Lexington Books.

Levy, M.R., & Windahl, S. (1984). Audience activity and gratifications: A conceptual clarification and exploration. *Communication Research, 11*(1), 51-78.

Lincoln, Y.S., & Guba, E. G. (1985). *Naturalistic inquiry.* Newbury Park: Sage Publications.

Lipsky, M. (1972). Protest as a political resource. In G. Zaltman, P. Kotler, & I. Kaufman (Eds.), *Creating social change.* New York: Holt, Rinehart and Winston.

Lowrey, S. (1991, November 6). Sharing secrets. *The News and Observer,* pp. 1-2D.

Lyotard, J. (1984). *The postmodern condition.* Minneapolis: The University of Minnesota Press.

MacAloon, J. (Ed.). (1984). *Rite, festival, spectacle, game.* Chicago: University of Chicago Press.

MacPike, L. (1989). *There's something I've been meaning to tell you.* Tallahassee, FL: The Naiad Press.

Mander, J. (1978). *Four arguments for the elimination of television.* New York: Quill.

Masciarotte, G. (1991). C'mon, girl: Oprah Winfrey and the discourse of feminine talk. *Genders, 11,* 81-110.

Matelski, M.J. (1991). *Daytime television programming.* Boston: Focal Press.

McClellan, S. (1992, December 14). Look who's talking. *Broadcasting,* pp. 22, 24, 26, 30, 38.

McCroskey, J.C., & Richmond, V.P. (1990). Willingness to communicate: Differing cultural perspectives. *The Southern Communication Journal, 56*(1), 72-77.

McLuhan, M. (1964). *Understanding media: The extensions of man.* New York: McGraw-Hill.

Merton, R.K., Fiske, M., & Kendall, P.L. (1990). *The focused interview: A manual of problems and procedures* (2nd ed.). New York: The Free Press.

Meyrowitz, J. (1985). *No sense of place: The impact of electronic media on social behavior.* New York: Oxford University Press.

Michaels, E. (1987). My essay on postmodernity. *Art and Text, 25,* 86-91.

Miller, L.N., Berg, J.H., & Archer, R.L. (1983). Openers: Individuals who elicit intimate self-disclosure. *Journal of Personality and Social Psychology, 44*(6), 1234-1244.

Miller, L.C., & Read, S.J. (1987). Why am I telling you this? Self-disclosure in a goal-based model of personality. In V.J. Derlega & J.H. Berg (Eds.), *Self-disclosure: Theory, research, and therapy* (pp. 35-58). New York: Plenum Press.

Mincer, R., & Mincer, D. (1982). *The talk show book: An engaging primer on how to talk your way to success.* New York: Facts on File Publications.

Monaco, J. (1978). Celebration. In J. Monaco (Ed.) *Celebrity* (pp. 3-14). New York: Dell.

Morris, A.D., & Mueller, C.M. (Eds.). (1992). *Frontiers in social movement theory.* New Haven, CT: Yale University Press.

Munson, W. (1993). *All talk: The talkshow in media culture.* Philadelphia: Temple University Press.

Noelle-Neumann, E. (1984). *The spiral of silence.* Chicago: The University of Chicago Press.

Ollove, M., & Zurawik, D. (1994, March 27). How a madman became a star. *The Baltimore Sun,* pp. 1A, 20A.

Ono, K.A. (1991, November). *The economic and political impact of Oprah.* Paper presented at the meeting of the Speech Communication Association, Atlanta, GA.

Parkin, F. (1972). *Class inequality and political order.* London: Paladin.

Patton, M. Q. (1980). *Qualitative evaluation methods.* Newbury Park, CA: Sage Publications.

Pennebaker, J. W. (1989). Confession, inhibition, and disease. In L. Perkowitz (Ed.), *Advances in experimental social psychology* (Vol. 22, pp. 211-244). San Diego: Academic Press.

Percy, W. (1960). *The Moviegoer.* New York: The Noonday Press.

Postman, N. (1985). *Amusing ourselves to death.* New York: Penguin.

Prager, K.J. (1986). Intimacy status: Its relationship to locus of control, self-disclosure, and anxiety in adults. *Personality and Social Psychology Bulletin, 12,* 91-110.

Priest, P.J. (1992). *Self-disclosure on television: The counter-hegemonic struggle of marginalized groups on "Donahue."* Unpublished doctoral dissertation, University of Georgia, Athens.

Priest, P.J. (1993). Toll-free numbers: A tool for qualitative research. *Feedback, 34*(1), 29-30.

Procidano, M.E., & Heller, K. (1983). Measures of perceived social support from friends and from family: Three validation studies. *American Journal of Community Psychology, 11*(1), 1-24.

Prone, T. (1984). *Just a few words: How to present yourself in public.* London: Marion Boyars.

Rachlin, A. (1988). *News as hegemonic reality: American political culture and the framing of news accounts.* New York: Praeger.

Rapping, E. (1987). *The looking glass world of nonfiction TV.* Boston: South End Press.

Rapping, E. (1991, October). Daytime inquiries. *The Progressive,* pp. 36-38.

Raphael, S.J., & Proctor, P. (1991) *Sally: Unconventional Success.* New York: William Morrow.

Rein, I.J., Kotler, P., & Stoller, M.R. (1987). *High visibility.* New York: Dodd, Mead and Company.

Reynolds, C. (1986). *"Donahue": A rhetorical analysis of contemporary television culture.* Unpublished doctoral dissertation, University of Minnesota.

Rubin, A.M., Perse, E.M., & Powell, R.A. (1985). Loneliness, parasocial interaction, and local television news viewing. *Human Communication Research, 12,* 155-180.

Rubin, Z., & Shenker, S. (1978). Friendship, proximity, and self-disclosure. *Journal of Personality, 46,* 1-22.

Sanger, K. (1992, October). *Definitional protest: The reclamation of identity.* Paper presented at the meeting of the Speech Communication Association, Chicago, IL.

Scheier, M.F., & Carver, C.S. (1981). Private and public aspects of self. In L. Wheeler (Ed.), *Review of personality and social psychology* (Vol. 2, pp. 189216). Beverly Hills, CA: Sage.

Schickel, R. (1985). *Intimate strangers: The culture of celebrity.* Garden City, NJ: Doubleday & Company.

Schorr, D. (1977, October). Is there life after TV? *Esquire, 88,* p. 105-106, 156, 160, 164.

Schwartz, T. (1981). *Media, the second God.* New York: Random House.

Shaffer, D.R., & Ogden, J.K. (1986). On sex differences in self-disclosure during the acquaintance process: The role of anticipated future interaction. *Journal of Personality and Social Psychology, 51*(1), 92-101.

Shaffer, D.R., Smith, J.E., & Tomarelli, M.M. (1982). Self-monitoring as a determinant of self-disclosure reciprocity during the acquaintance process. *Journal of Personality and Social Psychology, 14*, 215-220.

Simons, H.W., Mechling, E.W., & Schreier, H.N. (1984). The functions of human communication in mobilizing for action from the bottom up: The rhetoric of social movements. In C.C. Arnold & J.W. Bowers (Ed.), *Handbook of rhetorical and communication theory* (pp. 792-867). Boston: Allyn and Bacon.

Slobin, D.I., Miller, S.H., & Porter, L.W. (1968). Forms of address and social relations in a business organization. *Journal of Personality and Social Psychology, 8*, 289-293.

Snow, R.P. (1983). *Creating media culture.* (Vol. 149, Sage Library of Social Research). Beverly Hills, CA: Sage.

Snyder, M. (1987). *Public appearances/Private realities.* New York: W. H. Freeman.

Sohn, D. (1976). David Sohn interviews Jerzy Kosinski: A nation of videots. In H. Newcomb (Ed.), *Television: The critical view* (pp. 137-152). Oxford University Press: New York.

Steenland, S. (1990). Those daytime talk shows. *Television Quarterly*, 24(4), 5-12.

Stewart, C.J., Smith, C.A., & Denton, R.E., Jr. (1989). *Persuasion and social movements* (2nd ed.). Prospect Heights, IL: Waveland.

Stiles, W.B. (1987). I have to talk to somebody: A fever model of disclosure. In V.J. Derlega & J.H. Berg (Eds.), *Self-disclosure: Theory, research, and therapy* (pp. 257-277). New York: Plenum Press.

Stocking, B. (1994, October 1). Confession may be costly. *The News and Observer,* pp. 1A, 10A.

Stokes, J.P. (1987). The relationship of loneliness and self-disclosure. In V.J. Derlega and J.H. Berg (Eds.), *Self-disclosure: Theory, research, and therapy* (pp. 175-201). New York: Plenum Press.

Strauss, A.L. (1987). Qualitative analysis for social scientists. Cambridge: Cambridge University Press.

Tardy, C.H. (1985). Self-disclosure: Objectives and methods of measurement. In C.H. Tardy (Ed.), *A handbook for the study of human communication* (pp. 323-346). Norwood, NJ: Ablex.

Tichi, C. (1991). *Electronic hearth.* New York: Oxford University Press.

Tomasulo, F.P. (1984). The spectator-in-the-tube: The rhetoric of Donahue. *Journal of Film and Video, 36*(2), 5-12.

Trice, H.M., & Roman, P.M. (1981). Delabeling, relabeling, and Alcoholics Anonymous. In E. Rubington & M.S. Weinberg (Eds.), *Deviance: The interactionist perspective* (4th Ed., pp. 472-479). New York: Macmillan.

Tuchman, G. (1978). *Making news.* New York: Free Press.

Tucker, M. (1990). Director's forward. In R. Ferguson, M. Gever, T.T. Minh-ha, & C. West (Eds.), *Out there: Marginalization and contemporary cultures* (pp. 7-8). New York: The New Museum of Contemporary Art.

Untrue confessions of a devious duo. (1988, September 12). *Newsweek.* p. 80.

Warhol, A., Konig, K., Hulten, P., & Granath, O. (Eds.). (1969). *Warhol* (2nd ed.). New York: Worldwide Books.

West, C. (1990). The new cultural politics of difference. In R. Ferguson, M. Gever, T.T. Minh-ha, & C. West (Eds.), *Out there: Marginalization and contemporary cultures* (pp. 19-36). New York: The New Museum of Contemporary Art.

Williams, R. (1977). *Marxism and literature.* New York: Oxford University Press.

Wood, M., & Zurcher, L.A., Jr. (1988). *The development of postmodern self.* New York: Greenwood.

Worthy, M., Gary, A.L., & Kahn, G.M. (1969). Self-disclosure as an exchange process. *Journal of Personality and Social Psychology, 13,* 59-63.

Yoo, P. (1993, August 16). *New yack city.* Detroit News, pp. D 1, 3.

Young, J. (1981). Beyond the critical paradigm: A critique of left functionalism in media theory. In S. Cohen & J. Young (Eds.), *The manufacture of news: Social problems, deviance, and the mass media* (pp. 393-421). London: Constable.

2, 73
by outgroups, 57-69, 83, 114
and self-disclosure, 58-69, 70n.
1, 82
as social activism, 105-12
strategies for, 86, 91, 107, 171
talk shows as forum for, 73, 78,
101, 111
see also impression management; self-presentation
stigmatized groups, *see* outgroups
Strike It Rich, 2, 6n. 2
studio audience, 58, 66
and experts, 17
on *Donahue*, 17, 82
expectations of, 1
involvement of, 7n. 4, 17, 41,
49, 82, 89, 129, 142, 171
self-disclosures by, 3, 159n. 3
swingers, 31, 61
media treatment of, 80
see also evangelicalism; outgroups

T

talk show genre, 4, 5, 177, 179n. 26
access to, 9n. 9, 12-13
authenticity of, 127-130,
133n.27
characteristics of, 4, 13, 46,
160n. 12, 188
as courtroom, 49, 52, 186, 199n.
29
daytime placement of, 18
discourse patterns of, 14, 15,
16, 17
and gender, 16, 132n. 12,
history of, 2-4, 11-12, 14-19

literature review of, 14-19
norms for 1, 14, 83, 132n. 6,
182-184
outgroup use of, *see* outgroups
participant perception of, 81-87
participant viewing of, 77, 81-
87
and postmodernism, 14
profitability of, 11, 22n. 2
as publicity, *see* marketers
ratings of, 3-4
and self-disclosure, *see* self-disclosure
sensationalism of, 18, 81, 83-
84, 85, 90, 118, 191, 193, *see
also* commodification
as stigma management forum,
73, 80, 101, 108, 111, *see also*
outgroups
as support group alternative, 74,
85
television, 75-91
hyperreality, 6, 172-73, 176-77,
182, 189
participant attitudes toward, 73-
87
participant viewing levels of,
75-80
as a resource, 73-74, 78-87
see also certification; talk show
genre
television disclosure, definition of,
14
see also self-disclosure
therapists, 21, 26n. 45, 100
therapy, 36
participants' prior experience
with, 7n. 3, 37, 43n. 6